DATE DUE			
MAY 7 '78			
APR 24 1991			

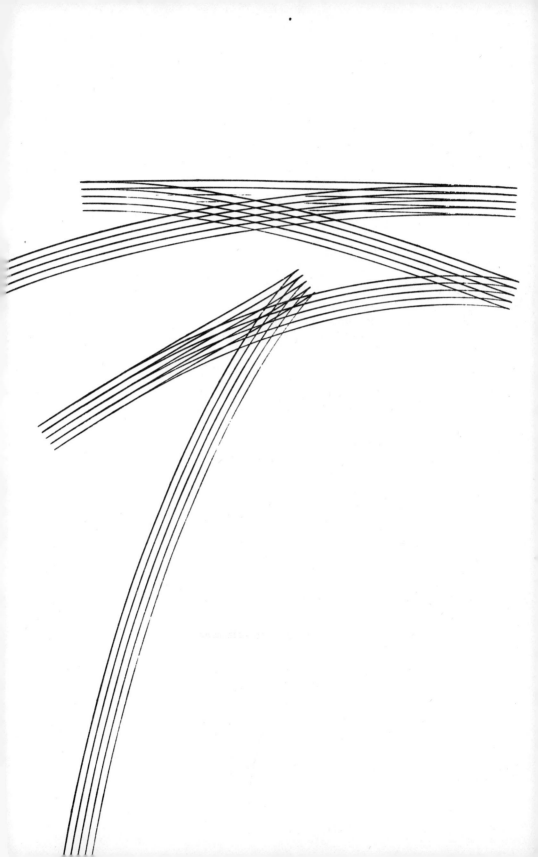

An Introduction to Electronic Music

by HERBERT RUSSCOL

Prentice-Hall, Inc.

Englewood Cliffs, N. J.

THE

LIBERATION

OF

SOUND

The Liberation of Sound: An Introduction to Electronic Music
By Herbert Russcol
Copyright © 1972 by Herbert Russcol

Printed in the United States of America

Prentice-Hall International, Inc., London
Prentice-Hall of Australia, Pty. Ltd., North Sydney
Prentice-Hall of Canada, Ltd., Toronto
Prentice-Hall of India Private Ltd., New Delhi
Prentice-Hall of Japan, Inc., Tokyo

Library of Congress Cataloging in Publication Data

Russcol, Herbert.
    The liberation of sound.

    Bibliography: p.
    1. Electronic music—History and criticism.
I. Title.
ML3817.R88   789'.9   72-1897
ISBN 0-13-535393-9

Again, to Margalit

Other Books by Herbert Russcol

The First Million Sabras
Guide to Low-Priced Classical Records
Philharmonic, A NOVEL

Acknowledgments

I wish to express my thanks to Louise Varèse for giving me some absorbing insights into the life of her late husband, Edgard Varèse, and for correcting my chapter on him; to Milton Babbitt, for reading much of this manuscript, and for his dazzling conversation; to Jacques Barzun, who quite innocently launched me on two years of work by suggesting that I write a short article on electronic music for the AMERICAN SCHOLAR and for reading a portion of the manuscript of this book.

And finally, my special thanks to Otto Luening, the Grand Old Man of electronic music in America, who valiantly read and criticized the entire book.

Credits

The author wishes to thank the following authors, or their representatives, or publishers, for their kind permission to quote from copyright material: Otto Luening and the *Music Educators' Journal*, for excerpts that appeared in the *Journal* in 1968; Broadcast Music, Inc., for the "Electronic Music Discography" which appeared in the BMI "Electronic Music Special," 1970; Bell Laboratories, for various writings by Dr. J. R. Pierce; The University of Toronto Press, for excerpts by composers which appeared in *The Modern Composer and His World*, University of Toronto Press, 1961; Dover Publications, Inc., for permission to quote from *The Essence of Music, and Other Papers* by Ferruccio Busoni.

Also, the introduction "Why Electronic Music?" first appeared under the title "Music Since Hiroshima: The Electronic Age Begins," in *The American Scholar*, XXXIX, No. 2 (March 11, 1970).

A REQUEST FOR THE LOAN OF YOUR EARS

by Jacques Barzun

NOTE: The following remarks were made by Jacques Barzun at the two initial concerts of the Columbia-Princeton Electronic Music Center at Columbia University's McMillin Theatre on May 9 and 10, 1961. The invited audience included music luminaries from New York and elsewhere, and the concerts were generally received as being of some historical importance. But the performances were damned by Paul Henry Lang, then music critic of *The New York Herald-Tribune*, as "Dictatorship of the Tube." Barzun answered him in a letter published in the *Herald-Tribune*, and Lang thereupon delivered another Sunday salvo entitled "Music and Musicians: The Chaos Machine."

A decade later, electronic music is taken for granted as a field of musical composition. It has achieved a place among the working materials of serious composers, and its role becomes more prominent each year. The sounds produced by electronic means are neither a panacea for the ills of modern music, nor are they the outlandish playthings of eccentric experimenters. Rather, they are materials for the music of our time.

Dr. Barzun's "request" remains the best summation of why we should "lend our ears" to this very exciting development in the art of music.

YOUR PRESENCE HERE, AT A CONCERT OF ELECTRONIC MUSIC, IS A compliment to the composers, as well as to the two universities that sponsor their work; and while I extend to you a welcome on behalf of those universities, I also wish to convey the composers' hope that you will be as gratified by hearing their works as they are by your willingness to listen.

No doubt your expectations are mixed. You are ready to be surprised, to have your curiosity satisfied, and possibly even to experience snatches of enjoyment as you would at an ordinary concert. If that is your state of mind I am fairly sure you will not be disappointed. But it may be that you are here in a mood of combined trepidation and resistance: this, after all, is the Age of Anxiety. . . . Or you may be bent on proving that electronic music is not music—doing this by the most painful test of endurance; or else you may be feeling caught because you have been brought by a friend and friendship is dearer to you than prudence.

If for these or any other reasons you are ill at ease, allow me to suggest a few considerations which should make you more serene, while leaving you your full freedom of opinion, your entire right to dislike and reject. I suggest, to begin with, that we are not here to like or approve but to understand. And the first step to understanding a new art is to try to imagine why the maker wants it the way it is. That attempt is interesting in itself, even if we ultimately disown the product. To understand in this fashion does not mean to accept passively because someone says that the stuff is new and therefore good, that many believe in it, that it's going to succeed anyway, so it's best to resign oneself to the inevitable. This kind of reasoning has gone on about modern art for some thirty years, and nothing has been more harmful to culture itself. It is an inverted philistinism, which eliminates judgment and passion just as surely as did the older philistinism of blind opposition to whatever was new.

What then is the decent, reasonable attitude to adopt? Very simple: make the assumption, first, that the old style—whatever it is— has exhausted its possibilities and can only offer repetition or trivial variations of the familiar masterpieces. I am not saying you should believe that the style of your favorite music is obsolete. I invite you to *assume* that it may be: for by trying to think that it is, as the new composer obviously has done, you will begin to discover what he is up to. By way of encouragement let me remind you that you make this very assumption automatically four or five times in every classical concert, in order to adjust your ear to the changes in style between Bach and Mozart, Mozart and Richard Strauss, and (if you can) between Strauss and Alban Berg. If styles and genres did not suffer exhaustion, there would be only one style, one genre in each art from its beginnings to yesterday.

But, you may say, electronic music is something else again; it is out of bounds; the jump is too great. There is no semblance of scale, the sounds are new, most of them are in fact noises. Ah, noise. Noise is the most constant complaint in the history of music. In the heyday of music it was not only Berlioz and Wagner who were damned as noisy; it was Mozart before them, and Haydn, and even earlier Lully and Handel. I suspect that the reason Orpheus was torn to pieces by women is that he made horrendous new noises on his lyre while they were washing their clothes at the river in what they thought was melodious silence.

The argument of noise is always irrelevant. The true question is: does this noise, when familiar, fall into intelligible forms and convey notable contents? To supply the answer takes time. One hearing, two, three hearings are not enough. Something must change in one's sensibility as a whole, in just the way that permits a foreign language suddenly to break into meaning and melody after months or years of its being mere noise. As a veteran of the premiere of Stravinsky's *Sacre du Printemps* in Paris, I can testify to the reality of the transformation. At the end of the work, in 1913, the conductor Pierre Monteux turned around amid the furious howls of the audience and said that since they had liked the piece so much he would play it again. The response was no better, and the police had to come in to quell the tumult. But now, fifty years after, the young accept those hammering rhythms and dissonant chords as if they were lullabies. They relish them while dallying in canoes, at the movies to accompany Disney's abstractions, and at the circus, where the music is used for the elephants to dance to.

Associations, in short, and assumptions and expectations rule our judgments. They govern our feelings, which we think are altogether spontaneous and truthful. But our sensibility is always more complex and more resourceful than we suppose, and that is why I have ventured to bring to your conscious notice what you knew all the time, but might not sufficiently allow for in listening to electronic music for the first time.

The word "electronic" suggests a final objection with which it is well to come to grips. Most people of artistic tastes share the widespread distrust and dislike of machinery and argue that anything pretending to be art cannot come out of a machine: art is the human product par excellence, and electronic music, born of intricate circuits and the oscillations of particles generated by Con Edison, is a contradiction in terms. Here again the answer is simple: the moment man ceased to make music with his voice alone the art became machine-ridden. Orpheus's lyre was a machine, a symphony orchestra is a regular factory for making artificial sounds, and a piano is the most appalling contrivance of levers and wires this side of the steam engine.

The application of this truth is obvious: the new electronic devices are but a means for producing new sounds to play with. What matters is not how they are produced but how they are used. And as to that we are entitled to ask the old questions—do we find the substance rich, evocative, capable of subtlety and strength? Do we, after a while, recognize patterns to which we can respond with our sense of balance, our sense of suspense and fulfillment, our sense of emotional and intellectual congruity? Those are the problems, beyond the technical, which our composers have tried to solve. We shall now attend to their handiwork with pleasure and gratitude (I hope), and certainly with a generous fraction of the patience they have themselves invested in their efforts to please us.

THE ARTIST AS WITNESS AND SEER

by Herbert Russcol

THE ARTIST IS THE WITNESS OF HIS TIME; IN OUR DAY, IN A WORLD that seems to be coming unhinged, he has taken on even greater importance. More and more we feel bewildered by the convulsions that have seized our age; more and more we turn to the artist's vision for answers to our troubling questions. He has been restored to his central tribal role as seer. As Malraux remarks, art for twentieth-century man is a vital and nourishing force, much as his edifice of religion sustained medieval man.

The artist, then, as witness, whose creative response delineates his era. Around 1900 a new kind of science and a new kind of art emerged together in Western Europe; Albert Einstein and Paul Klee were exact contemporaries; both were born in 1879. Arnold Schönberg, was born five years before them. It is Klee, the painter, and Schönberg, the composer, who intuitively express the dislocation of the world that Einstein discovered by cold reason. As scientists smashed the atom, painters smashed traditional forms and composers repudiated established musical frameworks.

The past seventy years have seen the completion of the Industrial Revolution, the beginnings of new revolutions, social upheavals, displacements of peoples, fascism, two world wars, the release of atomic energy, the onslaught of computers and automation—all at a riotous rate of speed.

We feel ourselves threatened, our preconceptions shattered. All that was once complacently accepted as "reality" has been destroyed or discredited. Our sense of cultural continuity has been rent. We feel that we are different from the generations before us, divorced from the traditions of the past. Desperately we turn to the modern artist in the hope that his vision can explain the chaos and sterility of our time, the dehumanization and the hateful technological trap.

Artists began in the last century to denounce the condition of modern man.

"During the past hundred and fifty years," Jacques Barzun has written,

> the one great attempt to stop the dry rot of the soul produced by the conditions of life in the modern world has been the handiwork of the artists of the West. Not the humanistic scholars and

gentlemen, not the critics, historians, philosophers, and students of society, but the artists have had the intuition, if not the total vision, of what we are now all able to describe. The artists have caught from one another the tragic message that something essential to human life was in mortal danger and with singular unanimity they have uttered warnings, improvised defenses, administered what they hoped were antidotes. They themselves have been driven by the obsessive conviction that to live under the industrial order and remain a man in the ancestral sense was impossible. Something pervasive that makes the difference, not between civilized man and the savage, not between man and the animals, but between man and the robot, grows numb, ossifies, falls away like black mortified flesh when technology assails the senses and science dominates the mind.*

Shortly after 1900, the artists began signaling the breakup more urgently. In painting, dance, theater, poetry, literature, and music they issued their warnings—shamans in loincloths, crouched around the tribe's campfire.

In music the discontinuity, the break with the past, has been more decisive than in any other art but painting. Hallowed musical conventions have been thrown overboard in what we now recognize as a revolt of the collective unconscious. Melody, tonality, harmony, and rhythm deliberately have been discarded. The consensus that had governed Western music for long centuries is no more. Traditions that had seemed sacrosanct and indestructible proved to be transitory; what had appeared to be inviolable, even eternal, crumbled rapidly.

New instrumental and vocal techniques emerged, along with a revolutionary new aesthetics of music. The breakup of the tonal idea that had held music together for centuries accelerated, first with the new interest in sound and acoustics, and later with the exploration of a wealth of new materials such as electronic music.

As a result, today's composer stands uncertainly in the midst of a turmoil of new ideas and a rejection of the old such as music has not experienced since the seventeenth century.

Ours is a time of many questions and few answers. In music, it is

---

*Jacques Barzun, *Science: The Glorious Entertainment* (New York: Harper & Row, 1964), p. 229.

a time of agitation, speculation, experimentation, and above all, a passionate search for a new basis. It is certainly not an age of musical masterpieces. Compared to the towering accomplishments of previous eras, since World War II we have thus far achieved only meager artistry in new music. Instead, composers have expended fierce energies shouting to each other and to us about which path music should take. But we must forgive them; after all, in a dark forest one may need to spend a good deal of time groping about and improvising escape routes.

The composer today is acutely aware that he has entered a strange new forest in which he must slowly, even painfully, stumble about to find his way. It is a land in which the old maps are useless. Moreover, being lost in this way results in a total freedom about which one cannot be entirely happy. By his own new code he must seek in every new work *the total possibility of experience*. The act of musical creation itself, rather than being the means of making a supreme statement, has become itself the core of his work. As in painting, experimentation and novelty themselves are now worthy goals in music. All possible materials, all conceivable relationships between creator, creation, performer, and listener are accepted and approved, because we no longer have any certainties.

Lost. No one knows where he is, everyone is bewildered by the swirling upheavals about him. That is the essence of our century's situation.

A discontinuity, then, an awareness of vanished certitudes—an awareness that was infinitely more deeply felt after World War II and Hiroshima.

Art, even music, when all is said and done, is fundamentally a record of people in a time, and this is the time of technology. The alarmed composer seeks to make his terrible vision clear and intelligible. In his tribal role as Witness and Martyr, that is his duty. For artists must be, in Antonin Artaud's haunting phrase, "like victims burned at the stake, signaling through the flames."

WHY ELECTRONIC MUSIC?

THE GROWTH OF ELECTRONICS HAS BEEN SO RAPID THAT THE WORD "electronic" is not to be found in any dictionary published before 1940. This is Robert Moog's definition of electronic music:

> *Electronic music consists of electronically generated sounds and natural sounds that are modified electronically, assembled into music by magnetic tape manipulation, or performed alive. Electronic music is a medium of expression, not a specific type of music. In fact, electronic music includes music as diverse as Carlos and Folkman's* SWITCHED-ON BACH, *the newest Coca-Cola commercial, some of the currently popular rock 'n' roll, and representative material from all camps of the musical avant garde.*

Perhaps a brief explanation of some of the tools employed in creating electronic music will provide a context for further discussion.

Tape Studios: Sounds on magnetic tape can be played backward, fragmented by splicing, subjected to reverberation, superimposed by overdubbing, and altered in speed and volume. Moreover, the exact correspondence between tape length and time means that the time dimension of the resulting "tape music" can be controlled with great precision. Some of the early techniques used in the preparation of tape music resembled the experiments of amateur tape hobbyists of today. Virtuosity with splicing block and recorder controls gave the composer additional resources, but making use of them was at first a laborious process involving hours of synchronization, re-recording, and splicing. To alleviate this drudgery, new kinds of equipment are constantly being added.

Synthesizers: Essentially a synthesizer is a unit combining sound generators and modifiers with a unified control system in one package. In size, such a device may range from the extremes of the mammoth RCA machine at Columbia University to Paul Ketoff's portable Syn-Ket, designed as a live-performance instrument, and the new bantam Putney. Between these extremes fall the most popular systems in use today—the Moog, Buchla, and Arp, among others. At present, synthesizers offer the composer one very great advantage over the otherwise more sophisticated computer—instant monitoring of the sound he is producing.

Computers: Some composers are now becoming seriously interested in the computer as a composing tool. The shape of any sound wave, however complex, can be precisely described by a series of numbers representing the amplitude of that sound wave at successive points. Such a number series can be run through a conversion unit to generate the analogous series of electrical oscillations, and these can then be used to activate a loudspeaker. Through input facilities allowing more or less instant replay, computers will soon have the same monitoring feature that is now available on synthesizers.

The composer of electronic music flips a switch and programs the dimension of a sound he has in his mind: frequency (pitch), octave, volume, timbre, duration, and envelope (degree of attack and decay). He faces a remarkably sophisticated machine that costs anywhere from $750 to $250,000, and that can produce any kind of acoustical event perceptible to man. He flips another switch, and the machine obliges at once with the requested sound. If the composer, who may also be a physicist, an acoustician, or a trained mathematician, is dissatisfied, he can reprogram. Or he can alter, transfigure, or refine the sound in mathematically precise gradations.

When he is pleased, he flips another switch and easily superimposes, or "patches," his specific sound onto combinations or layers of other sounds that he had stored on tape at an earlier time.

Eventually, after months of laborious splicing, the composer walks out of the studio with his new opus on a real tape under his arm. He has had control of executing his musical intentions to a degree undreamed of even a generation ago. He knows exactly what his new piece is going to sound like because he has been his own copyist, proofreader, publisher, conductor, and orchestra; and his orchestra has consisted not of strings and winds and percussion, but of the entire spectrum of sound.

What is more, he can dispatch his creation at once, to anyone who cares to hear it, anywhere in the world, as easily as an author can mail a book.

This, in a nutshell, is what electronic music is all about. For the first time in history, composers work directly on a medium, a concrete material, without the expensive and usually unwilling aid of interpreters. Thus they can establish the fixed and final form of their music on a simple storage device. This development has been termed, with good reason, The Revolt of the Composers; it brings to a close a 350-year-old epoch in which composers could give only approximate indications of their music on a manuscript, after which they had to go hat in hand to search for performers who would turn the symbols back into music.

This is the most staggering breakthrough in the art of music since the invention of counterpoint, and it may prove to be of even more far-reaching significance. Whether or not it can produce a Bach or Beethoven remains to be seen.

Paralleling this revolution is another one more difficult to sum up. The availability of electronic soundmaking machines has made composers impatient to wrench themselves out of the musical straitjacket of tonality, C Major scales, time signatures, violins, pianos, and everything else connected with what Western music lovers have long tended to regard as the divinely ordained requisites of musical creation. For the last fifty years, the era dominated by Stravinsky and Schönberg, composers have sought new roads and have avoided well-trodden paths. With his twelve-tone system of serial writing, Schönberg proposed a new language for music. Yet, as the English critic Peter Hayworth has pointed out, we can now view Stravinsky and Schönberg not as musical anarchists, but rather as men who tried desperately to hold the old order of music together, to keep the mainstream of music flowing *somewhere*. But "by postponing the break they inadvertently built up the pressure behind it."

That "pressure" came from the growing conviction among composers that their art should be allowed to encompass the entire range of aural possibilities. If a writer may use any word (or nonword), if a painter may draw any line or sign, why, they asked, must a composer be constricted by narrow, arbitrary, centuries-old assumptions defining the nature of "musical" sounds? A Bach fugue is, after all, only one particular organization of sound. There is an infinity of others.

And who is to say what is an acceptable sound? What about the intriguing, subtle sound discriminations of Eastern music? Why limit the composer to a few tones of the sound spectrum—roughly, the sounds produced on a piano? What about all the tones in between, the whole world of sound?

There is no definition of music that forbids a composer to use the sound of a steam shovel, or of an electronic machine, if he pleases.

You may agree with the description of music as "the art or science of arranging sounds in notes and rhythms to give a desired or pleasing pattern or effect," or you may prefer the definition favored by electronic composers, and set down by the eighteenth-century Polish philosopher Hoene Wronsky: *all* music, he decided, is "the corporealization of the intelligence that is in sound." Neither definition puts electronic music out of bounds.

The composer of electronic music is indeed searching for "the intelligence that is in sound." He is an artistic primitive and is feeling his way, groping for new forms of musical expression. Electronics is for him an immensely useful tool. The New Music, which includes electronic music, accepts any sound, produced by any means, as valid raw material to be worked artistically. Often the new composer substitutes the beauty of mathematical order for "inspiration," and it is not coincidental that Pierre Boulez, Yannis Xenakis, Karlheinz Stockhausen, and Milton Babbitt, formidable names in New Music, are all expert mathematicians.

The rupture in musical thinking began with Liszt, Wagner, and Debussy. The quest for the broadening of *sound materials* began as early as 1910 among the Italian musicians associated with the Futurist movement in painting. Around that time, the composer-pianist Ferruccio Busoni wrote enthusiastically about a crude progenitor of today's synthesizers, the Dynamophone. The twenties and the thirties also saw other exotically named electrical contraptions, such as the Trautonium and Theremin, all of which have wound up in the dustbin.

The attempts of composers to use these early inventions were frustrated for two reasons: first, the range of sounds the instruments could produce was limited; and then, it is one thing to be able to make weird sounds on an electronic device and quite another to get those sounds down in permanent form as you want them to remain forever. But as early as 1907 Busoni had postulated an electronic New Music; in 1922 Edgard Varèse, a pupil of Busoni whose influence on electronic music has been profound, wrote: "What we want is an instrument that will give us a continuous sound at any pitch. The composer and the electrician will have to labor together to get it." In 1937 John Cage, that Beckett clown and grand-Dada of us all, announced what was to become the credo of the New Music: "The use of noise to make music will continue and increase until we reach a music produced through the aid of electrical instruments that will make available for musical purposes any and all sounds that can be heard."

In the late 1940s, after the tape recorder had been developed in Germany during the war, the first "school" of tape music, *Musique concrète*, was founded in Paris. Pierre Schaeffer and others turned out what were essentially montages of random sounds gathered from traffic noises, bird calls, foghorns, the human voice, and whatever. These "junk sounds" were manipulated into a structural unity on tape.

At the same time, a group of musicians of West German Radio at Cologne rejected the *Musique concrète* method of working with prerecorded sound and experimented in the production of sounds by electronic means, rather than in their reproduction. Accomplished theoreticians and acousticians, they set out to design electronic equipment that would drive (activate) a loudspeaker or magnetize a tape to produce any sound at all. They followed the basic acoustical theorem that any tone consists of a combination of simpler partial tones called "sine" or "sinusoidal." These partial tones can be produced on a loudspeaker or a tape by an ordinary alternating electronic current, and they can be combined on tape in any way the programmer-composer desires.

In America, the electronic age in music was informally ushered in on October 28, 1952, at New York's Museum of Modern Art, in a concert led by Leopold Stokowski. (The vision and restless interest of Stokowski in electronic music developments has never been fully recognized, by the way. He can be considered today as the musical Marshall McLuhan.) A loudspeaker, mounted in a cabinet, was placed in the center of the bare stage, and there went a 350-year-old tradition. Music and musicmaking would never be the same again.

It is indeed significant that the electronic era in music—a cultural period as distinct and all-encompassing as the Renaissance or the Baroque era—coincides with the atomic age. The threat of thermonuclear holocaust, the dread reality of Us, has driven artists to a new sensibility and a search for a new tongue in which to utter the unutterable. The late forties and early fifties saw young composers everywhere seeking to discover and nourish the kinds of music that might express our transfigured age. And it was inevitable, as we shall see, that composers would seek an alliance with science and mathematics to depict the atomic age in sound.

Young musicians also have felt something of a revulsion against staid concert halls and performers in white ties in a world that produced the Bomb. Red-plush seats, white-maned conductors, and well-fed audiences waiting for a soothing musical massage—all the fixtures and symbols of the well-kept garden of music—one needed a confidence in Order and man's status to be a part of that establishment. Little wonder then that electronic music never sounds like a revelation of faith; it is more likely to be composed of creepy tones and glissando yelps and to sound absurd.

I do not suggest that when the Bomb fell, composers lined up to study voltage control and wave-forms rather than harmony and counterpoint. But Hiroshima does afford an authentic date from which to mark the death of one kind of twentieth-century music and the birth of another. The entire modern period in music, from 1900 through Schönberg, was cast overnight into the past, and all the violent arguments and theories about its authenticity were instantly made academic.

After 1945 young composers, especially those in Germany, found themselves without a valid past and embarked upon radical innovation; the Cologne studio was founded in 1950; Cage began his experiments in random music; Babbitt articulated a new theory of music that would have bemused Johann Sebastian Bach's "totally organized" music of mathematical exactness. The Bomb was, as the kids say in pop music, a New Sound. If a composer of the atomic age were to express the spirit of his time, he needed new tools, a new language, new sounds.

Since the end of World War II, composers in Europe and America have been engaged in a root-and-branch rethinking and restructuring of all ideas concerning music and artistic expression. (The revolution hit painting even harder, of course, and thus far with better-realized effects.) Music, abstract sound, was taken apart and reexamined in a way that had not been done since the seventeenth century when there had been another great upheaval in music; when monody—the melody-and-accompaniment style of writing—began to replace the earlier polyphonic style, in which all parts were held to be of equal importance (with none ranking simply as accompaniment). In the mid fifties, when magnetic tape became widely available, electronic music truly came into its own. The whole world of sound became the composer's oyster; any sound could be captured electronically, and innumerable new sounds could be created from electronic devices.

The cry went up at once that electronics was "dehumanizing" music. Actually, sound was being liberated, and the composer, for the first time in history, could create in sound precisely what he wished to create. It soon became clear that something radical had emerged. Perhaps it was a new art form altogether—an art of sounds rather than an art of related tones. And it is clear now that this art stemmed from the ideas of Busoni and Varèse more than from any other source. It has little to do with the grand tradition of music as it existed between Bach and Stravinsky.

Electronic music has been with us for a generation now, along with the new breed of musico-technocrats who think in the new language of frequencies, oscillators, and random generators; who no longer concern themselves with vague directions—*crescendo* or *diminuendo*—to faceless interpreters; but who control the *attack* and *decay* of a tone themselves, and with exquisite precision.

So how have they fared?

Most of their writing is abstract, in the sense that paintings by both Piet Mondriaan (controlled) and Jackson Pollock (random) are abstract. They are overwhelmed with the rank fecundity of the machine, to paraphrase Lewis Mumford. Just about every young composer of any worth in the world today (including those in Russia, where until recently they were a quasi-underground) has accepted the artistic validity of writing electronically. In America, young composers have plunged into electronic writing like happy ducks, because American composers have always suffered an inferiority complex vis-à-vis the awesome European composers, and because Americans are born tinkerers. New, smaller, more easily operated machines, of which the Moog Synthesizer of *Switched-On Bach* fame is the most successful, sell for a few thousand dollars. Colleges and universities all over America have ordered their Moogs, and the machine will soon be as taken for granted on campus as the chapel organ. Hundreds, perhaps thousands, of eager would-be composers are impatient to get started on their Moogs, and it is certain that in the next five or ten years we are going to be deluged with electronic music.

In the scathing words of the liveliest music critic of our times, Igor Stravinsky, "Electronic music . . . has moved into and conquered academe. The young musician takes his degree in computer technology now, and settles down with his Moog or his mini-synthesizer as routinely as in my day he would have taken it in counterpoint or harmony (see dictionary) and gone to work at the piano."

Nonetheless, the availability of synthesizers will bring about a profound change in how we learn about music, and in what we regard as valid sound materials for the art of music. At the new University of California's San Diego campus at La Jolla, the music department teaches music appreciation not with records and diagrams of music history, but with tape recorders and synthesizers, and students learn both the performing and creating of music as basic elements of the arts curriculum.

For a serious medium, electronic music has had an astonishing appeal for young audiences. They have embraced it, along with rock, as their very own. By contrast, the kids of the sixties rejected serious jazz with a firmness that dismayed the over thirty who, in their own adolescence, had regarded Louis Armstrong and Duke Ellington as the very embodiment of bold, youthful music. But the kids of the seventies are turned on by the same new kind of music that is captivating the avant-garde adults. They are buying electronic recordings by the armload. Their enthusiasm for *Switched-On Bach*—an unnerving reconstruction of Bach on a Moog—sent it right to the top of the charts.

Our youth have new ears. They are children of the unblinking Electronic Eye; in Susan Sontag's terms, they are cool, emotionally neutral, free from prejudice about what music should sound like, and utterly lacking in cultural presuppositions. They have been flipping television channels since infancy and have been exposed to a fantastic sound spectrum of folk, classical, pop, rock music, and commercials. Their nervous systems are extended to receive messages from every corner of McLuhan's global village, and they groove with electronic music, the true voice of our "technotronic" age. For the young people who sense that ours is an age with a rootless past, the nonpersonal sound of electronic music is as *right* as the neurotic, expressionistic music of Schönberg's *Pierrot Lunaire*" and Berg's *Wozzeck* were right for the Vienna of a half century ago, and as right as Aaron Copland's upbeat, affirmative Americana-in-music was for America in the forties.

Of course, the ready acceptance of electronic music by young audiences does not mean it is all good music. On the contrary, one cannot avoid the suspicion that many composers turned on to it because the music they wrote in the conventional medium was atrocious. But is electronic music, as many believe, nothing but a copout by composers who shrink from battling it out with Stravinsky and seek to evade the ghostly competition of the masters? Or is this "controlled chaos," this "wild clumps of jagged sound, blips, squeals," "tonal ruptures and utter boredom," "this aural nightmare," to use the words of various outraged critics, really here to stay?*

It seems that the answer is emphatically yes. Many refuse to believe it, especially the music lovers who adore Mozart and have just made their peace with Bartok, and now find themselves in sudden exile. But the aural nightmare, the abyss of total freedom, is upon us, just like the Bomb. Neither is simply going to go away.

Perhaps wistfully, we must realize that all the passionate arguments about the ideas of Hindemith, Bartok, Schönberg, Stravinsky, et al. are passé. The question that really haunts music today is whether the "electronic post-modern period" is just another phase in the history of music, or whether it marks the end of an entire epoch of what we have known as serious music.

Some composers regard the synthesizer as merely a fascinating new instrument, much as the new pianoforte, displacing the old harpsichord, fascinated Mozart and Beethoven. On the other hand, we are not lacking in prophets who refuse to accept electronic music as part of the orderly flow of the musical mainstream in the way Brahms succeeded Beethoven and Richard Strauss became the inheritor of Wagner. These prophets are convinced that the end has come.

I believe that it is too early to announce that an entire epoch has been brought to a close. For example, consider the fact that electronic

*It is not only the critics and listeners who are often enraged by electronic music. At a concert of John Cage's *Atlas Eclipticalis With Winter Music* (*Electronic Version*), scheduled by Leonard Bernstein and the New York Philharmonic in 1962, some of the Philharmonic's musicians smashed the electronic equipment.

music, instead of turning all new composers away from live performers, has encouraged them to write "live" with fresher and freer ideas of what is permissible.

Furthermore, the serious electronic composer is interested in *supplementing*, not supplanting other forms of music. As Edward Tatnall Canby observes, "The new area is showing itself every day more clearly [as] a new medium for the continuation of the ground principles of the past, which are inescapable whenever sound is to be organized into coherence."

We are in a period of experimentation and research. What is most impressive is the *medium* of electronic music itself. The new composers working in it, fumbling for keys to the marvels locked within, are like the primitive men who first discovered that a taut string vibrates and produces sound.

They are curious tinkerers, still learning just how many different noises can be produced by their versatile new instruments, and counting every bizarre new sound a triumph. Inevitably, the musical geniuses among them will emerge one day to make the new media their own. Some electronic technique now being perfected by one of our unknown contemporaries will produce a master's work and will thereafter bear his stamp. You can't forget Chopin when you play the piano; our orchestra is still Beethoven's, despite Wagner, Debussy, and Stravinsky. That historical process will be repeated.

We are at the beginning of a beginning. We shall have to give up most of our cherished notions as to what is off limits, unplug our ears, and learn to live, however unwillingly, with the New Music. After all, music lovers have been complaining about Ars Nova since the fourteenth century.

CONTENTS

"We have Sound Houses where we practise and demonstrate all Sounds and their generation. We have Harmonies . . . of Quarter sounds and lesser slides of Sounds. Diverse Instruments of Musick . . . Some sweeter than any you have, together with Bells and Rings that are dainty and Sweet.

Francis Bacon, THE NEW ATLANTIS, 1627

TOWARD A MUSIC THAT WILL REALLY SING
The old masters could sing but lacked the teachings of science to supplement those of art—a noble union, which enables moving melody and powerful harmony to be at one. . . . What might we not accomplish if we discovered the physical laws in virtue of which—mark this well—we bring together in proportions as yet unknown the ethereal substance in the air and thereby not only produce music but also perceive the phenomena of light, vegetation, and life itself! Don't you see! Those laws would equip the composer with new powers by making possible instruments far superior to those we have, and perhaps result in a grander harmony than that which governs our present music. . . . Composers have so far worked with a substance they did not understand.

Honoré de Balzac, GAMBARA
(translated by Jacques Barzun)

I want to be as though newborn, knowing nothing, absolutely nothing, about Europe . . . to be almost primitive.

Paul Klee

Music was born free, and to win freedom is its destiny.

Ferruccio Busoni

Our musical alphabet must be enriched. Speed and synthesis are characteristic of our epoch. We need twentieth century instruments to help us realize these in music. . . . To reveal a new world is the function of creation in all the arts.

Edgard Varèse

It may well be—I take it upon myself to predict it—that the apotheosis of the machine age will demand a subtler tool than the tempered scale, capable of setting down arrangements of sounds hitherto neglected or unheard.

Le Corbusier

PART ONE

The Breakup of the Harmonic Era

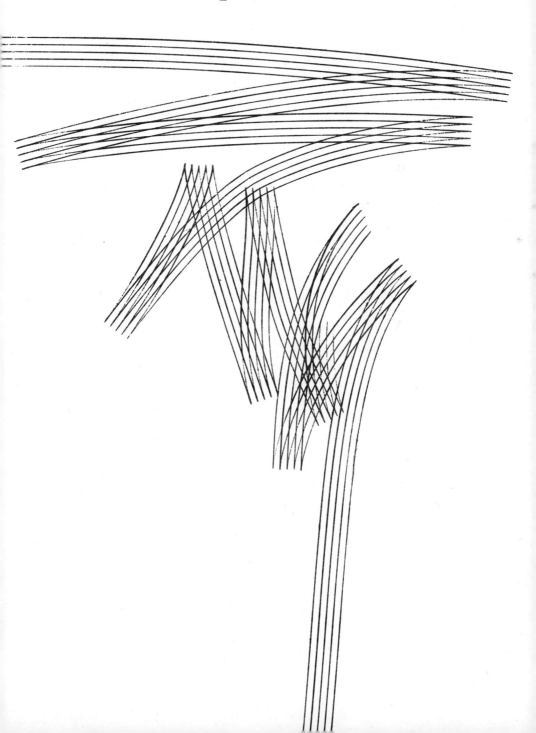

CHAPTER I

The First Revolution: 1900

Music has lost the mode of gravity and virtue, and has almost fallen to baseness.

Boethius, Roman philosopher, c. 475–525

Music is always in danger of falling apart.

Aaron Copland, 1962

THE ALMOST RIOTOUS EVENTS OF TWENTIETH-CENTURY MUSIC occurred in two great waves. The first, beginning shortly after 1900, involved the gradual annihilation of tonality. For centuries that particular system of organizing tones had been considered almost a preordained, God-given structure of arranging harmony and tonal relationships. No more. Wagner and Debussy had launched the attack; the composers who followed them at the turn of the century and after, finished the battle. Erik Satie, Busoni, Stravinsky, Schönberg, Anton von Webern, Alexander Scriabin, Varèse—these were the great revolutionaries.

The second revolution, a graver and more far-reaching one, was an outgrowth of the first. It took place after World War II. For the young composers who emerged at this time—Yannis Xenakis, Karlheinz Stockhausen, Pierre Boulez, John Cage, et al.—the old battle cries of harmony versus dissonance and tonality versus atonality were irrelevant. For them the old barriers were down, the old categories demolished. With great daring, they conceived a new music that knew no boundaries, no formal categories. For the new composers, as for the new painters and the new playwrights, all materials were acceptable and any kind of statement was possible. They knew that the Harmonic Era was dying, and that they themselves were ushering in a new era of sound, an entirely new aesthetic of music.

To understand the more recent of these revolutions in music, it is first necessary to examine the one that preceded it. The year 1900 can be seen in retrospect as the beginning not only of a new century but also of a distinctly new cultural era, one as clearly definable and as all-embracing as the Gothic period or the Renaissance. Between 1900 and 1913 alone, the world had absorbed the implications of Max Planck's quantum theory, Freud's *Interpretation of Dreams*, the Wright brothers' first powered flight, Einstein's theory of relativity, the first motion picture theater, Henry Ford's Model T, and Neils Bohr's theory of atomic structure.

Artists were aware that a new technological universe was emerging and that new work in the old traditional forms was pointless. They also knew that the great humanist tradition, which implied a confidence in a world order and man's dignity, was no longer valid. Between 1900 and 1913, Pablo Picasso and Georges Braque invented Cubism, thereby exploding a visual arts tradition that went back to Giotto; Vasili Kandinsky painted his first nonrepresentational pictures; James Joyce completed *Dubliners*; Frank Lloyd Wright put the finishing touches on his Robie house; Ezra Pound arrived in Italy; and Marcel Proust published the first section of *Remembrance of Things Past*.

In music, the Original Dixieland Jazz Band was formed and Stravinsky stirred up a riot in Paris with his ballet *The Rite of Spring*. Schönberg caused an upheaval by ceasing to write traditional tonal music and searching for a new tonal order. (He was to name it "the method of composing with twelve tones," and it is now commonly known as the twelve-tone technique, or dodecaphony.)

Schönberg was not alone in seeking a new method of composing; almost all composers after 1900 believed they were witnessing the decay of tonal music, the end of the line. Richard Strauss spoke of himself and his contemporaries as "triflers who had something to say in the last chapter." Arthur Honegger wrote, "The collapse of music is obvious . . . nothing is to be gained from resisting it." Paul Hindemith, Bela Bartok, and Sergei Prokofiev expressed grave doubts that music as they knew it—within the bounds of tonality, written in a key system, and employing major or minor scales—could survive.

What had gone wrong? The fact was that the awesome figures

from Bach through Wagner had exploited everything. The mine was exhausted, and composers were finding it more and more difficult to bring up new nuggets from the overworked lode.

Everything had been said in tonal music; everything had been tried. The noble structure of harmonic music that had triumphed from Haydn through Mahler, that magnificent expression of Western thought and humanism, had simply exhausted its possibilities. Music began to collapse not *because* of new ideas, but because new ideas no longer seemed possible within the old harmonic framework. As Roy McMullen has admirably put it, "Music as it was conceived in the Occident was at one time an immense continent of potentialities; but an army, officered by geniuses in each generation, moved across it, and by the close of the 19th century just about everything had been explored that seemed worth exploring. There they were—twelve semi-tones within the octave span, twelve seven-toned scales in the major mode and twelve in the minor, and a small number of basic types of chords, rhythms, and forms. . . . Evidence that the exploration was nearly complete can be seen in the fact that most of the traditional instruments had stopped evolving around 1850. Their makers were no longer being challenged by the discoveries of composers."*

The basic crisis was in tonality, which had evolved in the seventeenth century as a system of seven-tone notes in which one note is the focal point of a tonic key. The function of each of the other notes in this scale is determined by its relationship to that key. For several hundred years the seven-tone scale had been the dominant language of Western music. It was an artificial, man-devised language, of course, not a natural law; its grammar sounds "natural" to Western ears, but tonal music is no more "natural" than are Hindu Ragas or Gregorian chants. Each is a devised language for organizing musical sounds, precisely as English or Swahili is a language for organizing verbal sounds.

The revolution centered chiefly on harmony—that is, the system of musical principles concerned with the structure of chords (several notes sounded together) and the relationship between these chords, which usually support a melody. In music of the "classical age" har-

*Roy McMullen, *Art, Affluence, and Alienation* (New York: Frederick A. Praeger, Inc., 1968), p. 49.

mony forms patterns that seem to follow logically, because they are based on a regular framework in which some notes are more closely related than others. But during the past century, this framework gradually has been stretched or distorted to a point where it is drastically weakened or not there at all.

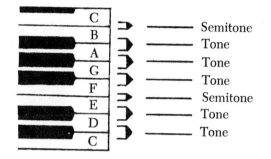

The diatonic scale

To put the matter more simply, if one plays on the piano all twelve notes, black and white, from, for instance, C to C, the result is called the *chromatic scale*. Out of these twelve notes a certain seven produce the scale that children (up to our time) first sing or play (the eighth note is a repetition of the first, higher up). These seven notes are called the *diatonic scale*, and this grouping of notes is the framework of the music of the classical masters—Bach, Haydn, Mozart, Beethoven, Schubert—and indeed of most composers before World War II.

The diatonic scale consists of a fixed pattern of intervals. (In the *major* scale it is tone, tone, semitone, tone, tone, tone, semitone; in the *minor* scale the semitones occur at different points on the scale.) Different keys are produced by starting on different notes, but the pattern remains the same. The starting (or key) note is always the chief "center of gravity": it is the note on which the music most naturally comes to rest. The pull exercised by the keynote is called *tonality* (music in which it is lacking is called *atonal*).

This seven-note scale produces the feeling of a pattern to which the other five notes of the chromatic scale do not "belong." The classical composers based their music firmly on it. But sometimes they used "chromatic" notes outside the diatonic scale, either structurally, to move from one key to another (modulation); or emotionally, to create a special effect—usually of unrest, movement or tension.

It was in this use of "chromatic unrest" that the crack in the entire system of tonality first appeared.

First, the Romanticists after Beethoven began distorting harmony to achieve coloristic and emotional effects. Later, by deliberately avoiding the keystones of traditional tonality—tonics (harmony based on the first note of the scale) and dominants (harmony based on the fifth note)—several early modernists, including Wagner, Debussy, Scriabin, and Charles Ives, challenged the established language of music. They and their successors evolved a more flexible music, one in which all notes in any combination could be regarded as viable material. With this stunning change, musical sounds that theretofore had been regarded as "dissonant" became, in theory, perfectly consonant in the tonal language—even if the ears of most listeners could not accept them. Influenced by these pioneers, nearly all our contemporary composers have explored the enlarged aural landscape. Thus was created a music vastly changed from traditional concepts, a music that enlarges our sense of what music *is*.

CHAPTER II

The Nineteenth-Century
Romantic Upheaval

A SYNOPTIC VIEW OF MUSIC SINCE BEETHOVEN MAY HELP TO CLARIFY what composers of today mean when they say that harmonic music has reached the end of the line.

The Romanticist idea—a counterculture, in effect—swept across Europe in the early decades of the nineteenth century. In the words of Marie d'Agoult, the famous mistress of Franz Liszt, the idea caught up "young people who deplored the increasing drabness and uniformity of existence, who preferred freedom to order, adventure to conformity, and imagination to correctness." The Romanticists called their movement "individualism, the liberation of human personality," and romantic composers sought liberation from traditional modes of harmony and tonality. In their world, music and poetry formed an intimate union, and music and painting drew closer as well. Color became a prominent aspect of Romantic music. A sensitive, refined new harmony, one of the main achievements of the Romanticists, contributed to the art of music an intensity and richness that it had never before known. But eventually, Romantic techniques undermined the old "classical" harmonic framework. From Schubert's time on, there was an increasing use of chromaticism, especially by Romantic composers with literary interests.

SCHUBERT

Franz Schubert (1797–1828) was a contemporary of Beethoven, yet he modulated (changed key) within his compositions more often than Beethoven did or than Haydn and Mozart had done. Consequently, he introduced chromatic notes for structural reasons with much more frequency. His great romantic songs were set to turbulent romantic poetry that demanded intense musical feelings; chromatic notes became for Schubert a dramatic tool employed for emotional effects. Schubert conquers us with his lyricism and the unexpectedness of his modulations.

CHOPIN

The tendency to use chromaticism for emotional effect was developed powerfully after Schubert by most romantic composers, particularly by Frederic Chopin (1810–1849). Romantic harmony *was* chromatic harmony. For Chopin it was a marvelous tool with which to exploit the new musical conceptions of light and shade, of fine gradations between lighter and darker colors—very new and radical ideas indeed in his day. He sought in his music those marvelous nuances of color that were also sought by Romantic French painters, especially Eugène Delacroix, his intimate friend. In the works of Gluck, Haydn, Mozart, and Beethoven, harmony gave color to the grand musical design but only in the sense of coloration; to them, melodic design was far more important. To Chopin, however, the concept of color as an independent, primary factor in music—was an important tool; as a result, he delineated a new tonal landscape of luminous shadows. Tonality for him was a technique of construction. The essence of Chopin's romantic music is melody conceived in terms of color, of constantly changing color, of color in motion and flow. He did not ignore or deny the constructive function of tonality, but his passionate delight was to veil or mask tonality, thus infusing it with those marvelously delicate nuances of color for which he stands alone and supreme. But when the idea of color became an indispensable factor in Romantic music, there was a price to be paid, for the frequent use of chromatic progressions *lessened* the distinction between major and minor tonalities—the very structure upon which tonal music was built.

BERLIOZ

Théophile Gautier remarked that the Romantic movement in France was wrapped up in a painter, a poet, and a composer—Eugène Delacroix, Victor Hugo, and Hector Berlioz (1803–1869). One of Berlioz' chief contributions to Romantic music was in the exploration of what is called program music. The aim of program music is to extend the possibilities of musical expression by interpreting musically a poem or a work of fiction. The idea was not exactly new, but the manner in which Berlioz developed program music was marvelously new.

As Jacques Barzun has written in *Berlioz and the Romantic Century*, "Unlike most of his contemporaries, Berlioz felt that true harmony should be a resultant of all the musical forces at work—not melody or structure alone, but rhythm, expression, dynamics, and most significantly timbre."

Berlioz himself put the matter clearly in his own vivid prose: "When I think of this realm of chords which scholastic prejudice has kept untouched to this day and since my emancipation [from the Conservatoire] I regard as my own domain, I rush forward in a kind of frenzy to explore it."

LISZT

The inclination to use chromaticism for romantic emotional effects was continued by Robert Schumann and Berlioz. Franz Liszt (1811–1886) sharply propelled the chromatic experiment onward. In his dazzling, experimental use of harmony, Liszt explored chordal combinations that foreshadowed atonality long before Wagner—who was deeply influenced by Liszt—began his own assault on the harmonic structure.

Liszt's works for piano, and above all his symphonic poems, were drenched in Romanticism. In these compositions Liszt abandoned most of the structural procedures of the classical symphonic form to seek new methods whereby music could follow a literary text. In his last period, he wrote bare, lean music that strongly hinted at the Impressionism of Debussy and the dissonances of Wagner which were to come later. In his symphonic poems, he pioneered the idea of allying music to poetry and painting with the aim of expressing in musical terms an originally extra-musical idea. This approach was later taken over by Richard Strauss in his own symphonic poems. With his wonderful sense of sound and color, Liszt enriched the sensitive new chromatic harmony pioneered by Chopin, and passed on to Wagner an admirable tool, which, as used in the opera *Tristan und*

Isolde, shook the very foundations of the tonal system. (Those famous iconoclastic opening chords of the opera, it is often argued, were taken over *in toto* by Wagner from a song of Franz Liszt.)

WAGNER

Richard Wagner (1813–1883) was a true revolutionary; by subordinating music to words, he gave the *coup de grâce* to the concept of form; he employed constant modulation to hold the listener's attention. Using ever freer harmony as a propelling force, he could accent or expose the drama he wished to evoke. Thus he toppled the very idea of tonality and brought chromaticism to its greatest heights.

Tristan und Isolde was the climactic work of Romanticism, and it marked the break from standard tonality. The chords in the opera are built with a harmonic vagueness that amounted to a virtual suspension of the use of a tonal home base as it was then understood.

Harmonically, *Tristan* is built upon the defeat of expectation; the listener expects that a given musical sound will lead to a predictable other, but Wagner, using chromatic freedom (but not atonality), confounds him.

Wagner's passionate, highly charged emotional music used chromaticism that was far more intense and systematic than it had ever been before. His use of notes that do not belong to the diatonic scale took his music to the brink of the agreed harmonic structure. *Tristan* approached the brink of atonality, and therefore marks the beginning of the great crisis in diatonic music; if Wagner had ventured any further, he would have demonstrated the expendability of the diatonic scale as a foundation of harmony.

However, the note of reference was still present in *Tristan*; one step remained to be taken—to detach the twelve notes of the chromatic scale from all bases of references, make them independent of the principle of tonality, and disregard the difference between those sounds "belonging" to the harmony and those foreign to it. This, as the composers themselves well knew, would bring music to the gravest crisis it had known in centuries. That is, to consider the twelve tones *as equal in value* would hurl music into a new world of sound with no further anchoring relationship to the tonal world that had served as the basis for musical rhetoric since the sixteenth century. The man who was to take this final step was Schönberg.

BRAHMS

The crisis brought on by Wagner was met with four-square resistance by many composers, above all by Johannes Brahms (1833–1897). Passionately convinced that Romantic music had to be counteracted, he sounded an eloquent recall to order. As a young man, he easily could have cast his lot with the revolutionary Liszt-Wagner party; but his ideals led him in another direction. In contrast to most Romantic composers, he never composed an opera or a symphonic poem, and, except in his songs, was not swayed by nonmusical influences.

In 1860, Brahms, along with some other musicians, signed a famous manifesto against "The Music of the Future," as the Liszt-Wagner school was called. As a result, German music was divided into two hostile camps for about thirty years. As a creative genius who would ultimately enjoy universal fame, Brahms was the leading spirit among those who regarded themselves as a countercurrent to the "Music of the Future." The history of German music in the second half of the nineteenth century may be summed up under two headings: Wagner and Brahms.

Music After Wagner

Despite the implacable opposition to Wagner of such conservatives as Brahms, after Wagner's death in 1883 most composers went on exploiting and extending his harmonic innovations more and more. Richard Strauss, Mahler, Debussy, Scriabin, and Bartok, to name only a few, come to mind in this connection. To the first post-Wagnerian generation of listeners, an increasing range of harmonic freedom was becoming acceptable. Thus the burning question: if any succession of chords or note tones is possible, why should one be preferable to another? With the posing of that insidious question, the whole structure of tonal order—in which harmonic exceptions make their effect precisely because they are exceptions—rapidly deteriorated.

DEBUSSY

Claude Debussy (1862–1918), by far the greatest French composer after Berlioz, was influenced by Chopin, Wagner, and the Russian nationalists—in particular, Modest Moussorgsky—in his approach to vocal writing and in his use of modal scales. He developed the use of the whole-tone scale. From Oriental music, which he loved, he borrowed yet another scale, the pentatonic (five-note). By personal experimentation with these nondiatonic scales, he ventured successfully into new harmonic territory without threatening the whole harmonic convention, as Schönberg was to do a few years later.

Twentieth-century music, as a generic term of reference, begins where Debussy ends. His impressionistic methods broke the grip of German Romanticism that had dominated nineteenth-century music, and were later absorbed into the international musical language as it moved on to new resources. Debussy was one of the greatest revolutionists in the entire history of music, because, as Aaron Copland once remarked, he was the first European composer in a long while to judge harmony by ear instead of by the rules.

"What rule do you follow?" he was asked. "*Mon plaisir!*" Debussy answered.

SATIE

If the rebellion against Wagnerian Romanticism that characterized musical activity in Paris during the first decades of our century could be symbolized by a single name, that name would be Erik Satie (1866–1925). His was the figure that *Les Six* (Darius Milhaud, Francis Poulenc, Arthur Honegger, Georges Auric, Louis Durey, and Germaine Tailleferre) rallied around, and his firm conviction that the idea of music as High Art needed deflation influenced such composers as Debussy and Ravel, and, perhaps more powerfully, Poulenc and Virgil Thompson.

A bizarre and dadaesque figure, Satie possessed a dry, mordant sense of irony that was the equivalent of that expressed in painting by his contemporary Toulouse-Lautrec. He often constructed deliberately absurd trivia pieces whose point is in their titles: *Disagreeable Impressions, Three Pieces in the Form of a Pear,* and so on. Satie was not greatly talented musically, but he had an immediate influence. Today he looms even larger and is more popular than ever; John Cage, to name but one New Music composer, adores him.

Satie is a spiritual godfather of today's avant-garde composers, and not only for his celebration of the absurd. He was also one of the first to use disconnected objectified sound—abstractly, quite divorced from tonal form and development. His piece *Vexations* demonstrates how up-to-the-minute his approach to music remains. Filling a single sheet of music, the piece can be played in eighty seconds. At the top of the sheet, Satie blithely noted, "To be played 840 times." The instruction was followed exactly when *Vexations* was first performed, in New York in 1963, by John Cage and nine fellow pianists.

SCRIABIN

Alexander Scriabin (1872–1915) is enjoying a small boom today. Like Schönberg, he took the harmony of Wagner's *Tristan* as his point of departure. A declared visionary, he wrote exotic, heady music which appeals to the sense rather than to the intellect—which may account for the contemporary interest in him.

A highly original composer whose ideas were more innovative than his actual achievement, Scriabin thought that music should be used as a means to propogate theosophic concepts. He envisioned music incorporated in a new religion, and indeed his mysticism may be one reason for the new interest in his music, for he believed in the "magic power" of music. He created a new esoteric harmony and used it in his works. He remains a curious figure; a composer of music of passionate lyricism and orgiastic turbulence, all combined with a strange mysticism and fatalism as well as a pantheistic religious ecstasy. (Scriabin's *Le Poème de l'Extase* was choreographed especially for Dame Margot Fonteyn in 1971. One ballet critic described the music as "nerve-tingling, sultry, perverse in its alternating currents of tonality and dissonance.")

STRAVINSKY

Igor Stravinsky (1882–1971) was a pupil of Nikolai Rimsky-Korsakov, and Russian nationalistic traits are much in evidence in his early music. He was also deeply influenced by Debussy. He gradually discarded Russian influences after leaving that country in 1914. As Picasso did in painting, he launched a variety of manners as proposed starting points for his music. There is not one Stravinsky style; there are ten. Also like Picasso (and Bach and Handel), Stravinsky took what he needed wherever he found it, on the grounds that the art of his predecessors is universal property.

In Stravinsky more than in any other modern master between the two world wars, we hear plainly the unrest, instability, and experimentalism that were later to become rampant in music after World War II. Unlike his great contemporary Schönberg, he never forgets the natural demands of the ear; he is never indifferent to acoustic effect, to sound itself.

With *The Rite of Spring*, Stravinsky broke loose from the past; the rhythmic scheme is extremely fluid, the orchestra at times becomes a huge percussive instrument, and both melody and harmony are subordinated to a chaotic surge of rhythm and exultant sound. No other music of our century caused the uproar that *The Rite* did at its premiere in 1913. It was like a sudden explosion, which, without warning, almost crumbled the whole edifice of music as it had been conceived before that time. *The Rite* is one of music's great trailblazing works, like the first operas and Beethoven's *Eroica* Symphony.

Stravinsky's great contribution is not in harmony, but in rhythm. He restored rhythm to its original meaning. Heartbeats, breathing, a naturally flowing tempo, work and dance motions—these are the first beats of life and the root of music. Stravinsky reinstated the primary function of rhythm and made it the thread of his musical fabric. Paradoxically, Stravinsky is viewed today as a great conservative as well as a revolutionary; the work of his neoclassicist period (which he later abandoned) implies that composers may exploit the new tonal freedom without yielding traditional ways and classical structures such as the sonata and the symphony.

SCHÖNBERG

The man who remorselessly brought the harmonic crisis to a head was Arnold Schönberg (1874–1951). He inherited a musical language on the brink of disintegration and created nothing less than an entirely new one—a revolutionary reordering of tonal possibilities.

After composing several extraordinary and most beautiful expressionist works between 1908 and 1912, Schönberg began searching for a radically new tonal scheme to replace the old one. In the 1920s he revealed his new method, referring to it as the "method of composing with twelve tones."

With Schönberg's twelve-tone equal-tempered scale, all the black as well as the white notes (to put the matter roughly in terms of the piano keyboard) are employed equally, without the special "more important" or "less important" significances assigned to certain notes by traditional tonality. He repudiated the all-importance of the tonic tone and declared the equal importance of the chromatic scale. Thus, in Schönberg's composing method, the twelve notes are related only to one another, and not, as in diatonic harmony, always to a keynote. He declared, "What we establish is the law. Earlier, when one wrote in C major, one also felt 'tied' to it; otherwise the result was a mess. One was obliged to return to the tonic; one was tied to the nature of the scale. Now we base our invention on a scale that has not seven notes but 12 and moreover in a particular order." It is this particular order, the row or "series" (hence the name *serialism*), of tones that determines the structure of the entire work. He also laid down basic tenets as to how the row may be presented.

Ironically, considering his reputation as the bogeyman of twentieth-century music, Schönberg aimed to revitalize tradition and considered himself the true twentieth-century classicist. "There is nothing I wish for more earnestly (if I wish for anything at all)," he wrote to the conductor Hans Rosbaud in 1947, "than to be regarded as a superior sort of Tchaikowsky ... or at the very most that my melodies should be known and whistled."

WEBERN

Two disciples of Schönberg who were deeply involved in the harmonic crisis sought a way out through serialism: Anton von Webern (1883–1945) and Alban Berg (1885–1935). Both Austrians, they were Schönberg's two greatest pupils. Berg, essentially an eclectic lyricist, sought to blend classical forms with serial technique. Webern was a far more radical figure; when Schönberg discovered how to organize atonal music by an arbitrarily arranged series of the twelve chromatic tones, Webern extended the serial principle to such areas as rhythm and dynamics.

As Stravinsky remarked, "Webern is the discoverer of a new musical distance between the musical object and ourselves and therefore of a new measure of musical time." Together with Varèse, Webern is a pivotal figure in the shift from the harmonic age to the age of sound. In many areas he took Schönberg's innovations and carried them to logical extremes. While Schönberg dissolved traditional tonality but continued to work with late Romantic forms, Webern dissolved the forms as well. He obliterated vertical harmonies, broke up melodies into one- or two-note fragments for each instrument, and swept away all sense of development and climax. "Once stated," he said, "a theme has expressed all it has to say."

Webern strived toward the isolation of *the single musical event*, dissociated from adjacent events. His music is concise and spare— a few notes set forth over a very short period of time. Such was the understated economy of his scores that his life's work amounts to a bare three hours of playing time. Most of his compositions take less than ten minutes each to perform, and he turned out works containing as much silence as music.

He is almost entirely free from the Romanticism that saturates Schönberg and Berg. By exalting the "isolated, individual event" he invented a new concept of expressive form. With this postulation he approached a state of total abstraction in which a piece would unfold entirely in accordance with the rules invented for it in advance by the composer, much as a computer responds to its mathematical programming.

Webern's new vocabulary has passed into the modern musical language to such an extent that it sometimes sounds like a lexicon of contemporary clichés: jagged leaps of melody, pointillistic instrumental textures, drily intellectual twelve-tone patterns. On the other hand, his musical vocabulary underlines qualities in his compositions that have remained fresh and inimitable to this day: delicacy, astringent lyricism, cold purity of craftsmanship.

BARTOK

A very great composer indeed, Bela Bartok (1881–1945) was not a revolutionary. Nevertheless, he stands with Stravinsky, Schönberg, and Varèse as a titan of the century and is included in this list to round out the picture.

A Hungarian, Bartok was the most important of twentieth-century nationalistic composers. Through the influence of Liszt and Debussy, superimposed on that of Eastern European folk music, whose harmonic and rhythmic possibilities he explored to the utmost, he forged an utterly original idiom. For a brief time, Bartok's style was extremely influential with the generation that followed him, but at the present moment it has waned in favor of his bolder predecessors. Nevertheless, Bartok's place remains secure; an intensely Hungarian and yet universal artist.

MESSIAEN

Olivier Messiaen (born 1908) is one of the two or three most important composers of his generation in Europe. A devout Catholic and a modern medievalist, he expresses his personal mysticism through his great static structures, his use of serialism, his adaptation of Eastern rhythmic modes, and his use of bird calls in his music. Messiaen's influence as a teacher has been enormous, for his pupils include, among many others, Boulez and Stockhausen. He and Varèse are the fathers of postwar avant-garde music in Europe. Messiaen was one of the first European musicians to teach twelve-tone technique, yet he himself was entirely free of the stern orthodoxies of the Schönberg-Webern school. For three decades he has both enthralled and antagonized audiences with his innovations in serialization, his unorthodox rhythms, and his attempts to give musical expression to the sounds of nature. An expert musical ornithologist, his bird songs have a most authentic quality. Everything under the sun can be heard in Messiaen —he is a "one-world" composer if there ever was one, convinced that all musical styles of all peoples are valid raw material. And that is the one irresistible idea among young composers today.

CHAPTER III

The American Experimental Tradition

THERE IS AN AMERICAN MUSICAL TRADITION THAT GOES BACK TO the Revolution and the composers Benjamin Franklin and William Billings. But until well into this century, almost every piece of music written in America followed strictly European—primarily German— antecedents. Charles Ives and Carl Ruggles, however, launched a radical movement that was largely indifferent to the European past and sought to incorporate styles from other cultures, including the primitive.

Horatio Parker's oratorio *Hora Novissima*, composed in 1893 and hailed as the great American masterpiece (at last!)—worthy of comparison with European music—pedantically followed European convention. On the other hand, the music of Parker's pupil, Charles Ives, commingled symphony with band music, Beethoven with Stephen Foster, and ragtime with his own abstract sound structures. Since Ives, there has been a remarkable group of native American composers— eccentrics, musical tinkerers, visionaries, some men of genius—who followed their own curious byways, instead of coursing along with the European musical tastes of their day.

The modern American experimentalists were fascinated with sound—sound itself. Restlessly searching for novel ways of using ordinary instruments, they also pioneered in the invention of new instruments, including electronic ones. They loved Oriental and primitive music and the Eastern metaphysical approach to the art. They represented the tinkering, pioneering tradition that had nurtured their forebears in the New World, and felt in their bones that continued imitation of imported German or French musical modes was mere subservience.

American experimentalists were anything but influential in their own day—except upon young radicals. They were largely isolated creative talents ignored by American Establishment composers who were dominated by the European conservatory tradition and outlook. The importance of Charles Ives, for example, has only very recently been recognized. Today, the radical experimental tradition, fierce as ever, persists through such admirable outlaws as Lou Harrison and Harry Partch, whose names are known only to a comparative handful of music lovers. The most famous of our present experimentalists, of course, is John Cage, who seems miraculously to have thrust all the radical ideas and attitudes into the public spotlight.

IVES

Charles Ives (1874–1954) was the first American composer to stand essentially apart from the great European tradition. A resourceful experimenter, he anticipated just about every important musical idea of the last half century. Astonishing ideas current today were perfectly natural to this remarkable iconoclast long before Schönberg and Stravinsky (to say nothing of Stockhausen and company) had stumbled upon them. He wrote what may be termed proto-serial and chance music before those terms had been coined; at various times he used tone clusters, polytempi, and free-form music. Amazingly, he also used a technique that is heralded as a dazzling innovation of contemporary composers: music that can be realized in a multiplicity of ways. He invented a new musical idiom that does not hesitate to employ tonality, atonality, and deliberate noise—the new world of *sound*. He cheerfully combined all known compositional techniques, from four-part elementary harmony to a partial use of the twelve-tone system. He also used microtones and double orchestras.

For long decades a prophet without recognition, let alone honor, Ives had the public face of a successful insurance executive whose hobby was composing. But this legendary "amateur" was nothing of the kind; he was a thoroughly trained musician and one of the most daring and original composers that ever lived. He is both the Emerson and Thoreau of American music. His music admittedly has an American rawness about it; but working alone, without a public, his works going unperformed, Ives embraced both the heritage and the potential future of American music.

Schönberg wrote, "There is a great man living in this country— a composer. He has solved the problem of how to preserve one's self and to learn. He responds to negligence by contempt. He is not forced to accept praise or blame. His name is Ives."

RUGGLES

Born in 1876, Carl Ruggles is in 1971 the oldest living American composer. Like Ives, Ruggles wants to create a new world of sound, traveling beyond the boundaries set up by the Western European tradition. He also clearly follows his close friend Ives as the classic type of rugged, isolated American individualist. (At ninety Ruggles was still living in his New England home, painting and composing.)

His works are short but immensely powerful, and suggest both the American wilderness and the austerities of Puritan New England. A self-trained composer, he writes music that is admittedly difficult, but of a clear, open resonance. His style is neither eclectic nor profuse. Throughout his long lifetime he has written and rewritten only a handful of works, all in a consistent style.

Wilfred Mellers has written of Ruggles, "He sought freedom—from tonal bondage, from the harmonic strait jacket, from conventional repetitions, from anything that sullied the immediacy and purity of experience—even more remorselessly than Schönberg."

Ruggles' voice is peculiarly American in both its surprising harshness and the sweep of its lyricism.

COWELL

In the 1920s and thirties Henry Cowell (1897–1965) was the most direct representative of the Ives tradition, and in a sense a link between Ives and the new avant-garde composers. This fact alone makes him a crucial figure in the development of truly native American music.

Like the music of Ives, his works abandon the nineteenth-century American custom of imitating European models. His music—again, like Ives's—mingles and juxtaposes both complex and appealingly simple elements. Cowell was one of the first composers of our age to be seriously concerned with the vast treasure of the primitive music and folklore of all peoples. A restless experimenter with new means of sound production, he attracted much attention during the twenties with his "tone clusters" on the piano. Cowell devised a method of achieving sonorous, unearthly sounds by pressing down a number of keys with his palm or forearm. Tone clusters are not a gimmick but an intriguing technique that involves melody and harmony, as well as sound-colors. Today, of course, Cowell's once outrageous outlook and experiments are taken for granted among the even more outrageous effects of the New Music.

Cowell had the idea of transforming the piano into a percussive stringed instrument by beating, muting, or sweeping the strings, years before John Cage invented his "Prepared Piano." Cowell was also co-inventor with Leon Theremin of the rhythmicon (see Chronology of Electronic Music, p. 71). The pioneering work of Henry Cowell is still to be fully appreciated by present-day composers, many of whom are barely aware of his name. His booklet, *New Music Resources,* was prophetic; *New Music* and *New Music Quarterly Recordings,* which he founded, brought out most of the composers of his era, including Varèse, Ruggles, and many others.

ANTHEIL

The 1920s was a period of heady exploration in all the arts, including music. George Antheil (1900–1959) achieved fame as a leader of the new young men who sought to create new ideas, new ways of organizing sound. The self-styled "bad boy of music," he began his career as "an anti-romantic, anti-expressive, coldly mechanistic esthete." Antheil's most notorious piece was the sensational "Ballet Mécanique" (1924), which created a furor in Paris and New York. It was scored originally for eight pianos, a pianola, and an airplane propeller. For the New York performance, Antheil doubled the number of pianos, and threw in anvils, bells, automobile horns, and buzzers. The musical worth of Antheil's compositions was not remarkable, but he deserves a footnote as one of the first American composers to coolly use whatever sounds he wished to express the machine age.

BRANT

The highly inventive Canadian composer, Henry Brant (born 1913), is the world's foremost experimenter in the field of antiphonal music—that is, music in which separate groups of performers are placed at some distance from one another so that the sounds come to the listener from several different directions. It is a concept that became more familiar to the general public with the increased interest in stereophonic recordings, which similarly depend for their effect on sounds being heard from different directions. Brant's sometimes absorbing efforts in "directional music" clearly antedate the work of Stockhausen and other experimenters.

HOVANESS

A composer of highly enjoyable music that strives to combine East and West, Alan Hovaness (born 1911) has immersed himself fully in Eastern music, especially that of Armenia, the land of his ancestry. His unique music sometimes sounds medieval, sometimes like pre-Christian art. His poetic music is scored for startling combinations and severely drawn forms, and is often based on Near Eastern melodic traditions. He is an exotic rather than an experimentalist, but he has not hesitated to speak to Caesar in Caesar's tongue: his seventeenth symphony, written for the American Metallurgical Congress, used entirely metallic instruments.

A Japanese critic wrote that Hovaness's compositions are "like Japanese scrolls, as they are rolled out, they reveal new images and their message bit by bit. Western classical music is in comparison like a photographic print."

PARTCH

One of the most challenging and yet generally ignored figures in American music today is Harry Partch (born 1901). As a musical outlaw usually working in isolation, he has had to wait many years for the times to catch up to his ideas. For many devoted listeners (mostly young people) that time has most decisively arrived today. Ironically, Partch is better known and respected in Europe than at home.

Along with Cage, he is a symbol of the rebel in music, a role filled by Varèse until his death in 1965. And like Varèse, but without his sheer genius, Partch has rejected ordinary scales and conventional instruments, and has built his own musical universe to play in. He is a musical loner, an artist of independent creative vision, a kind of modern Don Quixote of music, California-style. A hint of Partch's star-tling imaginativeness is suggested by the names of just a few of his instruments, which he builds himself: chromelodeon, eucal blossom, gourd tree and cone gongs, spoils of war, mazda marimba (rows of light bulbs), cloud chamber bowls, zymo-xyl, crychord, and so on. He cannot remember offhand how many instruments he has invented, but "It's in the printed list."

He is a naïf of music who has never grown up; he retains a wide-eyed simplicity. Peter Yates has described him as "one of those in-spired, stubborn radicals of creative thought who never exactly fit anywhere."

Partch's musical education was informal. He cites public libraries, Yaqui Indians, Chinese lullabies, Hebrew chants for the dead, Christian hymns, Congo puberty rites, Chinese music halls in San Francisco, lumber yards, junk shops, and *Boris Godunov* as basic influences on his creative output.

The basis of the Partchian language is a systematic and minute division of the octave into forty-three intervals. His music, say his many detractors, is more interesting for texture and pure sound than for ideas and artistic qualities. Nevertheless, he has a huge under-ground following; for a concert of Partch's work in New York in 1968, the Whitney Museum was jammed as though for a rock concert, and most of the hopeful auditors could not even get inside. The value of his controversial music is still much argued; meanwhile Harry Partch and the *Zeitgeist* of the 1970s fit each other admirably. Partch is also a pungent prose writer, as the following observation shows:

> *The profession of music is lacking in horse sense, not only be-cause the commonplace variety of horse is absent from its opera-tions, but because parts of the horses are noticeably present.... We accept without even a gesture of investigation any instru-ment, any scale, any asinine nomenclature, any rules, stated or implied, found in the safe deposit boxes of various eighteenth century Germanic gentlemen whom we and our immediate antecedents have been dragooned into idolizing.**

*Harry Partch, "Show Horses in the Concert Ring," *Circle 10*, Summer 1948, p. 43.

HARRISON

A one-time student of Schönberg and a fervent advocate of Ives's music, Lou Harrison (born 1917) is one of the more imaginative Americans at work today. He is a gifted melodist with a deep interest in Renaissance polyphony. He also has invented a Western elaboration of recondite Oriental scales. Like John Cage, with whom he has composed music (*Double Music,* composed in alternate sections), he is deeply immersed in Eastern music and in the search to elaborate upon it from a Western point of view. With Cage and another fellow composer, William Russel, he once put together a homemade gamelan of percussive sound producers, employing such un-Bali-like substitutes for bronze pots and bars as the brake drums from a Model A Ford.

Harrison himself has said, "I have been so bold as to try several of the ways in which I think classic Asian musics might of themselves, and together, evolve in the future, and have combined instruments of several ethnics directly for musical expression."

CHOU WEN-CHUNG

Chou Wen-Chung, born in 1923 in China, came to America to study architecture. He later turned to composition. He was one of Varèse's few pupils and also studied with Otto Luening. His early works, based upon traditional Chinese music, are subtle, extremely lovely transformations of ancient Chinese folk and art music; in his later period he seeks a broader, more comprehensive style that employs modern Western techniques as well, and he strives to fuse Eastern and Western musical rhetoric. His sensitive, delicate pieces subtly convey the feeling and color of Chinese poetry and painting.

The composer himself writes, "I am influenced by the philosophy that governs every Chinese artist, whether he be poet or painter: namely, affinity to nature in conception, allusiveness in expression, and terseness in realization."

CHAPTER IV

Revolution II: The 1950s

Serious music is a dead art. The vein which for three hundred years offered a seemingly inexhaustible field of beautiful music has run out. What we know as modern music is the noise made by deluded speculators picking through the slagpile.

Henry Pleasants, THE AGONY OF MODERN MUSIC, 1955

We are living in a pivotal period. We are witnessing the death-throes of an age-old art and the birth of new forms of thought and sensibility.

André Hodeir, SINCE DEBUSSY, 1960

The complacent assumption that what we are now witnessing is merely one more chapter in the uninterrupted evolution of music, with Cage and Stockhausen in the roles once played by Beethoven, Wagner, Debussy and Schönberg, seems increasingly glib and untenable.... We are confronted with the most decisive break in the development of Western music since the monodic revolution at the beginning of the seventeenth century. To put it crassly, we are living in a period when one music is dying as another is in the painful process of birth.

Peter Heyworth, THE FATEFUL SIXTIES, 1969

IN SPITE OF DECADES OF CONSTANT ATTACK AND PROPHECIES THAT it would soon vanish, the serial technique evolved by Schönberg and Webern surprisingly proved to be the dominant influence in Western music in the 1950s. A new group of disciples sprang up, very radical serialists who derived more from the austerity of Webern than from the new romanticism of Schönberg. Led by Pierre Boulez (born 1926),

Luigi Nono (born 1924), and Karlheinz Stockhausen (born 1928), this new school preached and practiced a post-Webernian technique of total serialization. They religiously followed an analytical, scientific approach, "the marriage of music and science."

At the same time, the period after World War II saw a resurgence of interest in pure sound and in a reexamination of the experimental tradition. Prophets and eccentrics (Satie, Ives, et al.) who had long been regarded as outside the mainstream of music, but whose ideas for "opening up" music were being constantly discussed, were accorded a new respect.

The theories of this second stream of rebels and outsiders are proving to be as influential in the New Music of the 1970s as those of the composers within the mainstream. There were other founding fathers in the Experimental tradition—Busoni, the Italian Futurists, and Varèse—who profoundly influenced electronic music, and who will be discussed at length in the next section of this book.

Thus the two streams—the Romantic tradition reaching its end with Schönberg and Webern, and the once derided outlaws of music, the Experimentalists—converged after the war and are proving to be the two great influences upon the music of the last third of the twentieth century.

The 1950s were a very exciting time in all the arts, painting in particular. American painters of the Abstract Expressionist and Action Painting schools shared common goals with the new composers—a common revolutionary *élan*, a common disengagement from middle-class values. They were determined to challenge modernist European tradition, which the six-year interlude of the war had proved they were no longer dependent on. Instead of the carefully calculated stroke, there was in painting the swirl of Pollock's drip paintings, the splattered brilliance of Willem de Kooning's terrifying women, Franz Kline's huge black-on-white compositions that showed no more sophistication than a Chinese ideograph.

In music there was an equal sense of exuberance. The barriers were down, the old fights had been fought. Young composers began to work with a complete disregard for the polemics of a few years before; the old problems no longer even interested them. Instead, they were out to create a New Music. The composer and critic Eric Salzman, a pupil of Luening at Columbia and Babbitt at Princeton, caught this spirit admirably when he wrote:

> *Beginning around 1948 and continuing through the '50's, an entire younger generation of composers in Europe and America took on the task of restructuring musical thought and expression from point zero. For the first time in three centuries composers were concerned not with the theater and its complexities but with the simplest, most basic units of abstract sound and silence. This experimentation was interrupted by the widespread availability of magnetic tape. Composers had been experimenting with sound collage and electronics for a number of years, but only in the mid-fifties did electronic music swing into high gear. Suddenly the world was the composer's oyster: any sound could be put to use, and vast quantities of new ones could be created electrically. . . . Instead of turning composers away from live performers, it sent them back with new and freer ideas about what they could do.*

Truly a revolutionary situation. Composers were liberated—what now?

Pierre Boulez, who is never at a loss for answers, wrote, "After the War, we all felt that music, like the world around us, was in a state of chaos. Our problem was to make a new musical language, seeking out what was good from the past, and rejecting what was bad."

To invent a new musical language—that was precisely what the champions of electronic music proposed to do, and what early prophets such as Busoni, the Italian Futurists, and Varèse had been saying for years.

PART TWO

The Search for a New Music

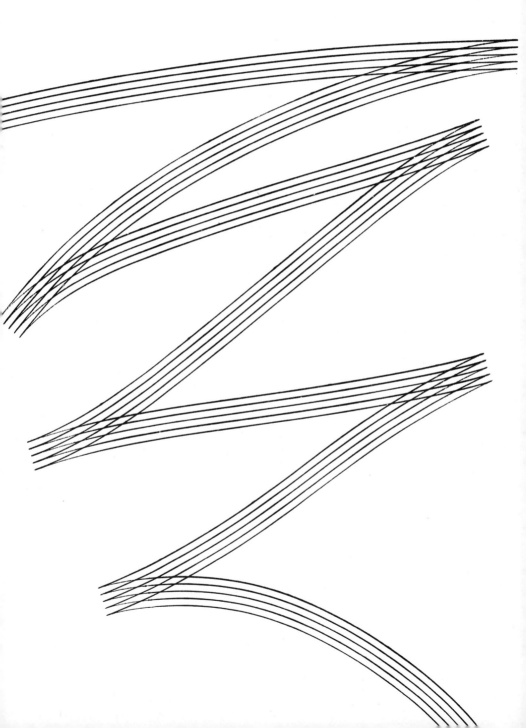

CHAPTER V

The Historical Background

THE ART OF MUSIC HAS A LONG HISTORY PARALLELING THAT OF civilization itself. The science of music—studies in sound—also began in antiquity. Chinese and Hindu philosophers were bemused by the natural laws that seemed to determine the nature of the sounds made when a taut string was plucked or a hollow gourd tapped.

The Greek scholar Pythagoras (about 500 B.C.) made a study of vibrating strings, and determined the conditions under which two musical tones sounded together will make a pleasing combination. And at least since Pythagoras, men have been arguing about what the "pleasing combinations" in music are, and whether new kinds of sounds can be accepted as "pleasing."

Man also has constantly sought new "tools"—instruments—with which to make music, and the argument as to which instruments are "acceptable" has raged continuously. Inventors and mathematicians produced an endless parade of musicmaking machines to push the boundaries of musical possibilities farther. Mechanically driven organs made their appearance around the year 1500; an instrument with 150 pipes was admired in the Schloss Hohensalzburg then. Hydraulically operated organs, along with all sorts of mechanical automata, adorned the parks of Renaissance princes.

The work of Hermann Helmholtz, a nineteenth-century German physicist and physiologist, presented the theoreticians with new avenues to explore. His *On the Sensations of Tone as a Physiological Basis for the Theory of Music*, published in 1862, is the basis of most modern theories of consonance and tone qualities. But it was only with the invention of electrical musical devices, around the turn of the century, that the exploration of the nature of sound itself was seriously undertaken.

The invention of the phonograph, which is technically both a storage and a retrieval machine, added enormous impetus to the study of sound. But the imaginations of early twentieth-century visionaries like Busoni and Varèse were fired by a more stirring prospect: an electrical instrument that could *produce*, not just reproduce, the whole "spectrum" of sound; an instrument that would give composers and musicians access to "a total world of sound."

BUSONI: "MUSIC WAS BORN FREE"

The first important musician to concern himself with what Edgar Varèse was to call "the Liberation of Sound" was Varèse's mentor, the Italian-German composer, pianist, and musical visionary, Ferruccio Busoni (1866–1924). A former child prodigy, Busoni was famous in his maturity as a piano virtuoso in the grand style of Franz Liszt. Many regarded him as the true successor of Liszt and the superior of Paderewski and Rachmaninoff.

Busoni's mother was German, and from 1894 he lived mainly in Berlin, where eventually he was to die. He won great renown as a pianist, composer, teacher, arranger of music for piano (in particular through his controversial arrangements of the organ works of Bach), and as a philosopher of art. He was also influential as a conductor, introducing the new music of Debussy, Gabriel Fauré, Jean Sibelius, and Bartok to Berlin. His artistic testament, however, is his opera *Dr. Faust*, an austere, lofty work, one of the masterworks of our century. He also wrote many searching essays about music, the most prophetic of which is his "Sketch of a New Aesthetic of Music" (1907).

Busoni was for twenty years the unswerving champion of all that was virtually new in art. His hospitable home in Berlin was the gathering place of fiery young artists from many countries. Almost nightly there were furious discussions there on the burning artistic problems of the day, Busoni presiding with scintillating esprit, charm, intellect, and kindliness.*

By birth and education half German and half Italian, Busoni

---

*The distinguished Harvard musicologist, the late Hugo Leichtentritt, as a student in Berlin was himself a member of the Busoni circle. He wrote nostalgically of the meetings of young artists at the master's home: "It is probable that in our confused, nationalistic, impoverished age such social intercourse no longer exists at all. Indeed, those gatherings were a sort of modern parallel to the Socratic symposiums of which Plato gives us so vivid a picture." (*Music History and Ideas* [Cambridge: Harvard University Press, 1938], p. 254.)

combined in his personality and in his versatile art the characteristic traits of both nationalities. Many of his theories were far in advance of his time. For instance, he constructed new scales because he refused to accept the limitations of major and minor modes (the ways of ordering the notes of a scale). He experimented with quarter tones. He was basically anti-Romantic, and he detested Wagner. Because he was out of sympathy with the Romantic aesthetic prevalent in Germany, his position there was curiously similar to that of Satie in France: many decades passed before the ideas of either man were accepted. He also fought for what was later known as neoclassicism in music— that is, a preference for small ensembles rather than the grandiose instrumental forces of Wagner, Richard Strauss, and Mahler; and an avoidance of heavy "emotionalism," to name just two features of this movement. His ideas can be perceived in the newly austere music of the 1920s and thirties, particularly in the works of Stravinsky, Bartok, Hindemith, and Ernst Toch, and of the Italian composers Alfredo Casella and Gian Francesco Malipiero.

But the most remarkable facet of Busoni's "adventure in music" —as he himself termed his life—was his deep, almost uncanny realization of where twentieth-century music (and all art, for that matter) was heading. To Busoni, each new influence in music, each new iconoclast, such as Debussy, heralded a liberation from some confining rule or other. He had a vision of music being freed from the shackles in which it had been placed for four hundred years by the concept of "tonality" and by a constricting system of major and minor scales.

Busoni also wrote, prophetically, of a problem that now absorbs us all. Addressing himself to the question of just where the mainstream of music can possibly flow after the towering artistic accomplishments of the last centuries of Western music, he wrote:

> *Exhaustion surely waits at the end of a course the longest lap of which has already been covered. Whither then shall we turn our eyes? In what direction does the next step lead?* To abstract sound, to unhampered technique, to unlimited tonal material. I believe that all efforts must be directed towards the virgin birth of a new beginning. . . . *Suddenly, one day, it seemed clear to me that the full flowering of music is frustrated by our instru-*

ments. . . . In their range, their tone, what they can render, our instruments are chained fast, and their hundred chains must also bind the creative composer.

These swirling ideas about the essential freedom of music are the burden of Busoni's little bombshell of 1907, "Sketch of a New Aesthetic of Music." Busoni's essay was read with smiles by almost all of his contemporaries, but today it reads like a precise catalogue of the road that music has traveled since the author's day. In "A New Aesthetic" he argues for freedom from rhythmic and formal conventions, freedom for composers from the limitations of conventional instruments, and freedom from our rigid system of scales. To provide new creative freedom in music, he proposed scales that arrange half steps and whole steps in arbitrary ways; he remarked that he was familiar with 113 such scales, and offered eight examples.

Busoni also referred enthusiastically to an electrical musical instrument called the Dynamophone, invented by an American, Dr. Thaddeus Cahill. Busoni had read about it in Ray Stannard Baker's article called "New Music for an Old World" published in *McClure's Magazine* in 1906. The article declared that this marvelous instrument could produce any combination of notes and overtones at any dynamic level—precisely the claim that has been made for the highly sophisticated electronic sound-producing machines developed since World War II. In fact, the Dynamophone was a primitive ancestor of the famous RCA Synthesizer installed at the Columbia-Princeton Electronic Music Center in the 1950s, and of the Moog and other synthesizers.

Busoni grasped at once what the Dynamophone might mean to composers who yearned for a broader base of sound materials.* He hoped that the invention would prove to be the means of putting music on a fully scientific basis:

*The Dynamophone excited other musical visionaries in addition to Busoni. On March 10, 1906, an enthusiastic editorial in the professional electro-technical journal, *Electrical World*, published in New York, described a demonstration of the Dynamophone in Mount Holyoke, Massachusetts. The editorial was signed L. Stokowski. (My source for this information is an article by Otto Luening, in *Journal of Music Theory*, Spring 1964. Leopold Stokowski arrived in America in 1905. H.R.)

I received from America direct and authentic intelligence which solves the problem [of tone production] in a simple manner. I refer to an invention by Dr. Thaddeus Cahill. He has constructed a comprehensive apparatus which makes it possible to transform an electric current into a fixed and mathematically exact number of vibrations. As pitch depends on the number of vibrations, and the apparatus may be set on any number desired, the infinite gradation of the octave may be accomplished by merely moving a lever corresponding to the pointer of a quadrant.

Only a long and careful series of experiments, and a continued training of the ear, can render this unfamiliar material approachable and plastic for the coming generation, and for Art.

But the Dynamophone, alas, was an unwieldy monster. It weighed over two hundred tons and looked like the engine room of a ship. Its principles were related to the later-developed Hammond Organ, but without its descendant's facility. It passed into oblivion.*

Busoni had a restless, inquiring, brilliant mind, and he was one of the boldest adventurers in music. He was also an uncompromising idealist, who helped to determine the direction in which twentieth-century music would flow. His prescience is evident in passage after passage from his "Sketch for a New Aesthetic of Music":

Music was born free; and to win freedom is its destiny. It will become the most complete of all reflexes of Nature by reason of its untrammeled immateriality. Even the poetic word ranks lower in point of incorporealness. It can gather together and disperse, can be motionless repose or wildest tempestuosity; it has the extremest heights perceptible to man—what other art has these? —and its emotion seizes the human heart with that intensity which is independent of the "idea." ...

*According to the phonetician Werner Meyer-Eppler, who in the 1950s was one of the founders of the famous Cologne Electronic Studio, the Dynamophone was built on the lines of the geared generators used in communications systems, and was used to broadcast concerts over telephone lines. This observation recalls the remark of Dr. J. R. Pierce of Bell Laboratories: "The application of electricity to the production of music goes back to ... the effort to bring signals from a primitive electric organ into homes over wires. This project was abandoned, partly because of the interference it caused to the telephone system."

Absolute Music! What the lawgivers mean by this, is perhaps remotest of all from the Absolute in music. . . . It reminds one of music desks in orderly rows, of the relation of Tonic to Dominant, of Developments and Codas. . . . The lawgivers, . . . being powerless to recreate either the spirit, or the emotion, or the time, have retained the Form as a symbol and made it into a fetish, a religion.

We are tyrannized by Major and Minor—by the bifurcated garment. . . . But the harmony of today is not for long; all signs presage a revolution, and a next step toward that "eternal harmony." Let us once again call to mind, that in this latter the gradation of the octave is infinite, and let us strive to draw a little nearer to infinitude. *So narrow has our tonal range become, so stereotyped its form of expression, that nowadays there is not one familiar motive that cannot be fitted with another motive so that the two may be played simultaneously.*

What we now call our tonal system is nothing more than a set of "signs," an ingenious device to grasp something of that eternal harmony; a meager pocket edition of that encyclopedic work; artificial light instead of the sun. . . . *Keyboard instruments, in particular, have so thoroughly schooled our ears that we are no longer capable of hearing anything else—incapable of hearing except through this impure medium. Yet Nature created* an infinite gradation—infinite! *Who still knows it nowadays?*

Music is part of the vibrating universe. . . . The creator should take over no traditional law in blind belief. . . . For his individual case he should seek out and formulate a fitting individual law. The function of the creative artist consists in making laws, not in following laws ready made. He who follows such laws ceases to be a creator. *Creative power may be the more readily recognized, the more it shakes itself loose from tradition. But an intentional avoidance of the rules cannot masquerade as creative power, and still less engender it. . . . Is it not singular to demand of a composer originality in all things, and to forbid it as regards form? No wonder that, once he becomes original, he is accused of "formlessness." Mozart, the seeker and the finder, the great man with the childlike heart—it is he we marvel at, to whom we are devoted; not his Tonic and Dominant, his Developments and Codas.*

Music as art, our so-called occidental music, is hardly four hundred years old; its state is one of development, perhaps the very first stage of a development beyond present conception. And we—we talk of "classics" and "hallowed traditions"! And we have talked of them for a long time!

We have formulated rules, stated principles, laid down laws— we apply laws made for maturity to a child that knows nothing of responsibility! . . . This child—music—it floats on air! It touches not the earth with its feet. It knows no law of gravitation. It is wellnigh incorporeal. Its material is transparent. It is sonorous air. It is almost Nature herself. It is free!

But freedom is something that mankind has never wholly comprehended, never realized to the full. Man can neither recognize nor acknowledge it. . . . He disavows the mission of this child; he hangs weights upon it. This buoyant creature must walk decently, like anyone else. It may scarcely be allowed to leap—when it were its joy to follow the line of the rainbow, and to break sunbeams with the clouds!*

Busoni's sweeping new proposals for unshackling music were carried out by Edgard Varèse who studied at one time with Busoni and who has left us a short memoir of his master. It is worth quoting in full here, because it sheds light on both of these great figures who so influenced the course of music in our century. Varèse wrote:

In 1907, still in my early twenties I went to Berlin, where I spent most of the next seven years, and had the good fortune of becoming (in spite of the disparity of age and importance) the friend of Ferruccio Busoni, then at the height of his fame. I had read his remarkable little book, A New Esthetic of Music, *a milestone in my musical development, and when I came upon,*

---

*Busoni's "Sketch of a New Aesthetic of Music" is included in *Three Classics in the Aesthetic of Music* (New York: Dover Publications, 1962). Collected papers of Busoni, which also make fascinating reading, are available in *Busoni: The Essence of Music, and Other Papers* (New York: Dover Publications, 1965).

"Music is born free; and to win freedom is its destiny," *it was like hearing the echo of my own thought.*

From the beginning Busoni took an interest in my work and let me bring him my scores for criticism. But one day—by then I had known him for three years or more—I brought him my latest score, whether it was Les Cycles du Nord *for orchestra, or an opera based on Hugo von Hofmannsthal's* Oedipus und die Sphinx, *I cannot remember. In any case he seemed surprised and expressed pleasure at the way I had developed. He went over the score with special attentiveness and asked many questions. At certain places he suggested modifications, which I found contrary to my conception. He asked me if I didn't agree with him, and I said emphatically: "No, Maestro," and gave him my reasons. "So," he said, "You will not make these changes." "No, Maestro," I repeated somewhat belligerently. He looked at me for a moment and I thought he resented my rejection of his recommendations as youthful conceit. But then he smiled and, putting his hand on my shoulder, said: "From now on it is no longer* Maestro *but* Ferruccio *and* Tu." *We spoke Italian or French when we were alone together.*

Having become acquainted with Busoni through his extraordinarily prophetic musical theories in his New Esthetic, *I was surprised to find his musical tastes and his own music so orthodox. It was Busoni who coined the expression, young classicism, and classicism young or old was just what I was bent on escaping. He could never understand how most of the works of such a master as Mozart, his favorite composer, could bore me as they did and still do. But it was also Busoni who wrote:* The function of the creative artist consists in making laws, not in following laws already made.

Together we used to discuss what direction the music of the future would, or rather, should take and could not take as long as the straitjacket of the tempered system (the diplomatic, 2 *semi-tone system, as he called it) continued to keep it immovable. He deplored that his own keyboard instrument had conditioned our ears to accept only an infinitesimal part of the infinite gradations of sounds in nature. However, when I said that I was through with to-*

nality, his quick response was: Tu te prives d'une bien belle chose. *["You are denying yourself a very beautiful thing."] He was very much interested in the electrical instruments we began to hear about, and I remember particularly one he had read of called the Dynamophone, invented by a Dr. Thaddeus Cahill, which I later saw demonstrated in New York. All through his writings one finds over and over again predictions about the music of the future which have since come true. In fact, there is hardly a development that he did not foresee, as for instance in this extraordinary prophecy: "... I almost think that in the new great music, machines will also be necessary and will be assigned a share in it. Perhaps industry, too, will bring forth her share in the artistic ascent." How right he was, for it is thanks to industry that composers today compose by means of electronic "machines," invented for industry's benefit but adopted by composers, with the assistance of engineers, for theirs. To musicians who have known Busoni only as a pianist, or through his scores, this ambivalence will come as a surprise. It was as though his heart, loyal to the past, refused to follow his adventurous mind into so strange a future. In any case I owe a tremendous debt of gratitude to this extraordinary man—almost a figure out of the Renaissance—not only one of the greatest pianists of all time, but a man of wide culture: scholar, thinker, writer, composer, conductor, teacher and* animateur—*a man who stimulated others to think and do things.**

Busoni continued to inspire and encourage Varèse, who in turn proved a great inspiration for many of our contemporary composers. One of them, Chou Wen-Chung, has declared,

"It is my conviction that we have reached the stage where a true re-merger of Oriental and Occidental musical concepts and practices—which at one time shared a common foundation—can and should take place. It seems to me that the music of China, India, Edgard

*This text was intended by Varèse to be given as part of the Ferruccio Busoni Centennial Celebration held at the *Casa Italiana* of Columbia University in 1966; but Varèse died the previous year, and his remarks were read by Otto Luening at the Celebration. The text was printed in the Columbia University Forum, Spring 1966.

Varèse, the Balinese *gamelan* music, the Japanese *gaguko*, the Korean *ah ahk*, and even our new electronic music all have much in common, sharing the same family traits."*

This is, of course, precisely what Ferruccio Busoni, who taught Varèse and Luening, who in turn taught Chou Wen-Chung, wrote in 1921:

"The time has come to recognize the whole phenomenon of music as a 'oneness,' and no longer to split it up according to its purpose, form and sound medium."**

Music and Sound, Timbre and Noise: The Italian Futurists

"Noise is any sound that one doesn't like" said Edgard Varèse. The exploration of the nature of sound, combined with the prospect that there soon would be available electrical devices capable of producing whatever sound their manipulators wanted, brought composers up against the old Pythagorean problem: When does music stop being music and become noise, and vice versa.

Even physics accepts several different definitions of noise, among them: "an accumulation of dissonances," and "an acoustical event in which a large number of frequencies and their associated pyramids of overtones are present simultaneously."

Some who are willing to grant that composers had the "right" to use "all the sounds of the world" in their music still preferred to restrict those who wished to violate the old musical canons to natural sounds—rain and thunder, the roar of the sea, the songs of birds— but there was no agreement as to whether even those sounds were technically music or just noise.

Instruments that produce noise—by anybody's definition—gongs, most kinds of drums, rattles, and the like, have an honored place in traditional Western music. Classical composers flirted with noise-makers; both Mozart and Beethoven now and then used the percussion effects of Turkish or janissary music, which were hardly known in Western Europe at the time. The short B-flat march in the finale of the Ninth Symphony suggests intoxicated joy by means of a bass

---

*In an interview taped for broadcast on radio WBAI, New York, 1965.
**From *Busoni: The Essence of Music*, p. 57.

drum, cymbals, and a triangle. But not before this century had it been suggested that a composer might be free to use "the sounds of the universe" as raw material.

The question that confronted Pythagoras more than three thousand years ago remains. What are "pleasing combinations of sound"? In painting, we take it for granted that a Jackson Pollock or a Picasso can employ harsh distortions or seeming chaos, and still, somehow, be "pleasing." What our contemporary composers are fighting for is the same right: to use raw materials that, while not mellifluous, may nevertheless be aesthetically satisfying—once we get used to them and to our composers' New World of Sound.

Two years after Busoni published his seminal booklet, the Italian Futurists came out four-square on the side of noise. The Futurists were an avant garde of writers, painters, and musicians who professed radical theories about all the arts and coined the term *Futurismo* to encompass them. One of their group, the painter Luigi Russolo, sketched out "a new music of noise." He had been influenced by the experimental poetry of Filippo Marinetti, who had written a war poem in which the sounds of weapons were depicted by syllables, vowels, and consonants. In 1912 Russolo, with Marinetti, wrote the manifesto of *Musica Futurista*, which many composers of today (some of whom have probably never heard of Luigi Russolo) have adopted almost instinctively as their own credo: "To present the musical soul of the masses, of the great factories, of the railways, of the transatlantic liners, of the battleships, of the automobiles and airplanes. To add to the great central themes of the musical poem the domain of the machine and the victorious kingdom of Electricity."

Russolo also called for a methodical investigation of noises and suggested distinguishing between six types: "Bangs, explosions, etc; Whistles and hisses; Whispers and murmurs; Screams, shrieks, and sounds produced by friction; Sounds produced by striking wood, metal, stone, etc; Animal and human cries—roars, howls, laughter, sobs, sighs, etc."

The first concert of Futurist music was given by Marinetti and Russolo in Milan in 1914. The program consisted of "four networks of noises" with the following titles:

1. Awakening of Capital.
2. Meeting of cars and aeroplanes.
3. Dining on the terrace of the Casino.
4. Skirmish in the oasis.

Among the instruments employed were bumblers, exploders, thunderers, and whistlers. The concert ended in a violent battle between the performers and the audience. This, of course, is in the grand tradition of modern music; a year earlier in Paris, at the first performance of Stravinsky's *Rite of Spring*—the most famous musical premiere of the century—members of the audience, infuriated by the composer's deliberate use of jarring, massed orchestral effects to suggest "noise," pummeled one another.

The Futurists must be regarded as family ancestors of electronic music; they argued for the introduction of what had been theretofore "unacceptable sounds" in music. Russolo wrote in 1913 of an "art of noises," suggesting that composers could validly employ "the most complex dissonances ... by the supplementary use of noise and its substitution for musical sounds."

Other Futurists were on the same track. Francesco Pratella gave a detailed description of a composition for an "orchestra" consisting of machine guns, sirens, steam whistles, and similar sounds. Futuristic music was introduced by Marinetti into the group of painters and poets who rallied in 1916 with the famous slogan "Dada." (Marinetti, who became an ardent follower of Mussolini, defined Futuristic music as "a synthetic expression of great economic, erotic, heroic, aviational, mechanical dynamism.") No composers were directly associated with the Dadaists, but the painter Marcel Duchamp composed a musical piece that consisted of random isolated pitches without any indicated durations. Similar notions of music, of course, can be heard today in the pieces of John Cage and others.

The Futurists were dismissed as lunatics, but one composer and music critic took them seriously. His name was Claude Debussy, and in a review he asked, "Will this [art] ever achieve the truly satisfying sonority of a foundry in operation? Let us wait and see, and refrain from ridicule."

Nothing much came of the Futurists and their *bruitsmo*; ironically, Pratella's own music was timid Debussyism, mingled with Puccinian idioms. The compositions of Pratella and Russolo are of meager artistic value—simple melodic ideas with an accompanying palette of noises. But their notions remained in the air for decades. They had provocatively raised the question: where do musical sounds end and noises begin? Only one composer of stature stepped forward to make a methodical exploration of that dark, unknown sonic territory. His name was Edgard Varèse.

CHAPTER VI

Edgard Varèse and "The Liberation of Sound"

I long for instruments obedient to my thought and which, with their contribution of a whole new world of unsuspected sounds, will lend themselves to the exigencies of my inner rhythm.

Edgard Varèse, in the periodical "391," June 1917

Your legend is embedded in our age. Farewell, Varèse, farewell! Your time is finished and now it begins.

Pierre Boulez's eulogy upon the death of Varèse, 1965

Varèse has been recognized at last, but his is a lonely figure still. This is partly because he, unlike so many other composers, preferred composing to the career of 'being a composer.' Instead of lecturing to ladies' clubs, writing articles on the state of music, and travelling on fellowships, Varèse stayed home and went his own way alone. Varèse's music will endure. More power to this musical Brancusi.

Some men, and Varèse is one of them, are like dynamite. That alone, I suppose, is sufficient to explain why they are handled with such caution and shyness. As yet we have not censorship of music, though I remember Huneker saying somewhere that it was surprising we hadn't censored certain masterpieces. As for Varèse, I honestly believe that if he were given a clear field he would not only be censored but stoned. Why? For the very simple reason that his music is different....

Igor Stravinsky, 1962

I remember vividly the first time I heard Varèse's music—on a magnificent recording machine. I was stunned. It was as if I had been given a knock-out blow. When I recovered I listened again. This time I recognized emotions which I had experienced in the first instance but which, because of novelty, because of the continuous, uninterrupted succession of novelties, I had been unable to identify. My emotions had piled up to a crescendo whose impact came as a self-delivered sock in the jaw.

Henry Miller, THE AIR CONDITIONED NIGHTMARE

Varèse never allowed us to follow our own tails. He was an insolent prophet, a negator of established values. . . . He will forever prevent those for whom music is always an eternal re-beginning from falling asleep. The sound of his music is begin-ning to awaken us now. . . . Away with scales, away with themes, away with melody, to the devil with so-called 'musical' music!

Yannis Xenakis, 1965

WE APPROACH THE LEGEND OF EDGARD VARESE WARILY; IT READS like popular fiction. It is too much, too romantic. All the cliché-ridden situations and stock characters are here: the revolutionary, unswerving hero-artist defying all obstacles in pursuit of his ideal; the charming, loyal wife steadfast by his side during the long years of ridicule and abuse; the small band of young followers; the en-couragement of a few older composers, who had survived their own bitter battles; the deaf critics, the jeering public, the riots and scan-dals at the premieres of his works; the support of one famous con-ductor; the spurning of a crass Hollywood offer; the lonely decades of neglect, and near oblivion; the black nadir of depression, and thoughts of suicide.

Much of Varèse's life reads like pages straight out of *Jean-Christophe*, and with good reason: he was actually one of the proto-types for Romain Rolland's great novel.* The climax of his career,

---

*Although Jean-Christophe was already published in part when Rolland met Varèse, he still used Varèse as a model for the rest of the book.

however, reads uneasily like *The Fountainhead*. The giant electrical corporation, Philips, approaches the world's most famous architect, Le Corbusier, and asks him to design a spectacular electrical exhibit for their pavilion at the Brussels World's Fair. Le Corbusier declares to the directors, "I will create for you an Electronic Poem. There is one man, and one man alone, to write the music for this, and his name is Edgard Varèse."

The directors are disappointed; they wanted a glittering, safe, "name" composer. They are appalled when they hear our hero's bold music and they try to sabotage his plans. Our hero battles them every inch of the way, writes his masterpiece—at the age of seventy-five— and world fame and homage come at last.

And finally, the long, enshrining obituary in *The New York Times*, "Edgard Varèse Dead: Pioneer Avant-Gardist Was Known as the 'Father of Electronic Music'; Championed Cooperation by Artists and Engineers."

Today Varèse is recognized as a composer of the same importance for this century's music as Stravinsky, Schönberg, Webern, and Bartok (the last three of whom were equally neglected and ridiculed during their lifetimes). Varèse is now a father-figure to many young composers all over the world. He is the poet of the technological world that more and more threatens to undermine the heady sense of human individuality that came to Western man with the Renaissance. Like Bartok and Schönberg, he is a symbol of our century—the loner, the uncompromising revolutionary, the seminal explosive force, the artist perfectly mated to his time. Edgard Varèse wrote music that takes us on an aural journey through some previously unimagined universe. Sound masses, magnificently juxtaposed, collide about us with frightening force. And Varèse achieves his effects through a remarkable, compelling logic that leads us from one idea to the next with irresistible power.

Varèse was nonconformity inflected by genius. He lived only to follow his ideal. Harold Schönberg wrote: "Varèse represented something bigger than life, and it was as much for this as for his actual accomplishment that he was hailed." Not that his accomplishment was minor—as Jacques Barzun has observed, "It is evident that Varèse is the man who solved in music the generic problem of the twentieth-century arts, the problem of creating a new idiom by creating new materials."

Varèse's dazzingly original concepts reach down to the very foundation of our new cultural style. His ideas and attitudes are to be felt everywhere—in television, in rock music and jazz, in underground films, in mixed-media presentations, and in the compositions of hundreds of young composers in America, Japan, Sweden, and Israel. One unlikely example: Charlie Parker, the great jazz saxophonist, appeared one night at the home of Varèse and begged the composer to accept him as a pupil. Varèse was willing, but was leaving for Europe; when he returned, Parker had died.* Parker's widow later told Varèse that her husband had followed him up and down the streets of Greenwich Village for two years without even daring to speak to him. "Varèse is the only man I'd be willing to be a servant to," Parker had told his wife.

Varèse's music—and the sheer force of personality we hear in it—speaks directly to young audiences in the language they want to hear. To the casual listener, it lacks human emotion, but this is precisely what appeals to many of us in our post-Hiroshima culture. His entire output was less than twenty-five works, but they are informed with an almost ferocious originality. Identifiable melodies and schematic harmonies are not here. Rather, sounds for their own sake surge and flow. Sounds succeed each other in so natural and forceful a manner that they seem to give birth to a new dimension in music, and his sounds often seem as palpable as physical objects. The way to hear Varèse's music is to think of it as "sculptured sounds," the sculpture of a musical Brancusi or of a Henry Moore. The three-dimensional sounds of Varèse almost cry out to be touched and caressed. They possess a natural life of their own, a physical shape in space.

Varèse was both child and father of his time. Born in Paris in 1883, he prepared for an engineering career by studying mathematics and the sciences, and weaned himself on the notebooks of Leonardo

*This incident was related to the present writer by Louise Varèse, the composer's widow.

da Vinci. He was quickly drawn toward music, and he used scientific principles as a battering ram against entrenched musical tradition. From the very outset of his career he was fascinated by the scientific study of sound as the foundation for new means of expression.

He was a born rebel, a smoldering new Berlioz, with thunderbolt eyes and a great shock of hair. He studied, unhappily, at the Schola Cantorum and the Paris Conservatoire. He haunted Montparnasse, and a list of his friends at that time reads like a roll call of genius: Romain Rolland, Erik Satie, Max Jacob, Amedeo Modigliani, Guillaume Apollonaire, Blaise Cendrars. His later friends and admirers included Paul Rosenfeld, Antonin Artaud, André Malraux, the Dadaist Tristan Tzara, the Futurist Luigi Russolo, Jules Pascin, Alexander Calder, Hector Villa-Lobos, Diego Rivera, Ossip Zadkine, Marcel Duchamp, Frank Stella, Joan Miró, Henry Cowell, Le Corbusier, Jacques Barzun, and Alexis Léger, who wrote under the name of St. John Perse. As these lists suggest, musicians themselves, with a few honorable exceptions, were among the last to recognize Varèse's achievement.*

He knew Lenin and Trotsky; he introduced Picasso to Jean Cocteau. Half-starving, he went to concerts that cost only ten sous. He drudged away at fugues and counterpoint, but hated "these places where the teachers are all ruled like music paper," as he once told Stravinsky. He told Camille Saint-Saëns during one showdown, "I have no desire to become an old fossil like you."

At the Conservatoire, he challenged the very existence and necessity of our hallowed tempered scale. "I refuse to submit to sounds that have already been heard," he declared. "I refuse to be shackled by predetermined intervals and frequencies." He dreamed of a return to music's primitive origins, a universal music of religious magic, of revelation, of timbres that reach out to infinity.

Two older composers—great revolutionaries themselves—were to be the inspirations of his life: Debussy and Busoni. "Rules do not

---

*Among the exceptions: the harpist and composer Carlos Salzedo, with whom Varèse founded the International Composers Guild (in the U.S.) in the 1920s; the composer Otto Luening, who was a close friend of Varèse. Luening suggested that Varèse teach a course in contemporary music at Columbia University and take Luening's own seminar there in the summer of 1948.

make a work of art," Debussy told Varèse to encourage his hope of a career as composer. "You have the right to compose what you want to, the way you want to, if the music comes out and it is your own. Follow the ear rather than the rule."

Debussy encouraged the young student's interest in music of other civilizations. Debussy himself had been riveted by the motionless tinkle of the Balinese gamelans at the Paris Exposition Universelle of 1889; when Varèse at a later exposition heard the tumultuous variety of rhythms and timbres of African drums, he sensed that here, rather than in the musty halls of the Conservatoire, he stood in the presence of musical truth.

In 1909 Varèse put two of his scores under his arm and introduced himself to the great French-Swiss writer, Romain Rolland. Rolland wrote to a friend, "A second Jean-Christophe has just recently appeared on my doorstep, an amazingly handsome one. Tall, with a fine head of black hair, pale eyes, and an intelligent, forceful face: a sort of young Italian Beethoven painted by Giorgione. Jean-Christophe really exists. I invent nothing."*

The writer and the composer became friends. "Draw on your passions, Varèse," Rolland wrote, "you are already the master of your musical language, with that virile youth and poetic talent I love."

Rolland introduced Varèse to Richard Strauss, and wrote to Strauss from Paris on February 21, 1909: "I talked a great deal this morning with one of the heads of the Orfeo of Barcelona and with a young French composer who has been living in Berlin for a couple of years and who admires you so much that he is afraid to call on you. His name is Edgard Varèse. He has great talent and seems to me particularly gifted as an orchestrator. I think you will find him interesting. He possesses what I believe you love as much as I do and what is so rare today—I mean *life*."**

In 1915 Varèse came to America and lived for most of the rest of his long life in Greenwich Village. He fell in love with New York and wrote, "Every age has its characteristic sounds. I have always listened to the sounds around me. There is always a sound in New

*Chère Sofia: Letters of Romain Rolland to Sofia Bertolini Guerrieri-Gonzaga (Paris: Albin Michel, 1951), II, 93.
**Richard Strauss—Romain Rolland Letters (Berkeley and Los Angeles: University of California Press, 1968), p. 88.

York. Be quiet and listen, and you will hear a roar. It keeps you company."

Manhattan, that man-made jungle that comes nearest of all cities to engulfing human individualism, obsessed him. And yet it offered exactly the atmosphere Varèse needed to develop his powerful musical instinct. "American music must speak its own language," he declared, "and not be the result of a certain mummified European music."

He was thirty-three when he arrived in New York, with thirty-two dollars in his pocket. He supported himself by odd musical jobs and was a first-rate choral director as well as conductor.* He courted an American girl, Louise Morton, and married her. In 1919 he founded the New Symphony Orchestra, the first ensemble in New York devoted wholly to modern music. Later he founded, with Carlos Salzedo, the International Composers Guild, which gave the American premieres of works by Debussy and Bartok, and of Schönberg's masterpiece, *Pierrot Lunaire.*

In 1920 Varèse began working on the music that symbolized his break with Europeanism: *Amériques* (first performed in 1926) was the ringing manifesto of Varèse's new world of sound. The premiere in 1923 of his *Hyperprism*, a short work as incisive as Picasso strokes on a drawing, created the first great scandal in New York musical circles. The audience rioted, and half of them left the hall when Varèse's fans insisted that the piece be played again.

Of *Hyperprism*, the American composer Charles Martin Loeffler wrote, "It would be the negation of all the centuries of music if I were to call this music. Nevertheless, I seemed to be dreaming of rites in Egyptian temples, of mystic and terrible ceremonies which history does not record. This piece roused in me a sort of subconscious racial memory, something elemental that happened before the beginning of recorded time."

For Varèse, all sounds were acceptable raw material for "the

---

*Jacques Barzun has pointed out to me that Varèse, early in his career in America, conducted a rare performance of the Berlioz *Requiem*. This took place at the old Hippodrome in New York, on April 1, 1917, "in memory of the dead of all nations." The rebel Varèse always felt an affinity to that great rebel Berlioz; after all, Berlioz too was passionately interested in *sound*, and wrote of one grandiose musical scheme, "As you may well suspect, entirely new means will have to be employed. . . ."

poetization of noise." The urban noise that increasingly had been inundating man since the nineteenth century—the sounds of airports, harbors, shrieking ambulances, airplanes, police sirens, air raids—all the cacophony of our age made the music of Varèse as unmistakably urban as Dvořák's is bucolic.

But there is much more to the music of Varèse than urban chaos. There is the sense of universality, of a world brought closer to jungles with chattering monkeys, shrill insects, and screaming birds; of the chants of India; of the prayers of Himalayan monks; and of Japanese *gagaku*. Today, Varèse's idea of pluralism in music has been totally accepted by young composers, and by pop musicians, who make collages, with equal aplomb, of rock, folk, Raga, and the idioms of Varèse himself.

Leopold Stokowski recognized Varèse's genius and played *Hyperprism* in Carnegie Hall and in Philadelphia. He was the only renowned conductor to schedule Varèse on his program. (Nicolas Slonimsky, Carlos Chávez and Waldman were other conductors devoted to both Varèse and his music.) There is no question that the unsettling appearance of Varèse, a stocky, vigorous figure, with strong blond features and hair flying in all directions, as well as his ruthless refusal to compromise in any way with taste and his open contempt of suave conductors and the whole sycophantic business of pleasing the socialites on the boards of directors of symphony orchestras, accounted in large part for the stone wall that divided him from an audience.

The harpist Lucile Lawrence, who had been married to Carlos Salzedo, another famous harpist and a passionate admirer of Varèse, once recalled,

> *People often asked why Koussevitsky, who played so many new works, never played Varèse's compositions. Some years ago Koussevitsky had an apartment in Paris where he went at the end of the Boston-Symphony season. Salzedo had tea with him there one afternoon, and was surprised to see two scores of Varèse—*Amériques *and* Arcana—*on the piano. Salzedo asked Koussevitsky if those works interested him. Koussevitsky replied that they interested him very much. "Why don't you play them?" asked Salzedo. Koussevitsky replied, "The day Varèse dedicates*

*a work to me, I'll play that one and all the others." Salzedo im-
mediately cabled Varèse to dedicate a work to Koussevitsky.
Varèse flatly refused. Apparently Koussevitsky had heard that
Varèse had dedicated a work to Stokowski....*

To Varèse, personal integrity was not a mere phrase, it was a
way of life. Years later, when he had gained a reputation as a composer of "shocking" avant-garde music, he was commissioned to write
music for a Hollywood film called *Carnegie Hall*, produced by Boris
Morros. Varèse wrote the music and was handed what for him was
an impressive check. When the time came for rehearsals in New York,
he went down to listen to what the producers were doing with his
music. When he heard the mangled performance, on which he had
not been consulted, he walked up and said, "Here is your check. Give
me back my score."

He once told a young composer, "You can't be both a virgin and
a whore." The young man asked, "What if I starve?"—a logical question in the days before universities fed composers. Varèse shrugged.
"Nobody asks you to compose music."

In 1925, Varèse composed *Intégrales*, in which the idea of "spatial
music," an idea that absorbs many composers today, was first proposed. *Intégrales* remains an extraordinary work, of which the Canadian poet Fernand Ouellette wrote, "Here Varèse found a way back,
beyond the area of musical form, to the very essence of song in its
most spontaneous manifestation: the sacred chant of man faced with
the mystery of God and the beyond, with the mystery of Nature."

In 1927, Varèse returned for a while to France.** His music still
provoked physical violence; at one of his concerts Tristan Tzara had
to be given four stitches after a battle in the hall. As always, other
artists sprang to Varèse's cause: Jules Pascin, Calder, Villa-Lobos,

---

*As quoted in Fernand Ouellette, *A Biography of Edgard Varèse* (New
York: Orion Press, 1968), p. 175. To anyone familiar with the egomania
of prima donna symphony conductors, with the busts and portraits of
Koussevitsky and the incense-laden atmosphere that filled Symphony Hall
throughout his era, this story carries the ring of truth.

**Louise Varèse told me that Leopold Stokowski saw Varèse off and pre-
sented him with a thousand dollars. It should also be noted (and saluted)
that Mrs. Harry Payne Whitney was the principal support of Varèse at
that period.

Artaud, and Malraux gathered round. Varèse collaborated at this time on a words-and-music scenario with Artaud, famous today for his "Theater of Cruelty." On a copy of one of his books Artaud wrote, "To my dear Edgard Varèse, whose music I love without having heard it, because hearing you talk about it has enabled me to dream of it."

Needless to say, Varèse was a great talker, bursting with ideas that he promoted ceaselessly. "We are quite satisfied that Boulder Dam expresses us better than the Egyptian pyramids," he said, "but in music we composers are forced to use instruments that have not changed for two centuries." When asked about Schönberg and Webern, he frankly confessed that the note-based organizational principles of the twelve-tone school did not appeal to him at all. "When every note in a composition has to be or can be explained, according to some system," he said, "the result is no longer music. Composition according to system is the admission of impotence." He spoke of "music as an art-science"; instead of saying that he was a musician, he declared that he worked with rhythms, frequencies, and intensities. "Most music sounds to me terribly enclosed," he said. "Corseted, one might say. I like music that explodes in space."

At another time he wrote, "I purposely do away with the 'note' in order to seek something deeper: 'sound.' I think of 'D' not as an artificial note of an imprisoning scale, but as a 'D' that is a number of frequencies in relation to other frequencies." It must be remembered that "neoclassicism" was all the rage in music at the time Varèse made these observations, and such notions seemed utterly absurd, the babblings of a mad artist.

Varèse wrote in Paris, prophetically: "New paths have been opened up for musicians by developments in the use of electricity, sound waves, etc. . . . The present tempered scale seems to me worn out. It no longer suffices to provide musical expression of our emotions or our conceptions. . . . *We are still in the first stammering stage of a new phase of music.* The instruments that the electrical engineers must perfect, with the collaboration of musicians, will make possible the use of *all* sounds, not only arbitrary ones—and also, in consequence, the perfection of any tempered scale music."

Those lines are a perfect description of the electronic musical devices of the 1960s and seventies, such as the RCA, Buchla, and Moog synthesizers. They were spoken by Edgard Varèse in Paris, in

1930, at a round-table discussion on the future of music. (Much the same ideas had been expressed a generation earlier by Busoni.) Toward the end of the 1930s Varèse wrote what may be called the manifesto of "The Liberation of Sound" and what is certainly a prophetic description of electronic music, which was as yet unborn:

The raw material of music is sound. *That is what the "reverent approach" has made most people forget—even composers. Today when science is equipped to help the composer realize what was never before possible—all that Beethoven dreamed, all that Berlioz gropingly imagined possible—the composer continues to be obsessed by traditions which are nothing but the limitations of his predecessors. Composers like anyone else today are delighted to use the many gadgets continually put on the market for our daily comfort. But when they hear sounds that no violins, wind instruments, or percussions of the orchestra can produce, it does not occur to them to demand those sounds of science. Yet science is even now equipped to give them everything they may require.*

And here are the advantages I anticipate from such a machine: liberation from the arbitrary paralyzing tempered system; the possibility of obtaining any number of cycles or, if still desired, subdivisions of the octave, and consequently the formation of any desired scale; unsuspected range in low and high registers; new harmonic splendors obtainable from the use of subharmonic combinations now impossible; the possibility of obtaining any differentiation of timbre, of sound-combinations, and new dynamics far beyond the present human-powered orchestra; a sense of sound projection in space by the emission of sound in any part or in many parts of the hall as may be required by the score; cross rhythms unrelated to each other, treated simultaneously, or to use the old word, "contrapuntally," since the machine would be able to beat any number of desired notes, any subdivision of them, omission or fraction of them—all these in a given unit of measure or time which is humanly impossible to attain.

Thus spoke the prophet, Edgard Varèse, long years before electronic music synthesizers had been invented.

The Depression years were unkind to Varèse. In the twenties he had been "temporarily famous," at least in avant-garde circles; but now musical taste swung toward the Americana populism themes of composers such as Aaron Copland and Roy Harris. And a new theme was heard: social consciousness. Varèse and his music went into eclipse. He became more moody and despondent; he toyed with the idea of suicide. For twelve years he composed no music and spoke bitterly of "changing his trade." Not only was he unwanted as a composer, he could find no one to engage him as a researcher in acoustics, a subject on which he was better informed than almost anyone in America. He applied to Bell Laboratories and, despite the good offices of Bell's Dr. Harvey Fletcher, was turned down. He applied repeatedly for a fellowship from the Guggenheim Foundation, once "for work on a musical instrument of electrical oscillations ... so as to obtain effects and high frequencies which no present instrument can give."

The Guggenheim directors, who have helped hundreds of now vanished composers, many of them unremarkable, had no allotment for Edgard Varèse. They also refused Arnold Schönberg's request for a grant that would give him the time and peace of mind to finish his masterpiece, the opera *Moses and Aaron*; thus the John Simon Guggenheim Memorial Foundation set up to nurture "creative work in any of the fine arts," holds the unique distinction of having refused two of the musical geniuses of this century.*

*Louise Varèse recalls that the Guggenheim Board turned down Varèse's application because he was "too well known." They turned down Schönberg's application for a fellowship in 1944. The grant would have paid Schönberg $2,500 a year; at that time the composer's basic income was his $38-a-month pension from the University of California in Los Angeles. Today, of course, the same University boasts a handsome Arnold Schönberg Building that probably cost several hundreds of thousands of dollars to build. So it goes. Stravinsky is reported to have remarked upon being told that Schönberg had once been rejected for the Guggenheim Fellowship: "Four more measures of *Moses and Aaron* would have been a greater contribution to music than all the works produced by all the recipients of the Guggenheim Fellowship."

In fairness to the Guggenheim Foundation, and those involved, I should like to add here a note from Otto Luening: "The attempt to downgrade the Guggenheim Foundation by saying they had helped unremarkable composers doesn't really work ... because at least seven of the people mentioned in the text received Guggenheim Fellowships. Louise Varèse is

In 1933, the painter Diego Rivera offered Varèse and his wife one of his houses so that they could live for a while in Mexico. They declined, however, and returned to their house in Greenwich Village. (Trotsky later moved into Rivera's house and was assassinated there.) That year, Nicolas Slonimsky conducted the first performance of Varèse's work *Ionisation*, scored for thirty-seven percussive instruments, including two sirens. *Ionisation* is today regarded as one of the signal masterpieces of our century. It was the first Western composition, other than folk music, to use only percussion instruments.

With *Ionisation*, Varèse presented the musical establishment with a bombshell: he challenged the very meaning of the term *music* as Western audiences had understood it until that time. *Ionisation* has nothing whatever to do with the traditional, "classical" music of the eighteenth and nineteenth centuries. The intense energies generated by the work must be experienced to be understood and appreciated. It was this piece that elicited Henry Miller's famous remark about an impact like "a sock on the jaw."

Paul Rosenfeld, who was almost the only music critic of the 1920s to grasp the importance of Varèse, wrote: "*Ionisation* sets living forces in action whose effects will never cease to be felt.... It suggests incandescent manifestations of material entities in space, and suggests the life of the inanimate universe."

Now the real tragedy of Varèse began to unfold. He simply could no longer compose, with the conventional instruments available to him, the fantastic music his mind's ear heard. Everything he had written until then was, by his thinking, for "make-do" instruments. He wrote to a friend, "I no longer wish to compose for the old instruments played by men. I am handicapped by a lack of adequate electrical instruments for which I can conceive my music."

---

correct in stating that the Guggenheim Foundation board turned down Varèse's application because he was too well known. Until recent years the Guggenheim Foundation concentrated more on younger applicants and this was the reason that both Varèse and Schönberg did not receive fellowships. Stravinsky's acid remarks, probably written by Robert Craft, are the privilege of an old man, but [they] don't help.... I suggested that Varèse apply for a Guggenheim Fellowship in the 1950s, and write to the secretary of the Foundation, Henry Moe, because the policy in regard to older musicians had changed somewhat, but he didn't apply."

Today one can hear the strained quality in much of Varèse's music, the work of a visionary artist trying to create his new world of sound, yet imprisoned by the seventy or eighty pitch levels of the orchestral instruments with which he was compelled to work. "The instruments we composers are forced to use reached their perfection in the eighteenth century," Varèse wrote. "By now they should be as obsolete for the transportation of our music as stage-coaches for the transportation of our bodies."

This was hardly a new notion to Varèse. As far back as 1917 he had written, in the New York Dadaist magazine *391*, "*I dream of instruments obedient to my thought, and which with their contribution of a whole new world of unsuspected sound will lend themselves to the exigencies of my inner rhythm.*"

Thus the tragedy of Varèse—a tragedy not experienced by any composer before him—was that his musical poetry and his thought were thirty years ahead of the technological discoveries he needed. He was a titan trying to reach beyond ordinary instrumental capacities into unexplored sonic territories, and as a result he was creatively paralyzed. "He was being devoured, as it were, by his own inner and unappeasable visions," Fernand Ouellette wrote. "He could not free himself from the sounds that were inflaming his soul, and there was just no way of producing those sounds. . . . He was to remain thus torn between his needs and the meagerness of his means."

Varèse's brain teemed with music composed in densities and volumes of sound, rather than in harmonies and melodies. He dreamed of music as sculpture in space—a newly imagined sound-space in which sonorous objects slowly revolved in a kind of acoustical geometry. He heard music which, instead of unfolding in time (that is, from the time of the beginning of the piece until its end), existed in *space*, as architecture and sculpture do. He heard music of three dimensions, with spatial objects hurling and colliding, sonorities moving in sweeping planes and levels. Indeed, Varèse's music has often been called "frozen architecture."

In 1936 he resumed work on *Espace*, which he had labored on intermittently since 1930, and the announcement of the event in *The New York Times* suggests the conflict that thwarted him: "Mr. Varèse's composition will be played conventionally, without the electrical appliances he foresees," the *Times* reported.

Much of Varèse's raging struggle at this time is perfectly presented in Romain Rolland's fictional account of a composer's life, *Jean Christophe*: "The difficulty began when he [Jean-Christophe] tried to cast his ideas in the ordinary musical forms: he made the discovery that none of the ancient molds were suited to them; if he wished to fix his visions with fidelity he had to begin by forgetting all he had heard...."

In 1937, Varèse's old friend André Malraux turned up in New York to solicit support for the Spanish Republic. Malraux spent an evening at the home of Varèse, and by the next morning the two had decided to collaborate. They held a press conference, announcing their plan to collaborate on a work to be called *A Symphony of the Revolution*. "For Mr. Varèse," the *Times* reported, "M. Malraux will become a poet, rewriting lyric passages of his novel *Days of Wrath*, reflecting what goes on in a communist's mind in the face of death of the cause."

The project was never completed. The only work that Varèse composed between 1934 and 1950 was *Densité 21.5*, a piece for solo flute, commissioned by the famous flutist George Barrere. This piece— "one long cry of tragic intensity"—had its premiere at a gala benefit concert for a French cause at Carnegie Hall. Lily Pons and Lucienne Boyer also appeared on the program, and all the New York critics were there; not one of them bothered to review the new composition by Edgard Varèse.

So it went. He became more and more bitter, cursing the musical life he had chosen. He refused even to attempt to compose music. He was not alone in suffering the musical establishment's indifference and neglect: another great, solitary voice, Bela Bartok, died in 1945.

After World War II, young composers in France and Germany turned enthusiastically to the newly developed medium of tape recording. Throughout the world there was a sudden interest in electronic devices as possible sources of a new musical language and in "the structuring of acoustical space." A scientific approach to music suddenly became fashionable. People remembered that a French composer living in New York had been predicting precisely this since 1916. Varèse was suddenly "rediscovered"; he was asked to lecture on his theories at Columbia, Princeton, Yale and other universities.

He was invited to work and compose at the Radio Television

Française research center, where Pierre Schaeffer had launched *Musique concrète*. Now seventy-one years old, Varèse arrived in Paris in 1954, loaded down with taped sounds and diagrams. He immediately plunged into work; at last, after nearly two decades of silence, he had the tools he needed.

He finished a remarkable work called *Déserts*, and Hermann Scherchen conducted the first performance of it in Paris, in the famous Théâtre des Champs-Élysées, where Stravinsky's *The Rite of Spring* had created a scandal some forty years before.

Varèse himself said explicitly—in words that have been echoed by hundreds of young painters and poets and composers who seek to expand their perceptions and our own—that the word "desert" is to be understood as suggesting not merely "all physical deserts (of sand, snow, sea, of empty city streets), but also the deserts in the mind of man; not only those stripped aspects of Nature that suggest bareness, aloofness, timelessness, but also *that remote inner space no telescope can reach, where man is alone, a world of mystery and essential loneliness."*

Déserts has been described by one critic as "tragic music, the tragedy of an age. It is a unique, frightening masterpiece of the atomic age; man's suffering, evil, despair, and nothingness are all here as in no other piece of music." Another wrote, "This is music that scrapes the listener to the bone." Most of the audience, however, was hostile, and there were cries of "Shame! Shame!" and "That's enough now!" One French critic wrote the majority opinion on Varèse: "What our electro-symphonist needs is a trip to the electric chair!"

Nevertheless, after *Déserts*, Varèse was reestablished as a significant force of the current musical scene. *Déserts* was the first important work of electronic music, "the opening gun in the battle for the liberation of sound." He was invited to the Bennington College and to Germany. The public was astounded that he was still alive, let alone so full of energy. The Italian composer Luigi Dellapiccola described Varèse at this time as "a giant, violent and very witty in conversation, a prince who enjoys dealing with the people." The critic H. H. Stuckenschmidt spoke of Varèse at the Darmstadt Festival: "This man of seventy-one has suddenly appeared on the horizon of the musical world, not as a twilight-shrouded figure, but rather as a living torch burning with creative musical ideas."

In 1954, André Malraux, who had become a powerful figure as De Gaulle's Minister of Culture, tried to persuade his old friend to return to France. "Your works intrigue all the young musicians here, and fascinate those who know them." Varèse demurred, explaining that he was content to remain in New York. Malraux wrote back, in effect, that "they'll put up that plaque on the little house on Sullivan Street whether you die there or not."

Varèse still preferred New York. He was famous now and was being interviewed endlessly. His ideas were always explosive. "Now that we have electronic instruments, the interpreter will disappear like the storyteller in literature after the invention of printing." "Conductors? They are middlemen. They are anxious to get first performances, and then never play the music again. What is it, a first performance? What does it mean? The tenth, the twentieth performance —that's the important thing." "The future composer of symphonies will consult the scientist in his laboratory instead of the violin maker in his garret." "The tempered scale is both a prison and an imbecility." "The electronic instrument is an additive, not a destructive factor, in the art and science of music. Just because there are other ways of getting there, you do not kill the horse."

In his old age he was still a promethean force, a determined-looking, heavy-set man, with the head of an Old Testament prophet. He was an awesome figure striding into a concert hall and there were always murmurs, "Varèse ... it's him, Varèse ..." One critic wrote that interviewing Varèse was like trying to encircle a geyser. "That goddam piano and organ are ruining music," Varèse told *The New York Times.*

"We must draw a line between entertainment and art," he said. "Art is from the shoulders up. The other is from the hips down." He hated to be called an experimenter. "I do not write experimental music. My experimenting is done before I make the music. Afterwards it is the listener who must experiment."

More recognition came. He was invited to work at the Columbia-Princeton Electronic Music Center. He was working at last with electronic sound resources, and was more convinced than ever of the enormous possibilities of the medium.

He said in an interview:

I am fascinated by the fact that through electronic means one can generate a sound simultaneously. . . . You aren't programming something musical, something to be done, but using it directly, which gives an entirely different dimension to musical space and projection. For instance, in the use of an oscillator, it is not a question of working against it or taming it, but using it directly without, of course, letting it use you. The same pertains to mixing and filtering. To me, working with electronics is composing with living sounds, paradoxical though that may appear. . . . I want to be in the material, part of the acoustical vibration, so to speak."

Later he said in a lecture:

The electronic medium is also adding an unbelievable variety of new timbres to our musical store. But most important of all, it has freed music from the tempered system, which has prevented music from keeping pace with the other arts and with science. Composers are now able, as never before, to satisfy the dictates of that inner ear of the imagination. They are also lucky so far in not being hampered by aesthetic codification—at least not yet! But I am afraid it will not be long before some musical mortician begins enbalming electronic music in rules.*

His music was admirably recorded by Robert Craft for Columbia records; he received the Brandeis University Creative Arts Award; he was honored in Japan. He was elected a member of the Swedish Royal Academy—"The Nobel Prize without the cash," as Alexis Léger observed. Although Koussevitsky had refused to play the music of Varèse during his lifetime, Varèse was now commissioned by the Koussevitsky Foundation, which also subsidized recordings of his compositions.

In 1956, Varèse was seventy-three, an age when most men are content to putter about and look back. But in this year a Monsieur

---

*From a lecture given at Yale University, 1962.

Kalff, a director of Philips, the giant electrical combine of Holland, visited Le Corbusier, the world-celebrated architect. He had come to ask "Corbu" if he would be willing to design and create the Philips pavilion for the World's Fair that was to be held in Brussels in 1958.

Corbu immediately started throwing off sparks. "Suddenly there sprang to my mind, out of the unknown, the notion of an 'Electronic Poem,'" he said later. "A work capable of profoundly affecting the human sensibility by audio-visual means ... to bring together on the creative level, by means of electronics, speed, number, color, sound, noise, unlimited power. Such was the sudden idea!"

In sum, Le Corbusier was using multi-media technique early in the game. "I will not create for you a pavilion, monsieur," he told the gentleman from Philips. "I will create a *Poème électronique* together with the vessel that will contain it. The vessel will be the pavilion, and there will be no façade to this vessel."

His brain was working feverishly five minutes after M. Kalff had introduced himself. Of course, there had to be music. Very bold, very special music. Who should he get to compose it? "Sounds, noises, unlimited power," Le Corbusier brooded, "a new creation opening all before it. . . . Suddenly I thought of Varèse, with whom I had had no dealings for nearly twenty-five years."*

The director had never heard of M. Varèse. He wanted a gold-plated big-name composer—say Aaron Copland or William Walton. But Le Corbusier would not budge. "My feeling on this was so strong that I was forced to say that I would not undertake to create this task except on condition that Varèse would create the music."

Meetings and consultations followed, in which representatives of Philips tried to persuade the great architect to agree on a more glittering name. "You must take it or leave it, as you wish, gentlemen," Corbu replied magnificently. "And, moreover, I make it a condition that Varèse shall be accorded a remuneration worthy of him."

Reluctantly, the officials of Philips agreed. Corbu at once wrote Varèse in New York, concluding, "I impose no scenario or condition of any kind. You will just do as you wish in the *Poème électronique*. I shall leave you quite free."

---

*This delightful episode is detailed in full in a letter of 1960 from Le Corbusier to Fernand Ouellette.

Rather dazedly, Varèse accepted. It was too good to be true. It was a miraculous gift from the gods at the end of his lifetime. He would not be merely collaging and interposing taped sounds, as he had done in *Déserts*; he would be creating music directly on magnetic tape—truly electronic music.

He was offered the use of the great Philips laboratory at Eindhoven, where he would have engineers and technicians to help him. Money was no problem. And above all, *mirabile dictu*, at the Brussels Fair he would write music that truly would move about in space, for his music was to sound from everywhere—on 425 loudspeakers!

Despite his age, he plunged into work with the energy of six men. He arrived in Holland for a preliminary visit to the Philips plant and found that Le Corbusier was off in India supervising a monumental project. Corbu had left his right-hand man, Yannis Xenakis, in charge of the pavilion plans. (Xenakis is better known today as a composer himself.)

The directors of Philips were openly hostile toward Varèse and his plans. Xenakis told him, "Don't let them make you give ground. Le Corbusier asked you to create this music, and he will stand up for you to the end. When LC returns from India, one bang of his fist on the table will bring the directors to heel."

Corbu returned and banged his fist on the table, and the directors reluctantly agreed to accept Varèse with no further objections. Varèse went ahead full-speed with the "480 seconds of music" that Corbu had commissioned. After eight months of hard work, he was ready. Philips asked to hear what he had written for their exhibition, in which they had invested $260,000. When they heard it, they were aghast. Cabals against him began anew.

"These gentlemen would be very happy to be rid of me," Varèse told Xenakis. "But I am not accustomed to being pushed around." Xenakis sent a grave warning to Le Corbusier, "More hostility against Varèse. There is definitely going to be an explosion."

Corbu cabled Philips, from his monumental architectural project at Chandigarh, that "The *Poème électronique* cannot be carried out except by Varèse's strange music. There cannot for a moment be a question of giving up Varèse. If that should happen, I will withdraw from the project entirely. Varèse is a great name in modern music."

The apprehensive officials were cowed once more, but they appealed to Varèse to write something more pleasant, to make concessions. The man whom the Nobel laureate Alexis Léger had described as "one of those artists for whom nothing has value in art but the truly creative work; his life is a noble lesson in integrity," looked at them.

"Make concessions?" Varèse said. "In music? That is something that has never happened to me."

Le Corbusier chuckled when he heard this story. "Varèse has a rotten character like my own," he said.

Just before the opening of the Exposition, Le Corbusier said in an interview: "After forty years of daily struggle, there is a combination made by the hands of the gods. Color, light, sound, and picture will be orchestrated. My friend Varèse has composed the music. . . . And then when the Exposition, that great ephemeral thing, has disappeared, the pavilion will be razed, because death is part of the things of life. . . . On April 17th, by pressing a button, we shall know what the pavilion is worth. Will the baby be beautiful? How can we tell before its birth? We are in the unknown, for all our tools surpass the existing ones. Varèse's music accompanies a poem whose performance lasts eight minutes—four hundred and eighty seconds. What will these minutes be worth? Ask a condemned man what he thinks of the last eight minutes of his life."

With the *Poème électronique*, Varèse entered the creative world he had anticipated decades before. It seems today an almost inevitable climax to his career, and it was accomplished with mastery and authority. The *Poème* is music that is fundamentally human, despite its large portion of nonhuman sounds. What it seems to demonstrate, more now than ever before, is the human condition—that condition that was always mysterious and terrifyingly strange in itself, and has been made more terrifying by man's diabolic inventiveness. The *Poème électronique*—a blend of pure tone, instrumental and vocal sounds, and noise—achieved a humanity that is not usually found in electronic compositions or *musique concrète*.

Varèse is not concerned with the passions of the human heart, with joy, grief, rage, laughter, or sentiment. Rather, he presents us with music that is indeed "completely divorced from the Good and the Bad." It is a new world of pure sound, of "organized sound," as Varèse himself called it, and it is now inhabited by Boulez, Stockhausen, Cage, and many more of today's composers of electronic music.

In this extraordinary piece, pitch itself—that is, notes being "high" or "low" in relation to each other—becomes not the ongoing, all-powerful generator of the form of the piece, but rather one aspect of timbre. Ever-moving color and accent predominate instead, and Varèse's play of potential and kinetic energies, his personal "imagined musical space" of invented musical shapes and powerful blocks of sound piled together in vast, spatial juxtapositions.

Howard Taubman reported on the Pavilion for *The New York Times*:

> *In a building that looks like an improbable and gigantic seashell frozen into silvered concrete, these men have attempted to unite light, color, imagery, rhythm, sound and architecture. The interior of this odd structure has three apexes. The walls are bare and lofty. In the dim lighting, one can discern a large-scale model of an atom hanging by what seems like a thread.*
>
> *From another apex there is suspended a nude figure. The 500 persons who crowded the floor-space—all is standing room—for each show, which lasts only eight minutes, wonder what is in store. They have every reason to suspect that they will encounter something different, and they are not disappointed. The lights go down. Out of the 400 loudspeakers situated in the walls in every part of the structure eerie sounds emerge. They are accompanied by washes of color that change and merge with imperceptible nuance. . . .*
>
> *One hears rattles, whistles, thunders and murmurs. At one point there is a sound that seems to emerge from a human throat. This score is not compounded of recognizable instruments. It is the work of a man who has been seeking for several decades to return music to a purity of sound that he does not believe possible in conventional music making.*

Two million people saw and heard the *Poème électronique* at the Brussels Fair. After the Fair closed, the *Poème électronique* was demolished, despite the pleas of art lovers throughout Europe who wanted to preserve Le Corbusier's and Varèse's magnificent and uniquely twentieth-century creation.

None of the musical establishment of America was interested in reproducing Varèse's music; it was left to the *Village Voice* to present a tape-recording of the *Poème électronique* in 1958, fittingly at "The Village Gate" in Varèse's beloved little province of Greenwich Village. But in the next few years honors and accolades poured in from all over the world; at last he was celebrated. The world had caught up with Varèse's concept of music: not harmonies and melodies, but rather volumes and densities of sound. A whole generation of young composers began to look at the musical piece as a "sound-object"—much as the new painters developed a cool, dispassionate concern with abstract art—and Varèse emerged as a major influence upon them.

This was the legacy of Varèse: he created a sound-universe that is half-scientific, half-magical, yet in which the ordering hand is always human. In the *Poème électronique* it is a human voice that cries out from the enormous prison of space and the physical universe. He also left us what the composer Elliot Carter, a lifelong friend, called "a special concern with sound, with music as a thing in itself. It is this compelling assertion which gives his work so much meaning."

Perhaps the importance of Varèse was best expressed in 1928 by Paul Rosenfeld, in words that sound amazingly contemporary in the 1970s: "In the music of Varèse, the impulse is one of unity, or perfection born of a wholeness in the psyche and moving towards a condition satisfactory to the entire man."*

After his Brussels triumph, Varèse's health began to fail. Disturbed by bronchial attacks, his lion's strength ebbed away. He waited impatiently to be strong again, and wrote to a friend, "I have plans for five projects. I shall have to make up for lost time." As he became weaker, he tried to hide his fatigue from visitors. Knowing his end was near, he muttered, "I loathe death, I hate it."

He died on November 6, 1965. At the time of his death preparations were being made in both New York and Paris to salute him on his eightieth birthday. But in fact Varèse was already nearly 82. The old revolutionist was always ahead of his time.

*Paul Rosenfeld, *Musical Impressions* (New York: Hill and Wang, 1969), p. 273.

CHAPTER VII

A Chronology of Electronic Music, From the Invention of the Phonograph (1877-1896) to the First "School" of Electronic Music, "Musique concrète" (1948)

THE FIRST PIECES OF ELECTRONIC MUSIC TO BURST UPON A STARTLED world shortly after World War II were the outgrowths of much pioneering work. It sometimes appears as though electronic music began in the 1950s, with the development of the tape recorder and electrically generated sound. Nothing could be further from the truth. Serious experimentation and the search for a means of direct production, reproduction, and manipulation of sound by electronic means had been going on for fully a half century. The following is a chronological list of musical visionaries and scientific researchers who prepared the way.*

1877–1896, USA Thomas Edison (1847–1931) and Emile Berliner (1851–1929) independently develop and patent the cylindrical and disc phonograph systems.

1876, Philadelphia At the Philadelphia Centennial, Elisha Gray (another inventor of a telephone along with Bell) demonstrates his "Electromusical Piano," transmitting musical tones over wires to a fascinated audience.

1880, Washington, D.C. Alexander Graham Bell (1847–1922) finances his own laboratory to promote research relating to sound and

*I am indebted above all to the admirable and indefatigable Lowell Cross, as well as to William Austin, Otto Luening, Henri Pousseur, Hugh Davies, and many others for much of the historical material that follows. Standard reference books and encyclopedias also have been consulted.

acoustics. Bell, with his early dedication to work in speech and hearing, had long been interested in the study of sound reproduction. Together with Charles S. Tainter, Bell devised and patented several means for transmitting and recording sound.

1895, USA

Dr. Thaddeus Cahill (1867–1934) applied for patent for "sounding staves," granted as U.S. Patent 520,667 in 1897.

1898, Copenhagen

Valdemar Poulsen (1869–1942) patents his "Telegraphone," the first magnetic recording machine.

1900, USA

W. Duddell describes the first (?) audio oscillator (negative resistance oscillator) in his article, "On Rapid Variations in the Current through the Direct-Current Arc."

1906, New York

Cahill's "Telharmonium" (or "Dynamophone," Holyoke, Mass.) is described in two articles in *Electrical World*, "The Art of Telharmony" and "The Generating and Distributing of Music by Means of Alternators."

1906, USA

Lee De Forest (1873–1961) develops the triode "audion," the first vacuum tube. This and his 300 other patents, have a deciding influence on modern communications.

1906, New York

Ray Stannard Baker discusses Cahill's work in "New Music for an Old World," an article appearing in *McClure's Magazine*.

1907, Berlin

Ferruccio Busoni (1866–1924) reads Baker's article and enthusiastically foresees the promise of Cahill's work in his *Entwurf einer neuen Aesthetik der Tonkunst*.

1910–1913, Italy

Francesco Pratella (1880–1955) and Luigi Russolo (1885–1947) publish their Futurist manifestoes for music in Milan and Florence.

1911, Vienna

Arnold Schönberg (1874–1951) completes his *Har-*

monielehre, which he concludes with the proposal of timbre-melody ("Klangfarbenmelodie").

1912, USA	Henry Cowell (1897–1965) introduces "tone clusters" in piano music, at the University of California. Cowell's tone clusters gave the impulse for further extension of piano resonance (later developed by Cage), and for other preparations of the piano and other instruments for experimental music.
1914, Milan	Russolo's first "art of noises" concert, April 21, is performed on his "Intonarumori." The "Intonarumori" were acoustical noise-instruments, whose sounds (howls, roars, shuffles, gurgles, etc.) were hand-activated and projected by horns and megaphones. Similar concerts took place in Paris during the week of June 17–24, 1921.
1915, USA	Lee De Forest patents three-electrode vacuum tube and also electric apparatus for producing music.
1916, New York	Edgard Varèse (1883–1965) calls for new musical instruments and enrichment of our "musical alphabet" (quoted in *The New York Morning Telegraph*).
1919–1920 (Leningrad and Moscow)	Leon Termen (name Gallicized as "Theremin," b. 1896), builds and demonstrates his "Etherophone" or "Thereminovox" (U.S. Patent, 1928).
1922, New York	Varèse insists that "the composer and the electrician will have to labor together" (quoted in *Christian Science Monitor*).
1922–1927, Paris	Darius Milhaud (b. 1892) experiments with vocal transformation by phonograph speed change.
1924, Berlin	Jörg Mager (1880–1939) publishes *Eine neue Epoche der Music durch Radio* and exhibits the "Sphaerophon," the first of his electronic performance instruments (others: "Elektrophon," "Kaleidophon," and "Partiturophon"). All were later destroyed in World War II.

1924, Rome	The composer Ottorino Respighi (1879–1936) calls for a phonograph recording of nightingales in his *Pini di Roma*.
1924–1925, Budapest	Dr. Endre Magyari constructs electronic devices for Radio Budapest's identification signal.
1925, USA	The composer George Antheil (1900–1959), in his unfinished opera *Mr. Bloom* uses motors and amplifiers.
1926, Donaueschingen	At the Chamber Music Festival in Donaueschingen it is proposed that recordings can be used as creative tools for musical composition.
1926–1927 Paris/New York	First performances of *Ballet Mécanique* (with decor by F. Léger), for which the composer Antheil required car horns, airplane propellers, saws, and anvils.
1927, New York	Varèse begins his discussion with Harvey Fletcher of Bell Telephone Laboratories concerning the development of an electronic instrument for composition. Varèse applied for Guggenheim Fellowships until 1936, so that he, René Bertrand, Fletcher, and others could collaborate. He was denied each time.
1927, Berlin	H. H. Stuckenschmidt, associate of Dada group and of Antheil, writes essay hailing "Machines, a vision of the future," and predicts that machines will transform the whole art of music.
1927, Berlin	Paul Hindemith (1895–1963) composes for mechanical organ to accompany cartoon film, "Felix the Cat."
1928, Paris	Maurice Martenot (b. 1898) demonstrates the "Ondes Martenot" at the Paris Opera, April 20. The instrument was later used by a long list of composers, including Honegger, Milhaud, Messiaen, Jolivet, Koechlin, and Varèse.
1928, Berlin	Friedrich Trautwein (1888–1956) completes the "Trautonium," an electronic instrument. Later, the instrument was used by Richard Strauss, Hindemith, and Werner Egk.

1928, Berlin	Robert Beyer (b. 1901) develops new attitudes on the spatial aspects of music in his article, "Das Problem der 'kommenden Musik,'" appearing in *Die Musik*.
1928, Germany	Walther Ruttmann (1887–1941) composes a soundtrack montage for film (sound only, no visuals).
1928, France	René Bertrand exhibits the "Dynamophone."
1929, Evanston, Ill.	Laurens Hammond (b. 1895) establishes his company for the manufacture of electronic musical instruments, which have included the "Hammond Organ," the "Novachord," the "Solovox," and reverberation devices.
1929, Frankfurt-am-Main	Bruno Hellberger and Peter Lertes collaborate on the "Hellertion."
1929, Paris	Givelet and E. E. Coupleux demonstrate a music "synthesizer" utilizing four electronic oscillators controlled by punched paper rolls (U.S. Patent 1,957,392).
1929, New York	Joseph Schillinger (1895–1943) composes his *First Airphonic Suite for Theremin with Orchestra*, performed with Sokoloff conducting the Cleveland Orchestra and Leon Theremin as soloist.
1929–1930, Berlin	Paul Hindemith and Ernst Toch (1887–1964) experiment with phonograph techniques at the Rundfunkversuchsstelle, Staatliche Hochschule für Musik. Their compositions included *Studie für instrumentale Klänge*, *Studie für vokale Klänge* (Hindemith), and *Fuge aus der Geographie*, phonograph version (Toch).
1930, Berlin	Trautwein publishes his *Elektrische Musik*.
1930–1932, Dessau	László Moholy-Nagy (1895–1946), Oskar Fischinger, Trautwein, Paul Arma (b. 1905), and other Bauhaus artists work with "drawn sound" and other sound-on-film techniques.
1931, Germany	Winifred Wagner commissions Mager to produce electronically synthesized bell sounds for the Bayreuth production of *Parsifal*.

A CHRONOLOGY OF ELECTRONIC MUSIC

1931, USA	Henry Cowell devises and has built by Theremin an electric instrument known as the rhythmicon, which can play metrical combinations of virtually unlimited complexity. He composes a concerto for it, *Rythmicana*.
1931, New York	Schillinger reviews and forecasts electronic applications for music in his article, "Electricity, a Musical Liberator," appearing in *Modern Music*.
1932, New York	Leopold Stokowski (b. 1882) addresses the Acoustical Society of America, calling for a collaboration among physicists, musicians, and psychologists, and predicting a time when the composer "can create directly into *Tone*, not on paper."
1933–1937, Paris	Maurice Jaubert (1900–1949) and Arthur Honegger (1892–1955) manipulate soundtracks for their motion-picture music.
1934, Paris	The Russian mystic and composer Nicolas Oboukhov (1892–1954) supervises the construction of his "Croix sonore," an electronic instrument in the form of a cross.
1934, New York	Edgard Varèse commissions two electronic instruments to his specifications from Theremin, for use in Varèse's piece, *Ecuatorial*. The instruments have a range up to 12544.2 cycles.
1935, Germany	The manufacturing firm Allgemeine Elektrizitäts Gesellschaft (AEG) builds and demonstrates the first "Magnetophon" (tape recorder), using magnetic tape developed by Fritz Pfleumer and manufactured by I. G. Farben AG.
1935, Leningrad	Yevgeny Sholpo (d. 1951) constructs "Variophones" (four models), which used graphic coding of films and were forerunners of the ANS (photoelectric sound synthesizer) of the Moscow experimental studio.
c. 1936, New York	Varèse experiments with phonographs that could be operated backward and at variable speeds.

1937, Mexico/N.Y.	Carlos Chávez (b. 1899) calls for a collaboration among engineers and composers in his book, *Toward a New Music.* He also prophesizes elimination of performers as middlemen between composers and listeners, through sound film.
1937, France	Olivier Messiaen (b. 1908) writes *Fêtes des belles eaux,* for six Ondes.
1937, Seattle	John Cage (b. 1912) foresees "the synthetic production of music . . . through the aid of electrical instruments which will make available for musical purposes any and all sounds that can be heard."
1938, Paris	Martenot, now a professor at the Paris Conservatoire, builds a special model of his invention, the Ondes Martenot, following specifications of Rabindranath Tagore and Alain Danielou, for the purpose of reproducing the microtonal refinements of Hindu music.
1938, Berlin	Harold Bode (b. 1909) builds the electronic "Melodium."
1939, Seattle	Cage realizes his *Imaginary Landscape No. 1* at the radio studio of the Cornish School. The work, to be performed as a recording or as a broadcast, calls for muted piano, cymbal, and two variable-speed turntables playing Victor test recordings of mixed and variable frequencies. Cage's article "Goal: New Music, New Dance" is published in *Dance Observer.*
1940, Germany	Richard Strauss (1864–1949) uses trautonium in his *Japanese Festival Music.*
1940, Ottawa	Hugh Le Caine (b. 1914) initiates his development of electronic musical instruments at the National Research Council of Canada.
ca. 1940, Princeton, N.J.	Milton Babbitt (b. 1916) experiments with film soundtracks.
1941, Paris	Georges Jenny constructs the "Ondioline."

1942, Chicago	Cage composes *March (Imaginary Landscape No. 2)* for percussion quintet and amplified coil of wire, and *Imaginary Landscape No. 3* for percussion, tin cans, muted gong, audio frequency oscillators, variable speed turntables, frequency recordings, buzzer, amplified coil of wire, and marimbula amplified by a contact microphone.
1942, New York	In the journal *Modern Music*, Cage writes an article, "For More New Sounds," and advocates "experimental radio music" to carry forward efforts so far limited to percussion.
1943, New York	Sydney Bechet, the great jazz saxophonist, experiments with superimposing, mixing, and performing on recordings.
1944, USA	Cage performs pieces for "prepared piano," substitute for percussion ensemble.
1944, New York	Percy Grainger (1882–1961) and Burnett Cross patent a device for "Free Music" employing eight audio oscillators and synchronizing equipment. Since 1895, Grainger had been developing a "Free Music," with eighth-tones and complete rhythmic freedom of the single voice, noted on graph paper.
1944–1950, Paris	Paul Boisselet (b. 1917) experiments with disc and tape procedures.
1945, USA	J. M. Hanert describes an electronic music synthesizer using punched cards to encode the electrical analogs of musical parameters (U.S. Patent 2,541,051).
1945–1948, Ottawa	Le Caine develops the "Electronic Sackbut," an instrument performed in the three space coordinates.
1947–1955, London	Tristram Cary (b. 1925) experiments with disc manipulations.
1948, Berlin	Oskar Sala (b. 1910) supervises the construction of the "Mixturtrautonium," an extended version of Traut-

wein's instrument. Henze, Orff, and Erbse later compose music for the instrument.

1948, Paris

Pierre Schaeffer (b. 1910) inaugurates *"Musique concrète"* at a Paris radio studio. This is the beginning of the "first school" of electronic music.

PART THREE

The First "Schools" of Electronic Music in the 1950s

CHAPTER VIII

The Breakthrough of the
Tape Recorder

OF THE MANY CHALLENGING DEVELOPMENTS IN MUSIC AFTER World War II, the three most significant were the revival of interest in the Schönberg-Webern serial technique; the legitimizing of chance and improvisation in musical works; and the advent of electronic music.

In Europe and America a generation of composers sprang up yearning to restructure musical thought as though from the Year One. Many of them astutely recognized that magnetic tape, which had been perfected during the war, was the tool they needed.

The tape recorder almost instantly became an easily handled medium for tonal manipulation, pointing to dazzling new possibilities in music.* Any sound could be captured, and undreamed-of new sounds could be created.

Three important pioneering centers of experimentation soon emerged. They were the *Musique concrète* group in Paris, led by Pierre Schaeffer; the Cologne studio in Germany (from which the composer Stockhausen emerged); and the collaboration of Otto Luening and Vladimir Ussachevsky in New York (which later evolved into the Columbia-Princeton Electronic Music Center). All three groups had different approaches to the new field of sound production, and all are of historical importance in music.

*The possibility of using magnetic fluctuations for recording and reproducing sound was known as early as 1898, when a patent was issued to Valdemar Poulsen of Copenhagen. The first magnetic tape recorder, the AEG magnetophon, was demonstrated in Germany in 1935. The tape was made of metal, and the device did not reach manageable proportions until plastic tape was developed, after World War II. The working side of this tape is coated with an emulsion containing microscopic metallic particles. As it passes the recording head, a fluctuating magnetic field, created in response to modulated electrical signals, causes the particles to align themselves in patterns which can later be made to create identical voltages in the playback head, whence they are fed to an amplifier and converted to audibility.

The Importance of the Tape Recorder

In the 1970s we are so accustomed to the marvel of the tape recorder that we take for granted its revolutionary properties. *Tape flows with the passage of time, and yet allows any instant to be picked up, captured, isolated.* Thus musical composition completely independent of physical sound production was now possible.

The importance to music of this invention cannot be overestimated. In a live performance all sounds immediately disappear. The fact that "music dies as soon as it is born" had always been a part of its poignant appeal. Thus, we had captured sound on phonograph records, but now, with tape, sound for the first time possessed plasticity. You could weld, mold, and blend it as a painter would his materials. In the words of the composer Hugh Le Caine, "The fleeting and transitory nature of sound was conquered. Now a sound could be criticized, considered, evaluated, could be multiplied and transformed, set to any desired time-relation to itself. The heart of the matter, of course, is the conquest of time."

It was now possible for anyone to make a permanent record of any sound he desired: voices, instruments, sirens, foghorns, trains, or whatever. As many amateurs know, a bit of patching and splicing can easily produce a "Symphony of Noises"—the aural counterpart of the painter's collage or the filmmaker's montage. Tapes can be speeded up or slowed down, thus producing not only a complete range of speeds, but also transpositions of register up to the highest peeps and squeaks and down to the lowest rumbles. With certain equipment it is even possible to alter speed without affecting pitch. And any pattern can readily be turned backward. Bits of tape can be chopped up and spliced in countless combinations. Big patterns can be juxtaposed; single sounds can be pared, or traced out with a razor blade in endless ways, each providing a different alteration of the original sound. In expert hands, sophisticated and ingenious manipulations can present a time-shattering continuity. Editing techniques also afford the composer an unprecedented freedom in the handling of rhythm. Irrational rhythmic structures that simply cannot be played by any orchestra or others that are beyond the grasp of even the most accomplished soloist can, by precise editing, be easily elaborated and heard in all their perfection.

With tape, the almost limitless range of "natural" and "artificial" sound material can be captured on a *permanent canvas*, so to speak, without the unwieldy limitations of phonograph recordings. The composer can control, with the greatest precision, duration and amplitude. He can create complex structures through dubbing. He can make "contrapuntal" superimpositions of any kind, and as he pleases. Through the use of filters, he can alter his basic material; he can also transform his basic material by reverberation techniques and other manipulations of the tape itself. Tiny bits of sound may be placed on circular strands—"tape loops"—thus providing the possibility of limitless repetition of particular patterns.

In sum, for musicians with vision, the tape recorder opened up a staggering new world of possibilities. It made the recorded piece of music itself a musical instrument—this was the achievement of the *Musique concrète* school. It also sparked a revolution in music of a scale unparalleled since the medieval discovery of organum, the principle that a plainsong could be harmonized by the addition of one, two, or three more parts. And it meant that the visionary ideas of Busoni, the Italian Futurists, and Varèse could be realized. With tape materials, the creative intelligence of a composer could at last manipulate sounds—*all sounds—into a communicative experience*. The limits of the musical horizon were no longer the limits of instruments and performers, but of human perception itself.

CHAPTER IX

"Musique concrète"

PARIS, THE CRADLE OF SO MANY AVANT-GARDE MOVEMENTS IN THE arts, was the center of the first "school" of electronic music—*Musique concrète*—essentially a school using sound montage concepts based on the use of recorded noises. Shortly after World War II, a young man by the name of Pierre Schaeffer discovered some of the tricks and effects that could be obtained by playing with recorded sounds. He was not a composer; he was experimenting out of sheer joy in sound for its own sake.

Schaeffer was an engineer, radio announcer, biographer, and novelist—not, significantly, a professional musician. He had received his training in radio broadcasting though later he became associated with the composer Pierre Henry. He had spent most of his life with the French radio service in Paris, and on August 24, 1944, he was responsible for the joyous broadcast announcing the liberation of Paris. He read from Victor Hugo and played *La Marseillaise*, to which the delirious French responded by throwing open their windows and singing along with their radios, and he asked all parish priests to peal their church bells in celebration.*

In 1948, Schaeffer revived the Futurists' attempt to find applications in music for mechanical, mundane, everyday noises. Tape recording had not yet become available—it was to be introduced in 1950—and Schaeffer worked with phonograph records instead. Utilizing the vast collection of records at his disposal, he made his own recordings of bits and pieces of noise and musical sounds from them. By using three phonographs at once, he was able to "compose" canons and other forms, manipulating them in inventive ways that drastically altered their character.

He christened his brand-new art form *Musique concrète*, distinguishing "concreteness," the physical presence of the music, from the ephemeral "abstractness" of sounds made by musical instruments.

*Larry Collins and Dominique Lapierre, *Is Paris Burning?* (New York: Simon and Schuster, 1965).

His methods seem fairly crude and amateurish today—the notion of making a new record from a group of old records, and then "fooling around" with the result hardly seems like a revolution. There is every likelihood, in fact, that the idea had been casually employed by previous amateurs, without their being conscious of the innovating principles involved.

In fact, in the middle 1920s some experiments were carried out at the famous Bauhaus in Weimar, in which records were deliberately played backward, scratched to alter rhythms, or actually cut in their grooves so as to produce howling *glissandi.* As was to be expected, several avant-garde composers flirted with that bemusing new machine, the phonograph. Ernst Toch recorded four speaking voices reciting the names of four cities in varying rhythms, and then re-recorded the original disk at a much higher speed so that the speaking was transformed into singing. Paul Hindemith composed music for a film by preparing the rolls of a mechanical piano without bothering to note down the music. Similar experiments were made at the broadcasting studios in pre-Hitler Berlin.

But before *Musique concrète,* these events were, comparatively, little more than tinkerings; there was no significant link between them and the search for an expansion of the raw materials of accepted sound.* They merely indicated how the imagination of some composers had been excited by a new tool of music. But with Schaeffer and *Musique concrète* the door was open to a new concept of music and musicmaking, precisely as Edgard Varèse had predicted.

Schaeffer's first piece of *Musique concrète* was "the exciting, sensational idea," he tells us, of "a concert of locomotives." He called it *Étude aux chemins de fer.* It is little more than a three-minute study of sounds usually associated with trains (or "traininess," as the painters would say), whistles, escaping steam, clicking wheels, and so on. Schaeffer had ransacked a huge catalogue of sound-effect recordings and collaged his selection into a composition. It was laborious work. He had to compile and "compose" his piece by use of a series of special phonograph records, re-recorded and mixed onto the final disk.

*I am grateful to Otto Luening for pointing out to me some noteworthy efforts prior to *Musique concrète*: the experiments of Toch, Hindemith, and Trautwein in the 1920s, and the cinema sound effects of Luis Buñuel and Orson Welles.

Étude aux chemins de fer is a simple sound montage, a modest little trifle, but it occupies a distinctive place in music history. It is significant on several counts: (1) the act of musical composition was accomplished by a technological process; (2) the work could be replayed innumerable times in precisely the same manner; (3) the replaying, or performance, was not dependent upon a human performer; (4) the basic elements were "concrète," (not ephemeral) thus offering the listener a mode of audition quite different from that employed in the perceiving of "abstract" music.

On October 5, 1948, the Radiodiffusion-Television Française (RTF) presented a program of Schaeffer's first five works of *Musique concrète* under the collective title, "Concert de bruits" (noises), which, in the best tradition, caused a famous scandal in Paris. Associated with this concert was Pierre Boulez, who had been asked to record a series of piano chords reminiscent of past musical styles (classical, romantic, impressionistic, atonal, etc.) which were to become the raw materials for Schaeffer's subsequent manipulations of the music.

In 1949, Schaeffer began the first of his musical collaborations with the composer Pierre Henry, a pupil of Messiaen. Together they composed one of the most interesting works of the *Musique concrète* school, the *Symphonie pour un homme seul*. It is not a symphony of course; it consists of ten short, powerfully atmospheric movements which represent the sounds that a man walking along at night hears about him. It was successfully used in a ballet by Maurice Béjart, who has used many *Musique concrète* scores in his ballets.

In 1951 the RTF established the first studio expressly designed for electronic composition, and stocked it with important new equipment such as continuously variable-speed turntables, a device for controlling sound in space, and single- and multi-channel tape recorders. The studio attracted a number of well known composers between 1951 and 1954. A catalog of their work produced there during this period (by composers other than Schaeffer and Henry) includes:

André Hodeir	*Jazz et Jazz* (piano and tape, 1951–1952)
Pierre Boulez	*Étude I sur un son* (1952) *Étude II sur sept sons* (1952)
Olivier Messiaen	*Timbres-Durées* (1952)

Monique Rollin	*Étude vocale I* (1952) *Étude vocale II* (1952)
Marius Constant	*Le joueur de flute* (1952)
Karlheinz Stockhausen	*Étude* (1952)
Michel Philippot	*Étude I* (1952)
Jean Barraque	*Étude* (1953)
Darius Milhaud	*La Rivière endormie (Étude Poètique*, Opus 333, for mezzosoprano, two narrators, orchestra, and tape, 1954)
Edgard Varèse	*Déserts* (winds, percussion tape, 1954; only a portion of the tape realization was done at the RTF studio)

The names of Messiaen, Milhaud, Boulez, and Stockhausen on this list are proof that *Musique concrète* at once attracted musicians of stature. But it is the last name on the list that is most provocative— Varèse. A clear and important relationship can be seen between the prophetic ideas of Varèse and the *Musique concrète* school, for Pierre Schaeffer and his colleagues had established conclusively, first with their re-recordings and then with the tape recorder, that all possible aural sensations are workable raw material for creative use. Varèse, like Busoni before him, had foreseen this many decades before the Paris group; he had also sensed that this new musical substance and sensibility would be needed to express twentieth-century experience.

Ironically, the most important pieces of *Musique concrète* did not come from the Paris group at all but from Varèse: his haunting *Déserts* of 1954, a pioneer work in its use of music written for tape and live instrumental ensembles; and his *Poème électronique*, commissioned for four hundred loudspeakers lining the inside of Le Corbusier's Philips Pavilion at the 1958 Brussels World's Fair. These impressive and powerful tape collages are superbly worked out of pre-existing recorded material built up into new spatial structures of extraordinary originality, breadth, and dimensions.

The 1958 Brussels Exhibition also presented the first performances of a number of works of *Musique concrète* by Yannis Xenakis, Schaeffer, Henry, and the Americans Luening and Ussachevsky. The possibilities of combining *Musique concrète* with other art forms was presented as a program at the Brussels Fair by the "Audio-Visual Research Foundation of San Francisco." Here, *Musique concrète* and electronic music were accompanied by visual images foreshadowing today's "multi-media" presentations.

The school of *Musique concrète*, based on processed natural sound, can be seen as a primitive first beginning, for its practitioners were limited by the variety of sounds available to them for what is basically collage, and the wearisome time-consuming process that pre-recording, splicing, and so on require.

The results of the *Musique concrète* school are, on the whole, disappointing. After some interesting experiments in the 1950s, it petered out and the thrust of electronic music composition was taken over by German experimenters such as Stockhausen. But the work of Schaeffer and other pioneers was extremely important. It was the first musical utilization of tape and music, and it pointed the way to the hundreds of electronic music centers and composers who are working in the medium of electronic music today.

Pierre Schaeffer wrote in 1952, "Photography, whether the fact be denied or admitted, has completely upset painting, just as the recording of sound is about to upset music. . . . For all that, traditional music is not denied; any more than the theatre is supplanted by the cinema. Something new has been added, a new art of sound. Am I wrong in still calling it music?"

Whether or not Schaeffer was wrong, his ventures in *Musique concrète* contributed much to an idea that was taking hold more and more—the concept of music as a "sound object."

The "Sound-Object" Idea in Music

In painting, the idea of the "found object" came as a reaction to Romantic nineteenth-century art. Music, too, was to be an abstraction, the negation of emotion and expression. In the early twentieth century many composers began to seek a kind of formal pattern-making in terms of pure sound; they rejected all ideas of an "emotional" approach to music. With the negation of emotion, they hoped to achieve "the purity of pure sound."

The notion that music perhaps may be, at times, a "sound object"—that is, music that can exist independently of any harmonic, melodic, or contrapuntal considerations—may be traced to that remarkable innovator, Claude Debussy. In the prelude to his *Martyre de Saint Sebastian,* he introduces a series of parallel aggregations that certainly cannot be comprehended as harmonic *chords*: rather, we can perceive them only as note groups, or note clusters, which are intended to enhance the melodic pattern.

Webern, later on, also foreshadowed the "objet sonore" (sound object) concept that was developed by Schaeffer and the *Musique concrète* group.* Within the framework of the row (serial) technique, Webern presents us with a *complex of notes* that are emphatically neither chords with precise harmonic functions nor melodic accompaniment. They are aural patterns—"sound objects." Webern developed the concept of "The individual, isolated, sound event," which is yet again the sound-object idea.

Boulez, particularly in his two *Études* also experimented with the sound-object idea. In these pieces, a sense of an organization of a musical space, a stereophonic dimension to this spatial organization, and *a filling up of that space with "sound objects"* (handled serially) seem to be the key elements of the composer's intent.

We may also hear the sound-object motif in much of Varèse, particularly in the percussive *Ionisation,* and in the savage cries of *Intégrales.* John Cage is another composer who went all out, at least in the 1950s, for this idea. His famous recitals, with David Tudor, for two "prepared" pianos (pianos that have been altered in tone-color by slipping wooden or metal objects between the strings) were often little more than play with sound objects, juxtaposed or superimposed against one another.

But it was that bold dilettante of music, Pierre Schaeffer, who enthusiastically—and successfully—embraced the "sound-object" idea as a basic concept and proved with his *Musique concrète* that it might, one day, become a new mode of musical art.

Music Without Adjectives and "The Sound Object"

In his book *A la recerche d'une musique concrète (The Search for a Concrete Music),* Schaeffer revealed himself as an intuitive poet

---

*The "sound-object" idea had been used sporadically by composers even before. For example, Otto Luening used it in a piano prelude as early as 1928.

of music. "The composer of *Musique concrète*," Schaeffer writes, "takes as his point of departure the *objets sonores*, the sound objects,* which are the equivalent of visual images, and which therefore alter the procedures of musical composition completely.... The *concrète* experiment in music consists of building sonorous objects, not with the play of numbers and seconds of the metronome, but with *pieces of time torn from the cosmos* (these pieces of time being grooves on records)."

Schaeffer also speaks of "a music without adjectives," and this intriguing concept has attracted composers more and more since World War II. This idea can be understood by recognizing that the "sound object" is analogous to the concept of the "visual object" in contemporary painting. When Gustav Mahler, early in this century, used snatches of haunting folk songs in his symphonies, he was employing precisely the affective device of memory-symbols that Chagall used with his juxtaposed rabbits and goats and fiddlers. The listener, or viewer, receives coded messages of artistic language that cause an effect. By the same analogy, when a composer of electronic music works with the sounds of trains or ocean liners or any of the sounds of our times, collaging and distorting them on tape, he is giving us a new awareness of the mutuality of art and life. Just as a Jasper Johns makes an American flag the subject of his painting, and thus invites a substantial number of questions about both the image of the flag and the way he painted it, so a composer working with aural symbols is often working along the same lines. Or he may have no intention at all, save for the symmetry of his "object," which may be as abstract and as coolly beautiful as the private statement of the geometric lines of a Mondrian or the convoluted configurations of a Jackson Pollock. Abstract art stresses basic formalized structures and ignores representation of objects; much of electronic music works on the same aesthetic principles, only in aural terms.

This concern with music as a "sound object" is most important. In our era there has been a shift in what may be termed musical

---

*"The found object" encountered in visual art is related to a notion cultivated in music by the composer Luciano Berio, who calls the third section of his much discussed *Sinfonia* "a found object (*objet trouvé*) recorded in the mind of the listener."

philosophy. Many contemporary composers have abandoned the nineteenth-century concept of music as an expression of subjective will and moral force. Along with painters, they are seeking out a new kind of abstraction, concerned with *sound and structure for their own sake and their own intrinsic beauty.*

Other writers besides Schaeffer have been fascinated by the aesthetic possibilities of *Musique concrète.* The French critic Serge Moreux has written, "The material of *Musique concrète* is sound in its original state as nature furnishes it, as machines establish it, and as handling transforms it. Between these particles and their multiplication, there are no other affective or acoustical relationships besides those which govern the scattered and twinkling physical universe."

Even the famous French anthropologist Claude Lévi-Strauss, has concerned himself with this subject:

> *Music, then, just as much as painting, supposes a natural organization of sense experience; but it does not necessarily accept this organization passively. . . . It follows that there is a striking parallel between the ambitions of that variety of music which has been paradoxically dubbed concrete and those of what is more properly called abstract painting. By rejecting musical sounds and restricting itself exclusively to noises,* Musique concrète *puts itself into a situation that is comparable, from the formal point of view, to that of painting of whatever kind: it is in immediate communion with the given phenomena of nature. And, like abstract painting, its first concern is to disrupt the system of actual or potential meanings of which these phenomena are the elements.**

Following the anthropological pattern sketched by Lévi-Strauss, we may venture to say that Western music (along with art) is showing signs of being polarized into the natural and the cultural, the "raw" and the "cooked." Culturally, nothing could be more raw than Schaeffer's noises of crashing bottles and the million other noises of our world; and nothing could be more "cooked" than the compositions put together directly on magnetic tape—which was the idea of the next school of electronic music, the Cologne Studio in Germany.

*Claude Lévi-Strauss, *The Raw and the Cooked* (New York: Harper & Row, Publishers, 1969), pp. 22–23.

CHAPTER X

The Cologne Studio

GERMAN RESEARCHERS AND MUSICIANS WERE AS CAPTIVATED BY the possibilities of tape music as were the French musicians in the *Musique concrète* group. They tackled the problem with Teutonic thoroughness, taking an almost reverent and metaphysical approach to the mathematics and physics involved.

The early efforts of the Cologne Studio* had an experimental air. Even the casual listener sensed that the composers were feeling their way into uncharted territories, and that the new discoveries were unorganized and shapeless. Still, they were exciting.

A triple collaboration met the challenge of purely electronic music. The collaborators were Werner Meyer-Eppler and Robert Beyer—experts in mathematic acoustics, physics, and electronics—and the composer Herbert Eimert. In October 1951, a broadcast from Cologne featured the "Sound-world of music created on an electronic instrument called the melochord." Much encouraged, the collaborators decided to establish an electronic studio in Cologne.

The studio was directed until 1953 by its spiritual father, Herbert Eimert. After Eimert, Karlheinz Stockhausen became the director. A number of theoreticians and acousticians with impressive credentials were associated with the group, and the affiliated composers were also knowledgeable about electronics and acoustics. All were unwavering followers of the Schönberg-Webern one-row approach to composition. In fact, some of them devoutly believed that there was an uncanny relationship between Webern's ideas and electronic music. Thus Eimert wrote of the new studio: "This is one of those turning points of electronic music, which is no longer copying Webern's inspired concept, but which "elevates," in both senses of the word. Many of Webern's constructions seem like premature electronic fragments. His permutations of sound lead directly to the question of shaping sounds by the grouping of sinusoidal tones, which has be-

*For a more detailed survey of the Cologne Studio, see Otto Luening's article in the Appendix, "A Documented History of the Cologne School."

come a current concern of electronic music. Timbre as a by-product of structural contours!"

In other words, the German groups proposed to develop Webern's "totally organized" row system, which is rigidly and mathematically constructed. To do this, they rejected the "prerecorded sound" techniques of *Musique concrète*. They concerned themselves not with the reproduction and alteration of sounds, but rather with the production of sounds electronically.

The Schönberg-Webern concept of twelve-tone technique had made a powerful resurgence after World War II. The war had interrupted serious musical investigations, and Hitler, of course, had frowned on the "decadent," "Jewish," ideas of Schönberg. But after the war serial music seemed to many composers to offer the only valid technique for expressing new ideas in new ways.

Schönberg's disciple Webern, even more than Schönberg himself, now seemed to point the way for young composers. Serialism, with its obsessive, mathematical approach, swept the boards in Europe as well as in America. In France, Olivier Messiaen wrote some of the first "totally organized" music in Europe; his influence on such younger men as Boulez, Stockhausen, the Italians Luigi Nono, Bruno Maderna, and Luciano Berio was enormous; all of them began as Webernists, and many of them studied with Messiaen.

Besides the mesmeric attraction of the serial principle, the younger composers were intrigued with Webern's concept of "the individual, isolated sound event." And no instrument or machine has ever been devised that can study an "individual, isolated sound event" as successfully as can electronic devices.

The link between Webernism and *electrische Musik* seemed portentous indeed. Eimert wrote euphorically of "The Opportune Moment of History. . . . The true nature of the electronic music media is recalled by the very fact that these media have become available for composition at the precise moment of history when they are needed.*

---

*Eimert was not the only one to perceive a divine hand in the invention of electronic music. The brilliant French critic André Hodeir asked rhetorically in *Since Debussy* (New York: Grove Press, 1961): "Was it mere coincidence that electrophonic techniques of sound production emerged at

Eimert had visionary hopes for electronic music: "The first step to real musical control of nature has been taken by electronic music. Its dependence for reproduction on the loudspeaker—which moreover has brought about an as-yet-scarcely-noticed subterranean revolution in hearing—at last permits risking the hypothesis that the symphony fixed on disk or tape may be the *surrogate* and electronic music *the true music*. Here, we may surmise, is the point at which the true order of music is revealed."

Ernst Krenek and the Cologne Studio

The Cologne experiments attracted one prominent composer of traditional music, Ernst Krenek (b. 1900). In the 1920s Krenek had become famous overnight with his jazz-idiom opera, *Jonny spielt auf*; in the 1930s he had been converted to Schönberg's twelve-tone method of composition. He became familiar with the work at Cologne in 1955, and at once decided to participate in it. In an article in which he outlined the reasons he was attracted to electronic music, Krenek wrote, "The composer is interested in the electronic medium for two reasons: firstly, it enables him to extend his control over a region of musical elements which remain inaccessible while he still uses conventional instruments. With the help of the electronic apparatus he can even bring timbres into construction."

In other words, the chance to employ an endless range of timbres, colors, and sounds heretofore never heard in music—this is one of the great fascinations of electronic music. After all, there are just so many severely limited timbres one can produce with violins, oboes, horns, and other conventional instruments.

Krenek continues, "Furthermore the composer can realize highly complex tone-relationships with a degree of precision that an en-

---

the same time that a related phenomenon, the sound object, made its first appearance under various guises in the instrumental works of Webern, Varèse, and Cage? Was it merely an accident that the possibilities afforded by tape-recording and editing were revealed at a time when rhythmic complexity threatened to confound human physical capacities, opening a breach between composer and performer? Was it not strange that composers should have begun to feel that they might one day exhaust the possibilities of the orchestra at the very moment when techniques were invented enabling them to transcend the orchestra?"

semble of human performers can never be guaranteed to provide, even after strenuous and protracted rehearsal."

Krenek's explorations in electronic music, utilizing *Musique concrète* techniques, as well as sound syntheses, note mixtures, and so forth, combined with human voices, including his own speaking voice, may be heard in his oratorio, *Spiritus Intelligentiae Sanctus.** The most successful pieces turned out by the Cologne group, however, have been those of Stockhausen, who is discussed in detail in Part Four of this book, "Some Leading Composers of Electronic Music."

The heavily intellectual Cologne Studio and Stockhausen himself were to become the chief influences on the many electronic music studios that soon proliferated in places as farflung as Milan, Warsaw, Stockholm, and Tokyo. Of these, the Milan group has thus far been the most significant; Berio, Maderna, and the Belgian composer Henri Pousseur have been associated with the Milan studio.

---

*Krenek also used electronic passages, reproduced on tape, in his opera of 1954, *Der Goldene Bock.*

CHAPTER XI

The Scene in America in the 1950s

John Cage and the Project of Music for Magnetic Tape

THE YEAR 1951, WHEN GERMAN INVESTIGATORS FIRST MADE PLANS to establish their electronic music studio at Cologne, also witnessed the beginnings of serious musical experimentation in America.

John Cage organized a group of musicians and engineers "for the making of music directly on magnetic tape, producing in that way works by Christian Wolff, Morton Feldman, Earle Brown, and himself."* The first piece to be completed in this project was Cage's *Imaginary Landscape No. 5* (1951–1952), described by the composer as "a recording on tape, using as material any 42 phonograph records." The score, composed "by chance operations derived from the I-Ching (the Chinese *Book of Changes*) is nothing less than a set of instructions for splicing together the recorded information." Cage has written about this piece:

> *This ... work, so far as I can ascertain, was the first piece of music for magnetic tape made in this country. The chief technical contribution of my work with tape is in the method of splicing, that is, of cutting the material in a way that affects the attack and decay of sounds recorded. By this method I have attempted to mitigate the purely mechanical effect of electronic vibration in order to heighten the unique element of individual sounds, releasing their delicacy, strength and special characteristics, and also to introduce at times complete transformation of the original materials to create new ones.***

*John Cage, with Robert Dunn, *John Cage: Catalogue of Works* (New York: Henmar Press, 1962).

**John Cage, in notes to the "25-Year Retrospective Concert of the Music of John Cage" New York, George Avakian, 1959 Avakian JCS–1. Whether Cage's claim that a recording of "any 42 phonograph records" constitutes "the first piece of music for magnetic tape made in this country" is valid or not depends upon whether the reader will accept this neo-Dada stunt as music. A much stronger claim for writing the "first piece in this country" can be made, perhaps, by Ussachevsky and Luening.

Cage composed a second piece as a member of his "Project of Music for Magnetic Tape." This was *William Mix*, created in 1952. Again the means of composition were based on *I-Ching* chance operations; about six hundred recordings, including city and country sounds, electronic sounds, songs, and music literature were employed.

The project was short-lived, lasting only from 1951 to 1953. Wolff, Brown, and Feldman composed but one work each as members of the group. But the demise of the project by no means signified the end of the participants' interest in electronic music. All of them became notable composers in both conventional and electronic media. In the early 1960s Cage went on (with David Tudor) to champion the trend toward "live," as opposed to taped, electronic sounds.

LUENING AND USSACHEVSKY

In 1951 Columbia University bought its first tape recorder, a professional Ampex, to record the concerts given at the University. Vladimir Ussachevsky, a member of the music faculty, was in charge of the machine. He took it home and began to work with it. Soon he was intrigued with the new sonorities he could achieve by recording musical instruments and then superimposing them on one another on tape.

"I suddenly realized that the tape recorder could be treated as an instrument of sound transformation," Ussachevsky has written. "Several months later, on May 9, 1952, I presented a few examples of my discovery in a public concert in New York together with other compositions I had written for conventional instruments."*

*According to Joan Peyser in *The New York Times*, "Until Ussachevsky was 40, he composed in a consistent, traditional style which he characterizes as 'pseudo-romantic Russian—very melodic, very harmonic and modestly dissonant.' Even Varèse's radical work for percussion, 'Ionisation,' which he heard at a Hollywood Bowl concert in 1933, left him unaffected. After World War II the composer's course suddenly changed; recognizing the potential that the tape recorder held for the manipulation of sound, Ussachevsky began to work in the new medium. Since then he has made a large contribution to what a French musicologist recently described as 'the total dismantling of music and its total reconstruction under new laws.'

"In 1951 while Ussachevsky was teaching 'traditional' music at Columbia University, the student engineer of Columbia radio station WKCR showed him how sound could be manipulated with tape. The composer

In 1951 the career of Mr. Ussachevsky—and the history of electronic music in America—converged with that of another composer, Otto Luening. We are fortunate to be able to have that story recorded authentically by Mr. Luening himself.

The Beginning of Electronic Music in the United States by Otto Luening*

Electronic music in the United States took quite a different turn from the paths it followed in Europe. The first public demonstration of the new medium was given by Vladimir Ussachevsky at his Composers Forum on May 9, 1952, in McMillin Theatre, Columbia University, shortly before Meyer-Eppler's lectures at the Summer School in Darmstadt. Ussachevsky, whose training has been traditional (Ph.D. in composition from the Eastman School of Music), is a brilliant contrapuntist and a superior vocal composer. Long before his Forum, he had had a predilection for electro-acoustical speculations. His experiments were quite independent of any in Europe. The equipment at his disposal consisted of an Ampex tape recorder (7½ and 15 ips.) presented by the Ditson Fund to the music department at Columbia University for the purpose of recording student concerts and a simple boxlike device designed by the brilliant young engineer, Peter Mauzey, to create feedback, a form of mechanical reverberation. Other equipment was borrowed or purchased with personal funds. The Forum attracted a great deal of attention and Henry Cowell in the *Musical Quarterly* (Vol. 38, October 1952) wrote a positive review of Ussachevsky's demonstration that ended, "Ussachevsky is now in the process of incorporating some of these sounds into a composition. The pitfalls are many; we wish him well."

The story of electronic music in the United States becomes at this point, in part, a personal narrative. I invited Ussachevsky to

---

began to experiment and discovered that, by superimposing sounds, he could produce complex and interesting sonorities. With tape one can record conventional sound, cut it up, slow it down, or erase it at any point. Ussachevsky experimented with these techniques until he produced something 'musical.' "

*From "An Unfinished History of Electronic Music," by Otto Luening, *Music Educators Journal*, November 1968. Reprinted by permission.

present his experiments at the Bennington, Vermont, composers conference in August 1952. My own connection with the medium began when I studied with Ferruccio Busoni in Zurich, Switzerland, from 1918 to 1920. My studies in acoustics continued during the 1920s when I was preoccupied with the problem of untempering a piano. I consulted the eminent physicist, Dayton Miller, in the early 1930s about new sound relations. In 1949, in the Introduction to Harry Partch's book, *Genesis of a Music,* I ventured to predict that we could expect a strange and beautiful music to develop if new musical ideas were used in conjunction with electronic and other scientific developments in sound.

At Bennington, Ussachevsky, at the controls of the Ampex, conducted a series of experiments involving violin, clarinet, piano, and vocal sounds. Equipped with earphones and a flute, I began developing my first tape-recorder composition. Both of us were fluent improvisors and the medium fired our imaginations. We played several tiny pieces informally at a party. After our demonstration a number of composers almost solemnly congratulated us saying, "This is it" ("it" meaning the music of the future).

The word reached New York City with lightning speed, and Oliver Daniel telephoned to invite us to produce a group of short compositions for the October concert sponsored by the American Composers Alliance and Broadcast Music, Inc., under the direction of Leopold Stokowski at the Museum of Modern Art in New York.* After some hesitation, we agreed to provide several pieces for the program. Henry Cowell placed his home and studio in Woodstock, New York, at our disposal. With the borrowed equipment in the back of Ussachevsky's car, we left Bennington for Woodstock and stayed two weeks.

*Stokowski's introductory remarks to that famous concert are still of interest: "I am often asked: What is tape music, and how is it made? Tape music is music that is composed directly with sound instead of first being written on paper and later made to sound. Just as the painter paints his picture directly with colors, so the musician composes his music directly with tone. In classical orchestral music many instruments play different groups of notes which sound together. In tape music several or even many tapes are superimposed; the tapes sound together the groups of tones that are recorded on them. So, essentially, it is a new way of doing what has been done for centuries by old methods."

Other equipment appeared almost magically from around the countryside. The folklorist, Eskin, produced an oversized speaker that resembled a large doghouse; carpets for sound-deadening appeared from somewhere.

Using the flute as a sound source, I developed an impressionistic virtuoso piece, *Fantasy in Space*, and *Low Speed*, an exotic composition that took the flute far below its natural range. *Invention in Twelve Tones*, with complex contrapuntal combinations, was also sketched. Ussachevsky began work on an eight-minute composition with piano as the main sound source, transformed by simple devices into sounds like deep-toned gongs and bells, tone clusters on an organ and a gamelan orchestra with metallic crescendos organized into an expressive whole.

In late September 1952, the traveling laboratory reached Ussachevsky's living room in New York, where we eventually completed the compositions. Peter Mauzey was then and has been all these years our invaluable collaborator and consultant. David Sarser, Arturo Toscanini's sound engineer, invited us to use the studio in the basement of Toscanini's Riverdale home to put the finishing touches on our compositions. These visits generally occurred between midnight and 3 A.M., but apparently never bothered the maestro. For the mixing of my *Invention*, we learned that the Union Theological Seminary had a collection of tape recorders, which we used for purposes other than those they were intended for.

The concert took place at the Museum of Modern Art on October 28, 1952. It was the first public concert of tape recorder music in the United States. Ussachevsky's *Sonic Contours* and my *Low Speed, Invention*, and *Fantasy in Space* were played. Ussachevsky and I with Mauzey transported the equipment to the hall, carried it in, set it up, and Ussachevsky operated the machine during the concert.

The public and professionals alike were cordial and astonished. Jay Harrison wrote in the New York *Herald Tribune* the next day, "It has been a long time in coming, but music and the machine are now wed. . . . The result is as nothing encountered before. It is the music of fevered dreams, of sensations called back from a dim past. It is the sound of echo. . . . It is vaporous, tantalizing, cushioned. It is in the room and yet not part of it. It is something entirely new. And genesis cannot be described." Nat Hentoff in *Downbeat* liked my

Fantasy in Space. Luciano Berio, writing for an Italian magazine, singled out Ussachevsky's *Sonic Contours* as the most significant piece and followed through by establishing the Studio di Fonologia in Milan, Italy. *Time* magazine said, "The twentieth-century instrument is the record machine—a phonograph or tape recorder."*

The first sound to emerge from the machine was a low rumble, rather like the very lowest notes of a piano. But after a few moments it became clear that this was no ordinary recording of a piano. No sooner was a chord struck, than it was cut off in a fashion that could never be achieved by any mortal pianist. For the next seven minutes the audience listened to a composition of music involving electronic manipulations of a piano, mixed here and there with the sounds of human voices.

The program was broadcast over WNYC in New York and WGBH in Boston, and we were invited to give a live interview demonstration on Dave Garroway's program, *Today*, on NBC television. The broadcasts were at 7 and 9 A.M. We arose at 4 A.M. and rehearsed at 5. As usual the three of us carted the equipment. We were met at the studio by a member of the Musicians Local 802, who asked if I had a union card. I said, "No, but if any flutist in the union can improvise the program, I will be glad for him to take over." That

---

*Of that famous concert, the conductor David Randolph wrote: "How many of those present in the auditorium of New York's Museum of Modern Art on October 28, 1952, realized that they were witnessing the beginning of a new era in the annals of music in America? As is the case with so many other important happenings—events that are later invested with a certain aura by the passage of time—this was announced with no special fanfare. In fact, the circumstances were becoming less and less dramatic as the evening progressed. The occasion was a concert of contemporary American music, conducted by Leopold Stokowski. The opening work had involved a small orchestra with piano; the next composition enlisted the services of only a quartet of wood-wind players. When they had finished, all the instruments, chairs, and music stands were removed; and a large speaker mounted in a cabinet, such as might be found in a high-quality phonograph, was placed in the center of the bare stage. Mr. Stokowski spoke briefly about the fact that the audience was now going to hear music conveyed directly from the composer to the listener, without the necessity of musicians to "interpret" it. Then he, too, left the stage, and the audience was left face to face with the speaker." (David Randolph, "Music from a Machine," *Horizon Magazine*, 1959.)

settled the matter. A crew of eight engineers tried to connect Mauzey's little box, but it would not work. Five minutes before the telecast, he was allowed to take over.

After Garroway's introduction, I improvised some sequences for the tape recorder. Ussachevsky then and there put them through electronic transformations. I looked up for a moment and to my astonishment found myself staring through a plate glass window with passers-by staring back. These included a mounted policeman on his horse. Somewhat startled, we finished the broadcast and repeated the interview at 9. Everybody seemed to have viewed it, for piles of letters arrived, many from friends and relatives we had not heard from in twenty-five years!

In April 1953, Radiodiffusion Française in Paris included "tape music," as our contribution was called, in their festival. It was introduced to the Paris listeners by Bernard Blin. Broadcast Music, Inc., sent Ussachevsky to represent us. Our contributions, stemming from a desire to extend the resonance of existing instruments, were different from the European compositions. Our works were received with interest and respect.

In that same summer, Stokowski commissioned us to do a two-and-a-half-minute piece for his CBS program, *Twentieth Century Concert Hall*. *Incantation* was the piece produced in the Ussachevsky living room by the two of us. We used woodwind instruments, voice, bell sonorities, piano sounds, and anything else available as sound sources. The piece was performed in October and was followed a month later by background tape music for CBS *Studio One*, "Crime at Blossom." Alfredo Antonini was musical director.

A concert with "Music in the Making" at Cooper Union under the partial patronage of the Music Performance Trust Fund and the Musicians Union established good relations with the union. The fact that the conductor, Broekman, announced that this probably meant the end of live music did not seem to detract from the audience's very real interest.

In late 1953, I received a commission from the Louisville Orchestra. I also received a small faculty grant from Barnard College. Ussachevsky consented to share these with me and to produce a joint composition to test the feasibility of combining the new medium with a symphony orchestra, even though we knew that we would have to purchase some materials and equipment from personal funds, a repeated necessity for a number of years.

Edward D'Arms and John Marshall of the Rockefeller Foundation became interested in the Louisville project and helped us to purchase another machine through Barnard College, where Henry Boorse had also shown interest in our work. William Kraft provided us with some percussion sounds for transformation.

Collaboration on the work *Rhapsodic Variations* was aptly described by Howard Shanet in program notes for our later composition *Concerted Piece*, played by the New York Philharmonic Orchestra: "... The nature and degree of their collaboration vary from one composition to another.... In general they work quite independently, the collaboration usually taking the form of criticism and suggestions offered to each other at frequent stages along the road." Sometimes we would actually exchange or borrow materials from one another. In the pieces from this period, we not only mixed the new sonorities with the timbre of the symphony orchestra but also devised a system of notation that would enable the conductor to follow the tape recorder and that would be acceptable for copyright in the United States, where every composition must be recorded in musical notation, often a trying and not too accurate technique.

Rhapsodic Variations, first performed on March 20, 1954, by the Louisville Orchestra, Robert Whitney conducting, is believed to be the first performance of tape recorder music with symphony orchestra anywhere.

A recording of our earliest music was released by Gene Bruck on the Innovations label in 1954. Reviewers said, "... The composers have entered this vast new realm in a sense of high adventure but also with a sense of responsibility." A recording of *Rhapsodic Variations* was released in 1955. Reviewers described the piece as a serious and fascinating listening experience. The worst comments pointed out that time would bring improvements, and the best ones said that the field already had ardent supporters.

To produce *Rhapsodic Variations* the traveling laboratory was transported to the Bennington Composers Conference and set up in a private living room. The score was tried out with the Conference Orchestra. In 1954, we packed up the mobile laboratory and took it to the MacDowell Colony, together with a projector, to make a score for a ballet, *Of Identity*, commissioned by the American Mime Theatre. The problem was that there was a voltage drop at certain times, but Ussachevsky, with mathematical meditations that I do not understand to this day, timed the score accurately enough so that we could deliver it just before the dress rehearsal, and it worked.

A new assignment came from Alfred Wallenstein for the Los Angeles Philharmonic Orchestra. The peripatetic equipment and professors took off from New York to the MacDowell Colony and produced *A Poem of Cycles and Bells*, an orchestral paraphrase of our two early pieces, *Fantasy in Space* and *Sonic Contours*. The transcription proved a post-graduate course in notation and ear training for the composers. The work was repeatedly performed in Los Angeles.

Commercial radio stations did not seem interested in setting up studios and research programs like those in Europe, so Ussachevsky and I decided that university auspices would best help electronic music to develop in the United States. Douglas Moore, executive officer of the Columbia University music department, gave us permission to deal directly with Grayson Kirk, president, and Jacques Barzun, provost. In turn, they helped us with space and with some outside contacts, which we were permitted to develop on our own. In addition to numerous demonstrations, lectures, and concerts, we wrote a report for the Rockefeller Foundation on the state of experimental music in Europe and the United States with recommendations about the best program to be followed here. The interest initially shown by Mr. D'Arms and Mr. Marshall was picked up by Mr. July and Mr. Fahs, who helped us to formulate further ideas.

In 1956, Doris Humphrey commissioned me to write a score for *Theatre Piece No. 2* to be performed at the Juilliard Anniversary Festival. Our studio in the Ussachevsky living room was by now so crowded with equipment and materials that it seemed desirable to move the portable laboratory to the back room of my apartment. Mrs. Ussachevsky had endured the perambulating laboratory without a murmur for years and it was time for a change. But our efforts did not settle the problem.

While I was busy with the ballet (assisted by Chou Wen-Chung), my house man and some neighbors became very suspicious about what was going on in the back room and reported their disturbance to the building management. I explained, but as my apartment was in a building owned by Columbia, we finally reported to President Kirk that unless we could have some space on the campus our whole program would be seriously jeopardized. Soon afterwards, we were provided with a suitable and charming Charles Addams-type house located on the site of the former Bloomingdale Insane Asylum on the campus.

The next major assignment came when, at the request of Mark Blitzstein, Orson Welles asked us to do an abstract sound score for his production of *King Lear* at the New York City Center. Welles came to the studio to listen to our basic sound materials, which we played for him after his stentorian command: "Proceed!" After five minutes' listening, Welles, who has an extremely musical ear, said, "This is the greatest thing to have happened in the theater since the invention of incandescent lights." We produced forty-four cues for *King Lear*. But at the first dress rehearsal there was trouble. Ussachevsky was not allowed to operate the machine but had to relay his suggestions to the regular union sound man, and this slowed up things considerably. Finally, all was straightened out and the show ran for three weeks. The press response recognized the great contributions the new medium could make in the theater.

In 1955, RCA demonstrated the Olson-Belar Sound Synthesizer. A recording on which existing instruments were imitated was released. The present director of the School of the Arts at Columbia University, Davidson Taylor, suggested that we try to get the synthesizer on loan. Because Ussachevsky had a great desire to pursue this possibility, I wrote to several RCA executives. We heard that Professor Milton Babbitt at Princeton University, who had been preoccupied with electronic music since the late 1930s, was also interested in working on this comprehensive machine. We joined forces! Grayson Kirk wrote to David Sarnoff, president of RCA and to Elmer W. Engstrom, then executive vice-president, who gave us permission to do research on the machine at the Princeton laboratories. The universities paid our expenses. Since I had to leave for Rome in three weeks, my colleagues suggested that I be the first to work with the machine.

Basic materials that I produced with the help of Mr. Belar, later greatly modified, became the material for my *Synthesis for Orchestra and Electronic Sound* and *Dynamophonic Suite.*

Babbitt, Ussachevsky, and I, in discussing the possible future development of electronic music, suggested first to the Rockefeller Foundation a University Council for Electronic Music with representatives from those institutions that had begun working in the field. Mr. Fahs wisely suggested that because Columbia and Princeton were able to work smoothly together we had better leave it that way.

The Luening-Ussachevsky report to the Rockefeller Foundation included a detailed description of the equipment and personnel needed for a representative center in the United States. It asked for technical assistants, electronic equipment, space, and materials to permit other composers to work there free of charge, and a concert setup consisting of a control console and nineteen loudspeakers for public concerts. One hundred seventy-five thousand dollars were needed for both universities for a period of five years. Our application was approved with the recommendation that we procure the RCA synthesizer.* At first

---

*In 1960 the Mark II RCA Synthesizer became an integral part of the Center's installation. This complex machine could produce, mix, and modify any desired sound in any desired manner through a complex series of electronic connections. One of its more sensational features was that any audible sound whatever, once present on the synthesizer, could be immediately tested by merely flipping a switch; the composer-engineer, if dissatisfied, could order any settings or adjustments he wished *before* the sound was committed to tape.

The Mark II Synthesizer, briefly stated, consisted of a battery of signal generators, followed by amplifiers, modulators, filtering devices, and "envelope" controls to shape the electronic waves before they emerged as sound waves. The method of control is a roll of paper tape, not unlike a player-piano roll, which is punched in predetermined patterns by the composer, and then unreeled over a "reader" to trigger the desired type and sequence of sounds. These are tape-recorded, segment by segment, until all the elements are on tape, and the segments are then spliced together in quite an ordinary fashion. As can be seen, the Mark II is a more complex and cumbersome father of the smaller synthesizers—the Moog, Buchla, etc., which are more portable and far more easily "playable." That is, a good deal of the incredibly complicated system of sound sources and modifiers have been ingeniously simplified and automated in the smaller machines. And the newer synthesizers are equipped with piano-type keyboards to trigger them.

we rented it. Then RCA loaned it to us. The press release in January 1959 announcing the grant caused a great deal of commotion in the world of music. The Committee of Direction consisted of Professors Luening and Ussachevsky of Columbia University and Professors Babbitt and Roger Sessions of Princeton with Professor Ussachevsky acting as chairman.

As soon as possible, we invited other composers to work at the Center. These included Muchiko Toyama from Japan, Bülent Arel from Turkey, Mario Davidovsky from Argentina, Halim El-Dabh from Egypt, and Charles Wuorinen of the United States, soon followed by many other distinguished composers from this country and abroad. Varèse revised the electronic part of *Déserts* in the Center and for a while worked there regularly.

In the midst of our new obligations, Ussachevsky and I were commissioned by Leonard Bernstein and the New York Philharmonic Orchestra to compose a work for tape recorder and symphony orchestra. Our *Concerted Piece* was first performed on March 20, 1960, at a youth concert that was televised, followed by four regular performances in Carnegie Hall and a CBS network broadcast.

The Columbia-Princeton Electronic Music Center gave its two initial concerts at McMillin Theatre, Columbia University, on May 9 and 10, 1961, before an invited audience that included music luminaries from New York and elsewhere. The program was well received by the two overflowing audiences; it consisted of an introduction by Jacques Barzun, *Electronic Study No. 1* (Davidovsky), *Leiyla and the Poet* (El-Dabh), *Creation—Prologue* (Ussachevsky), *Composition for Synthesizer* (Babbitt), *Stereo Electronic Music No. 1* (Arel), *Gargoyles for Violin Solo and Synthesized Sound* (Luening, Max Pollikoff—violinist), *Symphonia Sacra* (Wuorinen, The Hartt Chamber

---

It should be understood that the RCA synthesizer is *not*, properly speaking, a computer. However, it can be operated by a computer punch tape, that is, a sort of moving IBM punch-card system. This means, in theory at least, that a Milton Babbitt or any other person who has mastered the secrets and formidable complexities of the RCA synthesizer, can sit at home in his living room and punch out his score on a punch tape, for realization at a further time on the machine. In such an instance, the punch tape, roughly speaking, becomes the composer's score.

Players—Bertram Turetzky, director); technical assistants—Malcolm Goldstein, Edward Schneider, Peter Smith; Lighting—Richard Greenfield. A decade later, two of those composers—Wuorinen and Davidowsky—had received Pulitzer Prizes.

Countless foreign musicians, composers, and musicologists have visited or worked in the Columbia-Princeton Center.* We have considered it our duty to advise and help as much as we were able in promoting new developments, an attitude commonly accepted in the world of electronic music. For future guidance one can only paraphrase Busoni's statements of 1907: "Only further ear training and careful experimentation will continue to make this material plastic, artistically useful, and humanly satisfying." Novelty and tradition, methodology and complete freedom, systems and automation are by themselves not enough to bring music to new heights.

Only if we develop a sense of responsibility and a deep desire to bring human satisfaction to large numbers of individuals can our vision become penetrating enough to draw on the greatness of the past, add to it our new findings, and move forward into a future that even now promises beautiful new experiences as yet undreamed of.

Bon Voyage.

*Today the Columbia-Princeton Center is one of the two or three best-equipped centers in the world.

CHAPTER XII

A Chronology of Electronic Music, From "Musique concrète" (1948) to the Death of Varèse (1965)

AFTER WORLD WAR II, ELECTRONIC MUSIC, "THE TOTAL WORLD OF sound," became a sensational topic of conversation centering on the *Musique concrète* school of Paris and the experiments of Stockhausen and others in Cologne and of John Cage and his group in America.

After 1953, electronic music proliferated rapidly throughout the world. Important studios (some of which were later disbanded) were soon established in Milan, Tokyo, London, Geneva, Gravesano, Utrecht, Brussels, Berlin, Darmstadt, Warsaw, Toronto, and in Israel.

By the early 1960s, two new branches of electronic music had evolved—"live" electronic music and computer music. Some respected composers, however, such as Pierre Boulez, Morton Feldman, and Hans Werner Henze, turned away from electronic composition after having worked seriously in the medium.

Nevertheless, by 1967 Hugh Davies was able to compile a catalog of five thousand electronic compositions written throughout the world since 1948, and declared that another 2,500 works most likely existed.*

May-June, 1948, Paris	The first pieces of *Musique concrète* are produced by Pierre Schaeffer (b. 1910) and others in Paris, at the RTF Studio. The composer Pierre Boulez (b. 1925) assists Schaeffer, by recording a series of piano chords in various musical styles that became the raw material for part of the concrete manipulations.
1948	Schaeffer acknowledges the Italian Futurists and the American John Cage as his predecessors.

*Hugh Davies, "Repertoire International des Musiques Electro-acoustiques," *International Electronic Music Catalog*, 1967.

1948–1953, Berlin	Oskar Sala (b. 1910) produces electronic pieces with his "Mixturtrautonium."
1949, Germany	Near Munich, Bode builds the "Melochord," later installed in the NWDR Electronic Music Studio in Cologne.
1949	Schaeffer begins his collaboration with Pierre Henry (b. 1927), a pupil of Olivier Messiaen. The association lasts until 1958, when Henry became the leading composer at the new rival "Studio Apsome."
ca. 1949, New York	Abraham Frisch (b. 1900) initiates his series of numerous rhythmic studies, using for sound sources magnetized stencils placed directly on tape.
1949, USA	In the introduction to Harry Partch's book, *Genesis of a Music*, Otto Luening says, "If, in the future, these [Partch's] ideas are used in conjunction with electronic and other scientific developments in sound, one may expect a strange and beautiful music to result."
1949	Pierre Henry and Pierre Schaeffer compose *Symphony for a Man Alone*, an important work of *Musique concrète*. Messiaen writes *Mode de valeurs et d'intensité* for piano, a key work in the evolution of Boulez and Stockhausen.
1950	The Hohner firm, manufacturers of harmonicas, produce the Electronium.
1950	Varèse lectures in Darmstadt, August.
1950	Two lectures by Beyer, and one by Meyer-Eppler, on "The World of Sound of Electronic Music," presented by Darmstadt, August.
1950	Pierre Boulez writes quartet for Ondes and distinguishes himself as performer of Ondes.
1950	The first public performance of *Musique concrète* is given at the École Normale de Musique.

1951   The RTF establishes in Paris the first studio ex-
                               pressly designed for electronic composition.

1951   Schaeffer and Henry produce an opera, *Orpheus*, for
                               concrete sounds and voices, and open the research
                               studio to outside composers. These included: Messiaen,
                               Boulez, Jolivet, Delanney, Barraque, Barraud, and
                               Baudrier.

1951   In Germany, Robert Beyer (b. 1901), Werner Meyer-
                               Eppler (b. 1913), and Herbert Eimert (b. 1897) meet
                               and agree to establish an electronic music studio. It
                               was decided that the studio would be in Cologne, so
                               that the new facilities of Kölner Funkhaus could be
                               used. (The Cologne Studio becomes fully operational
                               in 1953.)

1951   On October 18th, a program of music called "The
                               World of Sound of Electronic Music" is broadcast
                               over the Cologne Radio System. Participating in the
                               forum are Beyer, Eimert and Meyer-Eppler, the last
                               providing the examples in sound.

1953–54   The commercial studio of Louis and Beebe Baron
                               provides electronic sound scores for films such as
                               Atlantis, Jazz of Lights, Forbidden Planet.

1951   John Cage (b. 1912) organizes a group of musicians
                               and engineers for the making of music directly on
                               magnetic tape, producing, on private recordings, works
                               by Christian Wolff, Morton Feldman, Earle Brown,
                               and himself.

1951, Tokyo   A group of Japanese composers established "Jikken
                               Kobo" (Experimental Laboratory) using equipment
                               furnished by the Sony Corporation.

1951–1953   Karlheinz Stockhausen studies composition in Paris,
                               under Messiaen and Milhaud. During this time he is
                               introduced by Karel Goeyvaerts to the properties of
                               sine waves, and makes the first attempts at a synthetic

	sound composition with sinus-oscillators in the Club d'Essai, Paris.
January, 1952	Cage's *Imaginary Landscape No. 5*, is "written" and, according to the composer, "so far as I can ascertain, this work was the first piece of music for magnetic tape made in this country." (The score was composed by "chance operations derived from the *I-Ching*, the Chinese *Book of Changes*," and was a "recording on tape using as material any 42 phonograph records." According to the composer, the piece was privately recorded.)
May 9, 1952	Vladimir Ussachevsky (b. 1911), working at Columbia University, presents a public concert of his "discovery that the tape recorder could be treated as an instrument of sound transformations."
1952	At the Bennington Composers' Conference, Ussachevsky and Luening compose and perform three small experimental compositions with flute as sound source.
October 28, 1952	Leopold Stokowski requests and performs four compositions for tape recorder (written by Columbia University's Vladimir Ussachevsky and Otto Luening on a program of contemporary music given at the Museum of Modern Art, New York. Luciano Berio was present at the performance.).
1952	Henk Badings (b. Java, 1907) produces electronic music for a radio play *De gravin Catalene* at the studios of Nederlandsche Radio Unie at Hilversom.
1952	Ussachevsky writes score for film, *No Exit*.
1952	The Cologne studio becomes fully operational. Stockhausen begins work at the Cologne Radio Station. Schaeffer publishes his book, *In Search of a Concrete Music*, Editions du Seuil, Paris.

THE FIRST "SCHOOLS" OF ELECTRONIC MUSIC IN THE 1950s

1952 | Bruno Maderna produces his *Musica su due Dimensioni*, and performs it at the Damstadt Summer School. According to the composer, the work is for "flute, percussion, and loudspeaker . . . and a first attempt to combine the past possibilities of mechanical instrumental music with the new possibilities of electronic tone generation." Messiaen composes *Timbres-Durées*, for tape.

1953 | On March 22, nine months before his seventieth birthday, Edgard Varèse receives an anonymous gift of a professional Ampex tape recorder and accessory equipment. He had been searching for decades for electronic instruments to fulfill his compositional needs; now he plunged immediately to work, collecting the materials for the electronic sections of *Déserts*.

1953 | The complete Schaeffer-Henry opera *Orpheus* is performed at the Donaueschingen Festival in Germany, to an outraged audience and press.
Paul Beaver (b. 1925) uses electronic sound in a film, *The Magnetic Monster*.
Hans Werner Henze (b. 1926) includes electronic music in his radio opera, *Das Ende einer Welt*. Sala composes *Concertino for Mixtur-Trautonium and Electric Orchestra, Concertante Variations*, for tape.
Luciano Berio (b. 1925) founds studio at Milan, where concerns of "Musique concrète" and "electronic music" are reconciled and developed.

1953 | Karlheinz Stockhausen *Electronic Study No. 1*, with sine waves as exclusive basic material.

1950–1954 | Varèse, *Déserts* for orchestra and five tracks of "organized sounds" on magnetic tape. (Varèse indicates on the score that the orchestra part can be played without the interpolation of the taped sounds.)

1954 | International Congress on Music and Electro-acoustics, at Gravesano, Switzerland, sponsored by UNESCO, reported in proceedings, and then pursued in periodical *Gravesaner Blatter*, with recordings. Milhaud, *Étude poètique*, for tape recorder. Stockhausen, *Electronic Study No. 2*, including nonstationary noises produced electronically.

1954   Cage, *Williams Mix*, with eight loudspeakers. The Cologne Radio presents a public concert in the series "Music of Our Time," using only electronically generated sounds by Stockhausen, Goeyvaerts, Pousseur, Gredinger, and Eimert.

Luening and Ussachevsky, *Poem for Cycles and Bells* for tape recorder and orchestra performed; recorded 1955.

Luening and Ussachevsky, ballet *Of Identity*, for the American Mime Theater.

Henk Badings (b. 1907) *Orestes*, incidental music on tape.

Ivan Vyshnegradsky (b. 1893), *Study* for electronic broadcast.

1954   Luening and Ussachevsky, *Rhapsodie Variations* (for the Louisville Symphony)—the first piece to combine orchestra and tape sounds.

1955   Toshiro Mayuzumi (b. 1929) founds studio at Tokyo. Luening and Ussachevsky receive Rockefeller Grant of $10,000 for creative research in electronic music and go to Paris, Germany, Switzerland, and Italy.

1956   Luening, *Theater Piece No. 2*, commissioned by Doris Humphrey; performed by José Limon and Doris Humphrey at the Juilliard School of Music.

Eimert and Stockhausen edit *Die Reihe I: Elektronische Musik*, a learned journal. Harry F. Olson and Herbert Belar exhibit RCA Synthesizer.

Varèse completes *Le Procession de Verges*, organized sounds on tape, for a sequence of the film, *Around and About Joan Miró*, by Thomas Bouchard.

Stockhausen, *Gesang der Junglinge* (Song of the Youths in the Fiery Furnace)—an outstanding example of "electro-acoustic" music, incorporating distorted vocal sounds.

Bruno Maderna (b. 1920), *No Turno*, for tape.

Giselher Klebe (b. 1920) *Interferenzen*, for tape.

Ernst Krenek (b. 1900), *Spiritus Intelligentiae, Sanctus*, for tape.

1955–56   Lejaren Hiller and Leonard Isaacson of the University of Illinois produce the *Illiac Suite* for String Quartet, the first complete piece of music produced with a computer. Counterpoint rules are employed.

1956   The first score of an electronic piece (Stockhausen's *Studie II*, written in Cologne, 1954) is published by Universal Edition.

1957   Studios founded in Rome, Warsaw, Brussels, Delft, and Israel.

1958   Varèse's *Poème électronique*, written in the tape medium, and produced at the Philips Laboratories at Eindhoven, Holland, is played over 400 loudspeakers in the Philips Pavilion of the 1958 Brussels World Fair. Luening-Ussachevsky, *Back to Methuselah*, for Theatre Guild.

Otto Luening creates material at RCA Sarnoff Labs, with Belar, to be used later for *Dynamophonic Suite*, and *Synthesis for Orchestra and Electronic Sound*. Modified and adapted in Rome and at Columbia-Princeton Studios.

Milton Babbitt (b. 1916) begins to work with the RCA Mark II Synthesizer in an RCA laboratory in New Jersey.

Pierre Boulez, *Poésie pour pouvoir*, combining electronic and instrumental music.

1958   Viktor K. Solomin, *Konstruirovanie Elektromuzykal'nykh Instrumentov*, indicates revival of Russian interest in electronic music.

January 8, 1959   The Columbia-Princeton Electronic Music Center is given a $175,000 grant by the Rockefeller Foundation. The following year the Mark II RCA Synthesizer becomes an integral part of its installation.

1959   Studio founded at Toronto, Canada.
RCA Synthesizer II installed at the Columbia-Princeton Electronic Music Center.
Henri Sauguet (b. 1901), *Aspect sentimental.*

1960   Luening and Ussachevsky, *Concerted Piece for Tape Recorder and Orchestra,* commissioned by Leonard Bernstein and the New York Philharmonic, first performed on March 20, 1960 at a televised youth concert, followed by four regular performances in Carnegie Hall and a CBS network broadcast.
Abraham Moles, *Les musiques expérimentales,* and Fred K. Prieberg, *Musica ex Machina,* provide comprehensive surveys of the field, one prescriptive and other journalistic.

1961   Milton Babbitt, *Vision and Prayer.*
Varèse is invited to the Columbia-Princeton Electronic Music Center, where he completes his realization of his *Déserts* material.

1961   The Columbia-Princeton Electronic Music Center presents its first public concert and receives much favorable mention, as well as the much publicized hostility of Columbia Professor Paul Lang.

1962   Luening, *Synthesis for Orchestra and Electronic Sound.*

1963   Hiller and Robert Baker produce their *Computer Cantata,* written in SCATRE, an IBM–7094 assembly language, and to a lesser extent in FORTRAN.

1964   A sound-producing program is started at Bell Telephone Laboratories under Max Matthews.

1964–65   Ussachevsky, *Of Wood and Brass.*

1965   Death of Edgard Varèse, father of "The Liberation of Sound."

Ferruccio Busoni, composer, pianist, and prophet of a "liberated" music.

Edgard Varèse and his wife, Louise, in 1965. *Photo courtesy of Louise Varèse*

Yannis Xenakis (right) when he was assistant to the architect Le Corbusier (left) and both were creating the Philips pavilion at the Brussels World's Fair in 1958. It was for this pavilion that Edgard Varèse composed his masterpiece, *Poème électronique*, despite the open hostility of many officials. Xenakis and Corbusier fought for Varèse and the *Poème*. *Photo courtesy of Yannis Xenakis*

Otto Luening, a pioneer of electronic music in America. *Photo courtesy of Otto Luening*

Another pioneer, Vladimir Ussachevsky, with Dmitri Shostako-vitch upon the latter's visit to the Columbia-Princeton Electronic Music Center. *Photo courtesy of Columbia-Princeton Electronic Music Center*

Milton Babbitt, a leading exponent of electronic music. *Photo courtesy of Columbia-Princeton Electronic Music Center*

John Cage. *Photo courtesy of John Cage*

Vladimir Ussachevsky. *Photo courtesy of Columbia-Princeton Electronic Music Center*

Several modern composers at the Brussels World's Fair, 1958. John Cage is the supine one, and in the front row (left to right) are Mauricio Kagel, Earle Brown, Luciano Berio, and Karlheinz Stockhausen. In the back row (left to right) are Henk Badings, Andre Boncourechlier, Bruno Maderna, Henri Pousseur, Mlle. Seriahine, Luc Ferrari, and Pierre Schaeffer. *Photo Faider, Brussels*

Karlheinz Stockhausen, the leading German composer of electronic music. *Photo courtesy of BMI Music Corp., New York*

John Cage and Karlheinz Stockhausen, about 1958.
Photo courtesy of John Cage

John R. Pierce of Bell
Laboratories. *Photo
courtesy of Bell
Laboratories*

Max Mathews of Bell Laboratories. *Photo courtesy of Bell Laboratories*

Graphic Console for composition of computer music, using a light pen as input. *Photo courtesy of Bell Laboratories*

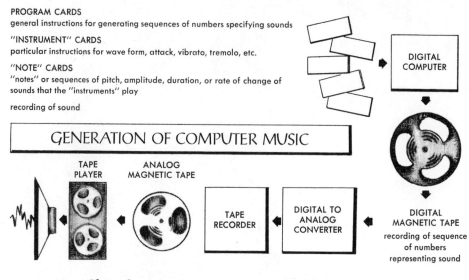

PROGRAM CARDS
general instructions for generating sequences of numbers specifying sounds

"INSTRUMENT" CARDS
particular instructions for wave form, attack, vibrato, tremolo, etc.

"NOTE" CARDS
"notes" or sequences of pitch, amplitude, duration, or rate of change of
sounds that the "instruments" play

recording of sound

DIGITAL
COMPUTER

GENERATION OF COMPUTER MUSIC

TAPE
PLAYER

ANALOG
MAGNETIC TAPE

TAPE
RECORDER

DIGITAL TO
ANALOG
CONVERTER

DIGITAL
MAGNETIC TAPE
recording of sequence
of numbers
representing sound

Chart demonstrating generation of computer music.
Courtesy of Bell Laboratories

Jean Claude Risset, French physicist and composer, demonstrates a
trumpet tune synthesized by a computer at Bell Laboratories,
Murray Hill, New Jersey. Twenty listeners were unable to distinguish
between M. Risset's computer tones and the real trumpet tones.
Here he follows a trumpet composition on the board while listening
to the computer-generated version played back on tape.
Photo courtesy of Bell Laboratories

PART FOUR
The Experimental Sixties

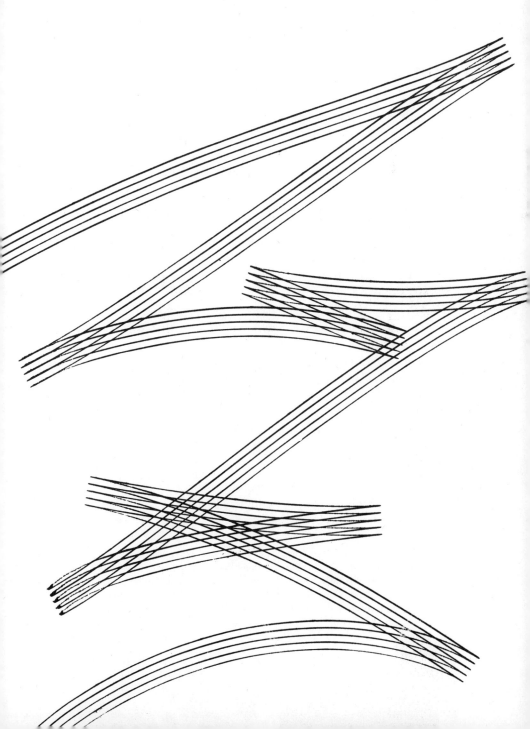

CHAPTER XIII

Some Leading Composers of Electronic Music*

By 1960, THE SWELL OF THE MUSICAL REVOLUTION HAD REACHED all corners of the Western world and into some communist countries. Warsaw became the site of a major contemporary festival, and an electronic studio was opened in Moscow in 1961.

The sixties were a time of ruthless experimentation—especially in electronic music. The experience of electronic music, of direct contact with the sound material—has affected the total work of every musician who has experimented, however casually, with the new medium.

The sixties also beheld the increasing importance of the performer's role in nonelectronic music. Many younger composers doubled as active performers, often also serving as organizers of the small ensembles mostly associated with universities that were common on the New-Music scene. Working on the spot with singers and instrumentalists, the composer can experiment with new performing ideas, new concepts of structure, and new notations, and he can make empirically based judgments about which notions are valuable and which should be discarded.

The decade also witnessed the proliferation of mixed-media compositions and the birth of a new kind of musical theater, a nondramatic genre in which the activities of the performers may form the major action. To be sure, some of this, such as the violin burnings of LaMonte and Young, for example, stretches out into regions dubiously related to music. "Rock operas" were conceived at this time and

*All the composers discussed here have written music for traditional, nonelectronic instruments as well. Some, like Xenakis and Brown, have written comparatively little music for the electronic media; others, like Subotnick, have declared that they "no longer attempt to deal with the concert hall as an institution."

enjoyed a certain vogue. By 1971, such works as *Tommy* and *Jesus Christ, Superstar,* while of uncertain value in themselves, were regarded by some as portents of a new kind of musical drama free from the stifling museum tradition of grand opera in its present state.

The distance between "classical" and "popular" music dwindled as electronic materials became available to all. Stockhausen praised the Beatles and vice-versa, while the Mothers of Invention quote Varèse.

With the advent of synthesizers, serious composers began to explore romantic vistas that their predecessors left largely untouched. Their work has been influenced by (and, conversely, is influential upon) recent developments in rock music. This radical young generation of electronic composers has been able to reap the benefits of all the experimentation that went on in the 1950s.

A new branch of electronic music was suggested when machines such as the Moog and the Syn-Ket opened up the possibility of *performable electronic music.* The potential is fascinating, and the 1970s certainly will see much more of "live" and "performable" electronic music. Incidentally, although serious composers do not like to admit it, this avenue was really pioneered in some respects by early jazz musicians—Sidney Bechet in particular—and later by the rock musicians of the sixties, with their arsenal of electronic organs, guitars, and basses.

The Syn-Ket, developed for the composer John Eaton, opens still other possibilities for composers of the seventies. This odd-looking instrument is equipped with three tiny keyboards, stacked like the manuals of a pipe organ, with vines of wires drooping down from their sockets. It rather resembles a child's toy piano hooked up to a telephone switchboard. But there is nothing childish about it. The Syn-Ket is the first machine capable of performing electronic music "live" in the concert hall. Like the various sound synthesizers that preceded it, Syn-Ket can approximate familiar instrumental and non-instrumental sounds, and can create a few that are not so well known. It does not have all the range and flexibility of the synthesizers, but it does have one advantage over them. Where synthesizers normally put their sounds onto tape, which is then brought into the concert hall and fed into a playback machine, the Syn-Ket eliminates the inter-mediate steps, for it is played like an instrument.*

The seventies surely will see many more "playable" electronic instruments of this nature, besides other startling developments such as the bantam Putney synthesizer, which stands only a foot and a half high and is extremely fast and flexible.

A Few Milestone Events in Electronic Music, 1965–1970

1967   Leon Kirschner's *String Quartet No. 3*, which used electronic sounds together with live performance of conventional instruments, is awarded the Pulitzer Prize for music.

1967   Dartmouth College institutes an annual award for the best electronic composition.

1967   J. K. Randall's *Variations for Violin and Computer* has its premiere.

1968   *Switched-On Bach*, devised by Walter Carlos on a Moog Synthesizer, becomes a national best-seller.

1970   The Pulitzer Prize for music goes for the first time to a purely electronic composition, *Time's Encomium*, by Charles Wuorinen.

1971   The Pulitzer Prize for music is awarded to an elec-tronic composition by Mario Davidovsky.

Also by way of milestones: The University of Toronto's recent *Bibliography of Electronic Music* lists 1,562 books and articles on the subject. English critic Hugh Davis has counted at least 150 electronic studios around the world and a total production in the medium's first twenty years of more than four thousand compositions.

*The Syn-Ket was developed by the engineer Paul Ketoff in Rome; the first model was made at the American Academy in Rome, where composers Eaton, Smith, Luening, and George Wilson worked on it. Ketoff developed an improved model for John Eaton who has used it as a performing instru-ment. (I am indebted to Otto Luening for this information.)

OTTO LUENING

Otto Luening, now a mellow septuagenarian, is not only a distinguished composer but also a living link with the great pioneering tradition of the past. He was a student of Ferruccio Busoni, the great visionary of a "liberated music" who was the first prophet of electronic music. Luening himself blazed trails in electronic music when monster synthesizers and electronic laboratories were undreamed of, and when electronic music in America was Otto Luening equipped with earphones and a flute, developing his first tape-recorder compositions together with Vladimir Ussachevsky. His accomplishments as a teacher also have been notable, in the best Busoni tradition. Two generations of composers, including Chou Wen-Chung, Harvey Sollberger, Vladimir Ussachevsky, Walter Carlos, Charles Dodge, Bölent Arel, and Pulitzer-prize winners Charles Wuorinen and Mario Davidovsky have attended Otto Luening's graduate seminars in composition at Columbia.

Luening's music—more than 250 substantial pieces, the bulk of it nonelectronic—stands as a bridge between the traditional and the avant-garde music of today.* Much of it is lyric and richly melodic, featuring accompaniments of a simple and moderately dissonant texture. As Oliver Daniel has written, "Luening's lyric gift is so strong that even critics who oppose the 'conservatism' of his style find his music 'important.'" Writing of Luening's opera *Evangeline*, an undertaking that took Luening seventeen years to complete, Virgil Thomson declared, "Nothing could be more deceptive than the taste and skill of this composer. His musical lines appear to move around in the most casual fashion. . . . Otto Luening is an original composer, and his textures are both highly personal and expressive. . . . They are thought through in every way; they are a master's work."**

Luening has written a great deal of music of a radical and experimental nature; his early compositions made use of polytonal, atonal, and near-serial techniques, and of course his electronic pieces were

---

*Luening has composed eighteen works for tape recorder, some using his own flute playing as the original sound score, others using "pure" electronically created sound.
**Virgil Thomson, *New York Herald Tribune*, May 16, 1948.

highly controversial when they were first heard in the early 1950s—sometimes for the mere fact that he had dared to use electronic techniques at all. Today, Luening notes wryly, he sometimes is regarded as controversial because he outrageously dares to use *traditional* sounds and styles in parts of his works.

Luening was born in Milwaukee, Wisconsin, on June 15, 1900. At the age of four he received his first musical instruction from the hands of his father, a prominent conductor in the Middle West. He began composing at the age of six, but he had no regular lessons until he was thirteen. His family moved to Munich before World War I.

In 1915 Luening became a student at the Royal Academy of Music in Munich, and the following year, at the age of fifteen, he made his first public appearance as a solo flutist. He is still an accomplished flutist, and has written extensively for the instrument in the traditional modes, as well as composing highly imaginative flute pieces in the electronic medium.

Otto Luening recalled recently:

> When the United States broke off diplomatic relations with Germany in 1917, I was expelled from the Academy as an enemy alien and I arrived in Switzerland just two weeks before I would have been interned. I went to Zurich to complete my musical education at the Municipal Conservatory. I concentrated in conducting and composing, studying with Andreae and Philipp Jarnach, and through the latter met Ferruccio Busoni, who became interested in my compositions. I became at this time flutist and percussion player in the Tonhalle Orchestra and the Opera Orchestra. At the age of seventeen my early compositions were first performed, and I also conducted for the first time that year.

The influence of Busoni upon Luening was profound, as it was upon other pupils such as Edgard Varèse, Kurt Weill, and Stefan Wolpe. (All four of this impressive covey eventually settled in America.) Luening absorbed from his teacher both the vigorous craft of neoclassic technique and his experimental bent.*

---

*According to Luening, Busoni described his "young classicism" concept as follows: "My idea (or rather feeling, subjective necessity rather than constructive principles) is, that the young classicism signifies a completion

119

SOME LEADING COMPOSERS OF ELECTRONIC MUSIC

For two years in Zurich, Luening also found time to be stage manager and to act juvenile leads and character parts under the direction of James Joyce with the English Players Company. He played piano at the famous Café Voltaire, founded by Tristan Tzara and other Dada artists who were in Zurich during the war.

Upon returning to the United States in 1920 (Busoni remarked, "Too bad; you have talent."), Luening became conductor of Chicago's new American Grand Opera Company, giving the first all-American opera performance in English. He also played piano in movie houses, taught, and conducted choral societies. In 1925 he moved to Rochester, New York, where he became Executive Director of the Opera Department of the Eastman School of Music, and a conductor of the Rochester American Opera Company. He won a Guggenheim Fellowship in 1930 (to compose his opera *Evangeline*), and two years later he was appointed Associate Professor at the University of Arizona.

At this period in Luening's career, his musical style began to lean more and more toward lyricism, a development to be heard for the first time in his *Fantasia for Orchestra* (1925). At this time Luening utilized his theory of acoustical harmony that involved the emphasis and manipulation of segments of the overtone row, using these as norms, instead of triads and seventh chords and without relationship to traditional key.

During the next two decades, his musical output encompassed a remarkably large number of works for all types of ensembles, climaxing in *Evangeline*, first produced in 1948 and eventually awarded the Bishpham Medal.

He went to Columbia University in 1947, where, as Musical Director of Brander Matthews Theater (1944–59), he conducted the world premieres of Gian-Carlo Menotti's *The Medium*, Virgil Thomson's *The Mother of Us All*, and his own *Evangeline*.

At this point, despite Luening's many impressive accomplishments, no one, probably including the composer himself, could have prophesied that he would soon become a trail-blazing pioneer, veering off into bold experimentation along the newly opened paths of elec-

in a double sense—completion as perfection and completion as the end and conclusion of previous experiments."

tronic music. But in fact Luening's interest in "the liberation of sound" began with his years as a student of Busoni, and continued throughout the 1920s when he was preoccupied with the problem of untempering a piano. In the early 1930s he consulted the physicists Dayton Miller and Edward Jordan about the problems of new sound relations. In his Introduction to Harry Partch's book, *Genesis of a Music* (1949), he predicted that "a strange and beautiful music would develop if new musical ideas were used in conjunction with electronic and other scientific developments in mind."

The first public demonstration of the potentials of the tape recorder was given by Vladimir Ussachevsky (a former member of Luening's composition seminar) at Columbia University in May 1952. Luening invited Ussachevsky to present the results of his experiments at the Bennington, Vermont, composers' conference in August.*

In such casual fashion was a revolution launched in American music. As Luening says today, "We still haven't seen the end of it." Luening's and Ussachevsky's absorption in the new medium also began at this time; so did their famous collaboration, which is one of the rare instances in history of composers actually composing together, and the only one of a long-lasting partnership.

When Orson Welles described the Luening-Ussachevsky sound score for his production of *King Lear* as "the greatest thing to have happened to the theater since the invention of incandescent lights," he may have been exaggerating, but the effect of electronic music on the theater and ballet has been enormous. Many people who are not attracted by electronic music as a listening experience thrill to it as a component of theater, ballet, or mixed-media performances.

As Hamard Shanet notes, "The first question asked by both the layman and the professional musician when the double composer, Luening-Ussachevsky, appears on a program is: 'How do two composers write a piece of music together? Who writes what?'"

Luening and Ussachevsky explain that the nature and the degree of their collaboration vary from one composition to another, but in general they work quite independently, the collaboration usually tak-

---

*For a detailed exposition of the events that followed, culminating eventually in the establishment of the Columbia-Princeton Electronic Music Center, see Otto Luening's own report, pp. 93–103, of this book.

ing the form of criticisms and suggestions offered to each by the other at frequent stages along the road. One of their joint efforts, *Concerted Piece*, consists of two distinct parts, quite separately created—a first part, lasting about 4½ to 4¾ minutes, by Luening, followed by a transition and concluding passage, of approximately the same length, by Ussachevsky.

"The next question," according to Shanet, "usually is: 'In a composition for tape recorder, where do the sounds come from in the first place?'" This question has three principal answers, according to the raw material that is preferred as a starting-point: (1) One may start by recording ordinary noises—railroads, turnstiles, the sounds of eating or walking. (The French "Musique concrète" originally began this way.) (2) Or one may use only electronically produced sounds, creating the raw material in the laboratory. (The Germans tend to regard the title of "Electronic Music" as properly applicable only to compositions made from such "pure" and precisely controlled sounds.) (3) Or one may mix the sounds of conventional musical instruments and human voices with the two types already described. The American "Tape Music" sometimes goes even further—combining sounds produced from such mixed sources with those of a standard symphony orchestra, as in Luening-Ussachevsky's "Rhapsodic Variations" of 1953–54.)"*

The Luening-Ussachevsky *Rhapsodic Variations* (1954), commissioned by the Louisville Symphony, was the very first work to combine tape-recorded sounds with those of a live symphony orchestra. The *Rhapsodic Variations* remain today one of the most expressive works in the electronic medium. The composers dared to try combining the traditional symphony orchestra with electronic sounds, and they succeeded. The music has, as one critic wrote, "an expressive life, too; strangely evocative of emotional states in the past tense. They are like profound experiences relived in one's memory—a remembered happiness, or a half-forgotten tragedy. It is provocative music and amazingly secure with its new materials."

European critics have been impressed with the work as well. *The Rhapsodic Variations for Tape Recorder and Orchestra* inspired

*Program notes of the New York Philharmonic, 1955.

the *De Nieuwe Dag* (Amsterdam), December 13, 1961 to aver: "In our opinion it seems to be a morganatic marriage, the assemblance of these two dissimilar sound units; the electronic novelties should not be seen as an expansion and enrichment of the rules of harmony and melody, but as a newly discovered territory, hardly to be overlooked, where the human mind is going to express itself in a completely different way, according to different standards. *Rhapsodic Variations* created a spatial effect which associates itself completely with the mind and development of this time."

Luening has been closely identified with the American Academy in Rome where he was composer-in-residence in 1958, 1961, and 1965. It was in Rome in 1958 that he suggested to Dmitri Shostakovich that he visit Columbia University during an American-Soviet cultural exchange mission the following year. When Shostakovich and a group of distinguished Russian composers and musicologists visited the Columbia-Princeton Electronics Center in 1959, they expressed curiosity and astonishment. Electronic music has since turned out to be one of the important areas of artistic communication between Soviet and American musicians.

At a testimonial dinner for Luening, the Pulitzer prize-winning composer Charles Wuorinen declared:

> *To his substantial accomplishments in composition, achieved during a lifetime of unceasing effort and continuous re-examination of basic musical issues, Otto Luening adds a truly remarkable record of unselfish devotion to furthering the cause of contemporary music, and to supporting its practitioners. His long-standing involvement with a multitude of musical organizations, his statesmanlike views on the musical scene, and his unfailing encouragement of the young, all bear witness to a figure of genuine breadth, to whom we gladly extend our congratulations. It is in his last role, as teacher, that I as his student most immediately regard him. His breadth, kindness, and sagacity will remain with me all my life.*

To this may be added the words of Chou Wen-Chung:

> *To Otto Luening, teaching is less a matter of imparting knowledge than stimulating the growth of the student as man and*

artist. His concern over his students therefore transcends the confines of the classroom, of technique and style. His students are legion; their commitments myriad, encompassing the whole spectrum of modern creativity. To them all, he remains always a wise counsel and friend in need. To know him as a teacher, following his own dictum, is to understand the man and artist, whose roots go back to the turn of the century and the folk tradition, whose imagination reaches for the future by way of electronic music and other areas of interest, and who is ever the advocate of new ideas, the moving spirit behind many an endeavor in behalf of composers today.

Luening is today a quiet, unpretentious man, his modesty like a fresh wind after the self-aggrandizement of so many contemporary composers. (He once described his own *Wisconsin Suite* as "unadulterated Wisconsin Baroque"—even though the *Herald Tribune* called it "sheer pleasure all the way through.") His great virtue is that he represents both the conservative and the revolutionary tendencies of contemporary music, fusing the two with great success.

He would probably wish no greater accolade. He himself wrote recently:

I believe that the music of our time will necessarily reflect in part the complexities and pattern of our age. It seems to me that a composer who is unaware of the most recent developments in his art and who does not use them when there is an artistic need for the use of such material is turning his back on his own age. This was never done in the periods of music which we venerate; I mean the Romantic movement of the last century and the Classical period before that. I do not feel that a composer need necessarily turn his back on everything that has been done before. That would be very unwise and bizarre. He needs to have the courage to explore and the desire to formulate those musical ideas which come to him because he is living today, and not living in memories and reminiscences of the glorious days of old.

VLADIMIR USSACHEVSKY

"Not far below the surface of Vladimir Ussachevsky's contemporary psyche lies a genuine romantic Russian soul," a *New York*

Times reporter wrote a while ago. "The composer's Morningside Drive apartment tells the story: photographs of his father—a bearded captain in the Czar's army and an honorary Mongolian Prince—stand in the bedroom and a grand piano presides over the living room. Persian rugs are scattered on parquet floors; original paintings, Oriental paintings, Oriental scrolls and medieval music manuscripts hang on the walls."

One would not gather from this *gemütlich* description that Ussachevsky is one of the Grand Old Men of electronic music in America.

He was born in China in 1911, of Russian parents. He received his earliest musical training from his family and did not begin formal study until he came to the United States in 1930. He earned his B.A. degree at Pomona College in California and his M.A. and Ph.D. at the Eastman School of Music. He taught in Los Angeles and Pasadena public schools in 1940–41, and was then inducted into the army. While he was in the army, he enrolled in a special Far Eastern Program at the University of Washington, and was subsequently assigned to Washington, D.C., as a research analyst. After his discharge from the army, he continued in this capacity for another year with the State Department, resuming his musical career in 1945. Two years later he joined the music faculty of Columbia University.

In 1951 Ussachevsky began to experiment with the tape recorder recently acquired by Columbia. His collaboration there with Otto Luening attracted nationwide attention in 1952 when their work was introduced by Leopold Stokowski at a concert in the Museum of Modern Art in New York.*

The story of the Ussachevsky-Luening collaboration is described in detail in this book by Luening himself, but it might be added here that their compositions predated anything else in the electronic field except the first *Musique concrète* efforts in Paris and some of the first experimental work of the Germans at Cologne. They pioneered in using live and live-recorded sound in conjunction with tape techniques.

Many of Ussachevsky's works, including *Sonic Contours, Piece for Tape Recorder, Linear Contrasts*, and *Of Wood and Brass*, have been widely performed in concert and on radio and television, both

*cf. above, pp. 93–103.

in the United States and abroad. His *Creation: Prologue*, the first part of a projected large work for four choruses, soloists, and electronic accompaniment, set to old Akkadian and Latin texts, and most of his other compositions in the tape medium have been issued on commercial records. He also has composed two electronic music scores for films: one for George Tabori's full-length adaptation of Jean-Paul Sartre's play *No Exit*, and the other for a forty-five minute abstract film, *Line of Apogee*, by Lloyd Williams, which had its premiere in New York in March 1968. (It has since been shown to professional groups and to the contemporary music audiences in New York, Hollywood, five South American countries, Czechoslovakia, Holland, Sweden, West Germany, and Great Britain.) Ussachevsky was the coordinator in charge and one of the composers of what was apparently the first completely electronic music score—a 1968 CBS television production entitled "An Incredible Voyage" in the 21st-Century Series. He supplied music and sound cues for the fall 1968 production by New York's American Place Theater of George Tabori's play *The Cannibals*.

Ussachevsky has appeared several times on national television network programs and has performed as tape-recorder soloist with many symphony orchestras in performances of his and Luening's compositions for tape recorder and orchestra. In 1967 the Bell Telephone Laboratories in New Jersey invited him to use their facilities, and he began investigating the possibilities of sound synthesis by means of computers. A composition produced there in 1968, with the aid of a GE–635 computer, was later used as the basis for another film by Lloyd Williams, *Two Images of a Computer Piece*. It was shown as a part of an electronic music and mixed media evening at the Whitney Museum in New York in January 1969. In the same year two concerts devoted entirely to his works were presented in Boston and New York.

Ussachevsky shares with many of his colleagues in New Music a faculty for which their predecessors were not notable: great verbal fluency. He is in demand as a lecturer not only in the United States, but also in Europe, the Soviet Union, and Latin America. (The State Department has sponsored several of his Latin American tours.)

Ussachevsky's electronic music for film has been particularly admired. Of his score for *No Exit*, the critic Charles Whittenberg wrote:

Ussachevsky's skill became apparent from the first bar of his film score. There was none of the naive "space-music" effects that spoiled an earlier attempt by others to combine synthetically generated sounds with a motion picture, in a grade-B science-fiction thriller called Forbidden Planet. *Both visual symbols and auditory devices, the latter skillfully intersticed with the screen-play, became for Ussachevsky structural springboards in a leit-motif relation of considerable subtlety: a call bell that rings or does not ring on the whim of the "management," a telephone that reels off an announcement of unchanging minute and hour, a bathroom in which the crucial events of earthly life are re-experienced as hallucinations, a weird series of flashbacks, and an attempted stabbing of one of the young ladies by the gentle-man who momentarily forgets that all three are eternally locked beyond the releasing power of death in Sartre's Danish-modern living room Hell.*

Speed transformations, juxtapositions of material, contrapuntal presentations of two or more motives, and various filterings of frequency relations produced something not unlike a latter-day Rondo form. The cardinal virtue of this film score seemed to be the advantage of any gesture that could be associated with gauche manipulations of sonic shock—qualities that are all-too-often associated with electronic music in the public mind due to the efforts of a few irresponsible composers.

Strictly musical logic guided Ussachevsky's choice of intensities, color, and relation of elemental shapes. A less cultivated musical intelligence would no doubt have "pulled out all the stops" avail-able in Columbia-Princeton's Studio 106 where the score was realized with the manual help of composer-technicians Bölent Arel and Mario Davidovsky. Ussachevsky gives us an unusual example of musical taste and acumen, strictly and correctly limited to the background of the aggregate event.

A listener whose acquaintance with the electronic medium is slight would do well to see No Exit *before moving on to Ussa-chevsky's absolute music and works by others such as Babbitt, Varèse, or Arel. The visual art of cinema has at least been served* *in mature fashion by one of the newest developments of the auditory art. To enhance and sustain the mood of Sartre's incisive play is not an easy task, but Vladimir Ussachevsky has accomplished it in a score of both historical importance and good no-nonsense musicality here and now.* *

Apropos of his popularity as a lecturer Ussachevsky has written:

It appears that while the medium of electronic music, in common with many musical advances of the past, has reached the point where its potential for survival seems well assured, the danger of the subject being talked to death is clearly with us. In my own case I became aware of this danger in the summer of 1960 when, following my talk on electronic music before the Convention of the American Symphony League, I next delivered twelve hours of lectures concerning music in tape medium to a class at the University of Colorado, and then proceeded to the Composers' Conference at Stratford with a similar purpose. Economic and publicity purposes aside, a composer who forsakes his tape recorder for a typewriter or a lectern is in one way succumbing to the inevitable necessity of propagandizing or defending his efforts. In doing so he is following in the historical footsteps of many composers, and, in common with them, he frequently shares the traditional uneasiness that to entrust an evaluation of his work solely to critical opinion may be precarious. Nevertheless, if he is free of a Messianic complex, a composer knows that in some respects it is premature to think that he has formulated judgments of lasting significance. The potential of the electronic medium is so vast that it is more important right now to parallel the rise of public interest with a proportionate growth of new compositions sufficiently varied in styles and materials to demonstrate the enormous richness of sounds and the opportunities for structural ingenuity with new materials. Even then, there certainly is already more than ample evidence that the existing interest in electronic music transcends mere curiosity. The emotional and the intellectual involvement

*American Composers' Alliance Bulletin, June 1963.

demonstrated by all types of audiences indicates that enduring values are present in the many compositions from the growing repertoire of the various schools.

On the problems of blending electronic sounds with a symphony orchestra, Ussachevsky writes:

The combination of a tape recorder and a symphony orchestra can be a fruitful one, and interest in audiences and among musicians is excited not so much by the novelty of this combination as by the discovery that this union of an electronic instrument and the orchestra serves not to diminish but to enrich the palette of orchestral sounds. In its long and glorious history, the orchestra has either absorbed or rejected countless instruments, but never before has it been possible to employ an instrument which is capable of reproducing sounds taken from the total world of natural or synthesized sounds.

. . . I should like to stress that there are no mysteries in this medium that will not succumb to the good musical sense which is the common property of all thoughtful and open-minded composers. In all fairness one must mention that there are obstacles yet to be overcome. The principal difficulties are with the availability of the technical facilities—a problem which can be solved only gradually. Commercially the new medium is handicapped by the traditional inflexibility of media which potentially could use what electronic music has to offer to a considerable advantage. On the other hand, there has been gratifying response from audiences; one is also inclined to believe that, in common with a good deal of contemporary music, electronic music already appears to have been immunized by repeated injections of criticism. This alone assures it a place in the next edition of Mr. Nicolas Slonimsky's Lexicon of Musical Invective.*

MILTON BABBITT

The musical genius who was neglected by his obtuse contemporaries is an all-too-familiar figure in the corpus of romantic legend. But in the 1970s we are presented with a new phenomenon

The Modern Composer and His World (Toronto: University of Toronto Press, 1961).

of neglect: the composer whose name is famous because of instant worldwide communications, but whose music remains largely unplayed. No American composer has ever been more famous while remaining more unheard than the genial, awesomely intellectual Milton Babbitt. One of the leaders of the "academic" school of composers that has sprung up in America since World War II, his music is almost completely unplayed in the concert hall and only a handful of his works has been recorded.

Some performances of his music have been almost traumatic. In 1969 Leonard Bernstein led the New York Philharmonic in the world premiere of Babbitt's *Relata II*. What should have been a happy event proved to be a disaster owing to the many serious mistakes made by the copyists, and because only six hours of rehearsal time had been allocated to the study of the formidable work. ("Dare we go ahead?" Bernstein asked Babbitt at one point in the rehearsals.)

Babbitt accepted the calamitous procedures with equanimity, then issued a scathing condemnation of our concert-going public:

> *Who will hear this piece? No one is concerned but my interested musical colleagues, those for whom I really offer it. There will not be a broadcast, a tape, a recording. There won't even be a published score. My associates across the country will not have any opportunity to hear it unless they get to Philharmonic Hall next week.*
>
> *On the other hand, the regular Philharmonic audience does not want to hear this piece. And why should they have to? How can it be coherent for them? It's as though a colleague of mine in the field of philosophy were to read his paper on the Johnny Carson show. The milieu is inappropriate to the event.*

Babbitt's further remarks after this fiasco shed pitiless light on the sad situation of the modern composer:

> *"Relata II" will not reach interested ears and minds. The performance won't be taped; because it is not being broadcast, taping is against union regulations. It won't be recorded; recording it would cost at least $20,000. "Relata II" won't even be published. The university presses are not publishing music. I have a Chair at Princeton, and no one there thinks of me as a second-class academic, yet Princeton publishes in all other fields,*

persistently ignoring that of music. My own publisher—a subsidiary of Schirmer—has not published any one of the eight works that I've written for conventional instruments and voice since 1957. Computers can be used for music publication; the process was offered to publishers at least four years ago. But nobody picked it up because nobody regards the propagation of music as being at all consequential.

In view of this appalling situation, it is little wonder that Babbitt, along with a host of other composers, embraces the medium of electronic music with open arms. Babbitt has no doubt about its great potential. "The medium provides a kind of full satisfaction for the composer. I love going to the studio with my work in my head, realizing it while I am there, and walking out with the tape under my arm. I can then send it anywhere in the world, knowing exactly how it will sound. My last electronic work, 'Ensembles for Synthesizer,' recorded by Columbia Records, has been played hundreds of times in universities."

Like Webern and Varèse, Babbitt is the son of a mathematician. He was born in Philadelphia on May 10, 1916, grew up in Jackson, Mississippi, and studied mathematics and science. His ancestry can only be termed bizarre: "No one will believe this, but one of my great-grandfathers was a rabbi and another was a Metropolitan of the Russian Orthodox Church." He came to Manhattan to attend New York University, and has lived there ever since. He now commutes twice a week to Princeton, where he is Conant Professor of Music.

At New York University Babbitt took courses in music theory and history; after leaving college he studied composition privately for three years with Roger Sessions, another much admired (and much unplayed) composer, though of an older generation. In 1938 Babbitt was appointed music instructor at Princeton at the instigation of Sessions, who had been asked by Princeton to form a graduate department of music. Sessions appointed his pupil Babbitt, then twenty-two, to the faculty. Babbitt considers this the most fortunate circumstance of his career, "If not for Roger, I might have spent my entire life teaching in South Dakota."

At Princeton, Babbitt began evolving the musical theories in which he extended the twelve-tone system of Schönberg and Webern into a serialism of his own. He freely acknowledges his great debt to Schönberg: "If not for Schönberg, I would have gone into mathematics. Schönberg hit upon a technique that made composition more interesting and challenging." Babbitt firmly believes that Schönberg's twelve-tone system is one of the great intellectual achievements of the age, "the result of a half-century of revolution in musical thought, a revolution whose nature and consequences can be compared only with those of the mid-nineteenth-century revolution in mathematics or the twentieth-century revolution in theoretical physics."

In the late forties Babbitt extended the twelve-tone technique by further serializing the dimensions of musical structure. It was this concept, which he called "total serialization," that first brought him recognition. To put it as simply as possible, Babbitt proposed an extension of twelve-tone and serial ideas of musical organization to include such nonpitch elements as rhythm, dynamics, instrumentation, register, and so on. (Incidentally, several prominent European avant-garde composers tried their hand at "totally organized" music, and either Olivier Messiaen or Pierre Boulez is usually given credit for the notion. The fact is that Milton Babbitt's *Composition for Four Instruments*, composed in 1946–47, predates any similar work by at least three or four years.)

It was almost inevitable that Babbitt would be drawn to the swiftly evolving field of electronic music, in which music could be mathematically controlled and regulated with a scientific precision hitherto unimagined. Electronic media were also ideally suited for what Babbitt terms "the multiplicity of function of every event." "Conventional instruments," he explains, "provide automatic or semi-automatic means of pitch control, but no compatible means of rhythm control." Another attraction for Babbitt was that the electronic media offered the composer total control over every facet of his piece, from its creation to its performance and its dissemination—thus fixing a "performance" for all time.

Toward the end of the 1950s Babbitt turned toward electronic media as his chief area of musical work. He became active at the Columbia-Princeton Electronic Music Center, which had been founded by Otto Luening and Vladimir Ussachevsky in 1951.* Babbitt had

*See Chapter XI.

been a consultant on RCA's David Sarnoff Research Center, and eventually RCA gave him unlimited access to its Mark II Synthesizer. For Babbitt, it was love at first sight.

He still loves the instrument, and it is quite a sight to see him at work with this leviathan in the rather depressing environs of New York's 125th Street. The Mark II Synthesizer, which is some twenty feet across, seven feet high, and a few feet deep, consists of an incredible battery of signal generators, frequency multipliers, and other parts, not to mention about 1700 tubes. Babbitt either can set any or all of the myriad switches by hand, or he can use a typewriter-like apparatus attached to the synthesizer to punch holes in a roll of wide paper tape that feeds into the machine. Once the composer has designated all the attributes of a sound (or "an acoustical event," as he prefers to call it), the machine can produce the sound at once, while an oscilloscope on the face of the synthesizer indicates a visual analog of the aural experience.

Babbitt loves the freedom the Mark II affords him and uses it now for most of his important writing. *Philomel* (1963–64) and *Ensembles for Synthesizer* (1961–63), two highly regarded compositions, were produced on it. "It's a wonderful opportunity to walk into the studio, close the door, and know that in one series of steps I'm going to be specifying what I have composed, copying the parts [all the more rewarding, no doubt, after the traumatic experience of the copyists botching his *Relata II*], proofreading, rehearsing, then walking out of that studio with the final performance, for which I am totally responsible. This is a unique and satisfying experience."

In an attempt to describe Babbitt's music, Richard Kostelanetz has written, "If the visual analog for the European (serialists) is the painting of, say, Paul Klee, Babbitt seems closer to the rich multiplicity of Jackson Pollock and Willem de Kooning."

Edgard Varèse shed light on both Babbitt's music and his methodology when he wrote, "Babbitt wants to exercise maximum control over certain materials, as if he were *above* them. But I want to be *in* the material, part of the acoustical vibration, so to speak. Babbitt composes his music first and then gives it to the synthesizer, while I want to generate something directly by electronic means.... I simply want to project a sound, a musical thought, to initiate it, and then let it take its own course."

For this listener, Babbitt's music has a mathematically determined kaleidoscopic quality; the basic musical material is not arbitrarily manipulated in a numero-mystical fashion, as is so common in the European serialist composers. With Babbitt the music is turned and rotated, as it were, so that it is viewed and contemplated from every possible angle. It is a little world of sound, a bordered and limited area, totally explored. One feels that not just a single course or line of sound is developing, but rather that a plurality of sound structures is unfolding.

On the other hand, the English composer-critic Wilfred Mellers, in his *Music in a New Found Land*, wrote in 1964, "Babbitt's abstraction is so extreme that he favors pure electronic sounds, not the processed natural noises that Varèse and Cage commonly employ. The result does not seem very meaningful in terms of human experience, though it is too early to tell whether this is due to Babbitt's deficiencies as a composer, or to his inexperience in handling a new medium."

Paradoxically, Babbitt established his reputation among the general musical public not with his music, but rather with a highly controversial article he wrote for *High Fidelity* magazine in 1958 entitled "Who Cares If You Listen?"* In this piece Babbitt rejects the popular notion that the composer must necessarily communicate with the layman. On the contrary, he regards the composer's duty as the advancement of new musical concepts. Of the present-day composer's isolation, he says:

> *I do not see how or why the situation should be otherwise. Why should the layman be other than bored and puzzled by what he is unable to understand, music or anything else? ... After all, the public does have its own music, its ubiquitous music: music to eat by, to read by, to dance by, and to be impressed by. Why refuse to recognize the possibility that contemporary music has reached a stage long-since attained by other forms of activity? The time has passed when the normally well-educated man without special preparation could understand the most advanced*

*Just to set the record straight, Babbitt has informed me that his original title for the piece was the far more innocent: "The Composer as Specialist." The editors of *High Fidelity* renamed it "Who Cares If You Listen?"

work in, for example, mathematics, philosophy, and physics. Advanced music, to the extent that it reflects the knowledge and originality of the informed composer, scarcely can be expected to appear more intelligible than these arts and sciences to the person whose musical education usually has been even less extensive than his background in other fields.

Such challenging, provocative words were not calculated to endear Babbitt to the music lover at large, let alone to Harold Schönberg and Henry Pleasants, the outraged critics who habitually reject our modern composers for the sin of being unpopular with audiences. Does Babbitt feel distressed over his unhappy "isolation"? Not a bit. *"It is my contention that, on the contrary, this situation is not only inevitable, but potentially advantageous for the composer and his music.* From my point of view, the composer would do well to consider means of realizing, consolidating, and extending the advantage."

Babbitt's name is almost inevitably linked with John Cage's, for they are the two magnetic poles of modern music, the two high priests of separate religions, each with his acolytes attending the True Cause. Babbitt's work is totally structured and rationalized, where Cage celebrates the irrational, the unpredictable, the randomness of art as resembling the randomness of life itself. Cage is the neo-Dadaist who has gaily abdicated artistic consciousness, even artistic responsibility. This is a course that would be inconceivable, even reprehensible, to Milton Babbitt, yet, ironically, both men are accused of being responsible for modern music's becoming increasingly incomprehensible to the casual music lover.

Does the future belong to Babbitt and his many adherents? Or to the untrammeled, undisciplined Cageans? Or to neither school? It is of course too early to tell, but American culture has always been a polyculture, and there is reason to believe that the future of the new American music will have followers in both schools, despite their conflicting (and complementary) approaches to music. Both Babbitt and Cage are pioneers of the expanding techniques and the new concepts and forms of today's music, which seeks "the totality of possible experience."

Does electronic music foreshadow the end of the live performer? Babbitt does not think so:

I know of no serious electronic composer who ever asserts or would want to assert that we are supplanting any other form of musical activity. We are interested, not in supplanting, but in supplementing. We're interested in increasing the resources of music. After all, the human voice was not supplanted by the musical instruments that came into being in the sixteenth, seventeenth, eighteenth, and nineteenth centuries, in spite of the fact that they introduced all kinds of flexible capacities that the voice doesn't have. Leaping four octaves on a piano is no great task; however, I don't know of many singers who can do this. These instruments all have their own unique qualities and attributes. Who wishes to supplant? Who wishes to do anything more than simply make music available in all of its maximal resources?

JOHN CAGE

John Cage is perhaps the most famous and controversial American composer to emerge since World War II. What is more, it can be persuasively argued that he has been one of the most influential figures in the arts for the last twenty years. His ideas, not necessarily his music itself, are admired by hippies and highbrows alike. Along with Marshall McLuhan, Buckminster Fuller, and Merce Cunningham—all friends of his—Cage is one of the super-gurus of today. His thought has been embraced by the young, who seem to be yearning for a new messiah and to delight in John Cage, a turned-on, sixtyish Pied Piper whose notions nevertheless seem just right. Indeed, so wide has been his acceptance that he is very much a part of the "Now" Establishment. Ironically, *because* of this acceptance, his radical ideas make far less impact now than they did a decade ago, when his pronouncements and creations seemed so startling.

John Cage clearly belongs to the American Experimental school, which traces honorably back to Charles Ives. He is a rebel, a true eccentric; Virgil Thomson has written, not very favorably, of Cage's "rigid schedule of beliefs and prophecies, his monorail mind and his turbine-engined, irreversible locomotive of a career."[*]

John Cage is a complex man. The number and range of his in-

---

[*]Virgil Thomson, "Cage and the Collage of Noises," *The New York Review of Books*, April 23, 1970.

terests are enormous. So is the number of people he generously credits with having influenced him. Of them, reflections of Charles Ives, Erik Satie, and Edgard Varèse are most apparent in his music. In allied arts, he recognizes the kinship of his own work with Marcel Duchamp's and Joan Miró's, and credits Jasper Johns and Robert Rauschenberg with having stimulated him. The science of mycology (mushrooms) fascinates him, and he spends considerable time pursuing that interest. Variations on the theories of Buckminster Fuller and Marshall McLuhan flare up in the pages of his writings like relay rockets.

A student of Eastern religions, he took up Zen Buddhism years before it became fashionable. The heightened awareness of ordinary events that Zen tries to instill, its serene acceptance of nature's randomness, served to mature Cage's own feelings about life and art. He is fond of the Zen aphorism: "We should imitate the sands of the Ganges. They are neither disgusted by filth nor pleased by perfumes." He feels that information and facts are the enemy of experience. "What we need is less information and more direct experience of life around us," he says. "It took pop art to show us that we've never experienced the commonplace."

One says his name with the knowledge that he has been a catalyst, teacher, and rallying point, as well as an inventory of the new anti-art, neo-Dada culture that is very much with us. Cage's composition classes at the New School for Social Research and at Black Mountain College in the 1950s were filled with painters, actors, poets, and dancers as well as musicians. An instinctive showman, he staged at Black Mountain College a simultaneous series of mixed-media improvisations with himself reading a lecture from the top of a stepladder, Merce Cunningham and his troupe capering through the audience, two poets reciting their work, while movies were being projected against the walls and ceiling. Cultural historians now recognize this as the first "happening." It gave courage to such as Allan Kaprow, reputedly the inventor of the happening; to the composer Morton Feldman, who realized the principle of chance in Western music; and to members of the influential mixed-media group called the Judson Dance Theater.

As Cage's influence has widened, and as each phase of his career has attracted greater approval and more and more imitators, it has been almost impossible for critics to categorize him or to describe the man and his work in sensible words. Some have seen in him a spiritual link with the Dadaists and Italian Futurists. His affinity with the Zen Buddhists has become famous since his own writings (*Silence, A Year From Monday*, etc.) began piling up in college and underground bookstores throughout the Western world. Yet despite his own books and many lectures and interviews, Cage himself eludes classification as his music eludes definition. With sunny optimism, Cage advises his listeners to "accept music for what it is: a way of life devoted to sound and silence, the only common denominator of which two is rhythm, rhythm."

A Californian who has the pioneering spirit in his bones, John Cage was born on September 5, 1912. Valedictorian of his Los Angeles high school, he entered nearby Pomona College (coincidentally, also Ussachevsky's alma mater) just before his seventeenth birthday. For a while, he considered studying to be a Methodist minister, as his grandfather had been. Instead, he soon dropped out of school (rather appalled, he says, at the regimentation of individual thought and curiosity), and traveled across Europe for a year before returning to Los Angeles.

In Europe he had toyed with the notion of becoming an architect, a painter, or a writer; he now decided to concentrate on music. He studied composition briefly with Richard Buling as well as with Henry Cowell, a leading avant-garde composer. Cowell was at that time in San Francisco, not only composing prolifically himself, but also arranging concerts of new music and publishing much experimental music in his *New Music Quarterly*. Cowell, who was the first to experiment with "tone clusters" produced by striking the piano keys with the entire forearm, himself had been a bold innovator, and he encouraged the dash and originality that Cage displayed in the scores he gave him to read.

In 1934 Cage became a pupil of Arnold Schönberg, who had recently come to America and was then teaching at the University of Southern California. Cage relates a touching story about their first meeting. Schönberg questioned whether Cage could afford to study with him. "I told him," Cage has said, "that there wasn't any question of affording it, because I couldn't pay him anything at all. He then asked me whether I was willing to devote my life to music, and I said I was. 'In that case,' he said, 'I will teach you free of charge.' " Cage has since gratefully repaid this debt by teaching his own students free of charge when they could not afford to pay, and sometimes when they could.

The choice of the radical yet rigid theoretician Schönberg as teacher, a man who proclaimed his own twelve-tone system as "The Law," may seem an odd one for John Cage, the future prophet of no-order in music. But Cage recalls that Schönberg was "a magnificent teacher who always gave us the impression that he was putting us in touch with the musical principles." Despite Schönberg's generosity, Cage found his convictions uncongenial. He could not relate to Schönberg's harmony or to his setting up of his own harmonic theories (the serial technique) as the tablets straight from Sinai. In short Schönberg, who insisted on top of everything else that a composer must have a sense of harmony, was not radical enough for Cage. Cage not only had no gift for harmony; he was emphatically uninterested in harmony. He left. Many years later he found out that Schönberg had confided to Peter Yates that "Cage was not a composer, but an inventory of genius."*

In 1943 Cage made his debut in New York City at a concert of his percussion compositions at the Museum of Modern Art. Under Cage's direction, a large group of performers displayed their talents with flowerpots, brake bands, electric buzzers, and other objects not primarily musical but capable of producing startling sounds.

In an interview that appeared in *PM* on March 24, 1946, Cage declared that his major contribution to the composition of music was the elimination of harmony. In his search for nonharmonic instruments that were not too unwieldy or too expensive, he started a percussion orchestra that included Chinese, Indian, and other Oriental instruments. He also developed instruments from pieces of junk, such as the scrapped hoods of old automobiles.

His experiments with improvised instruments—junk instruments in a sense—led Cage to his invention of the prepared piano. The list

---

*Cage also studied with Adolph Weiss, a former pupil of Schönberg.

of objects that he installed as dampers between the strings of the piano includes screws, bolts, spoons, clothespins, aspirin boxes, a doll's arm, and strips of felt, rubber, plastic, and leather. Cage has said: "Just as you go along the beach and pick up pretty shells that please you, I go into the piano and find sounds I like." By eliminating all sounds of precise pitch, Cage produced atonal music and substituted for the chromatic scale a gamut of pings, plucks, and delicate thuds. Virgil Thomson has described the sound as "a ping qualified by a thud." Cage has said that the prepared piano is, in effect, a percussion ensemble under the control of a single player. One wit has called it "the well-tampered clavier."

As the critic Arthur Berger pointed out, the Cage "prepared piano" is a conception not dissimilar to that of the one-man bands common to the jazz world. It would be more apt, perhaps, to describe it as a one-man gamelan. Nevertheless, in 1949 the National Academy of Arts and Letters awarded him $1,000 for inventing the "prepared piano."

Like Edgard Varèse, whose music he admires enormously, Cage was fascinated with the possibilities of electronic music long before the devices were invented that made them possible. In a lecture delivered in Seattle called "The Future of Music: Credo," he declared as early as 1937:

I BELIEVE THAT THE USE OF NOISE

Wherever we are, what we hear is mostly noise.* When we ignore it, it disturbs us. When we listen to it, we find it fascinating. The sound of a truck at 50 m.p.h. Static between the stations. Rain. We want to capture and control these sounds, to use them not as sound effects, but as musical instruments. Every film studio has a library of "sound effects" recorded on film. With a film phonograph it is now possible to control the amplitude and frequency of any one of these sounds and to give to it rhythms within or beyond the reach of anyone's imagination. Given four film phonographs, we can compose and perform a quartet for explosive motor, wind, heart beat and landslide.

*In Cage's printed version of his speech, the "Credo" is stated succinctly with the phrases in capital letters running diagonally across the page.

TO MAKE MUSIC

If this word, music, is sacred and reserved for 18th and 19th century instruments, we can substitute a more meaningful term: organization of sound.

WILL CONTINUE AND INCREASE UNTIL WE REACH A MUSIC PRODUCED THROUGH THE AID OF ELECTRICAL INSTRUMENTS . . .

. . . The special property of electrical instruments will be to provide complete control of the overtone structure of tones (as opposed to noise) and to make these tones available in any frequency, amplitude and duration. . . . It is now possible for composers to make music directly, without the assistance of intermediary performers. Before this happens, centers of experimental music must be established. In these centers, the new materials, oscillators, generators, means for amplifying small sounds, film phonographs, etc., available for use. Composers at work using 20th century means for making music. Performances of results. Organization of sound for musical and extra-musical purposes (theater, dance, film).

THROUGH THE PRINCIPLE OF ORGANIZATION OR MAN'S COMMON ABILITY TO THINK.

Cage's *Imaginary Landscape No. 4*, originally performed at Columbia University in 1951 before an invited audience, called for twelve radios playing simultaneously. Each radio was manned by two performers, one continuously twiddling the station selector, the other the tone and volume controls. Thus, what assailed the ears varied from moment to moment, according to the random positions of the dials, the programs being broadcast, and the static. The performance lasted merely four minutes, but that proved too long for the stupefied audience. Virgil Thomson, then the influential music critic of the New York *Herald Tribune* and generally an admirer of Cage's, warned him gravely never to subject a paying audience to such an experience.

In 1951, Cage organized a group of musicians and engineers "for the making of music directly on magnetic tape." Cage's own contribution, *Imaginary Landscape No. 5*, was described by the composer as "a recording on tape, using as material any 42 phonograph records." Cage has said, "As far as I can ascertain, this was the first work composed for tape made in this country." Cage's *Landscape* was played in January 1952; whether it was actually the "first tape piece in America" is debatable, and depends on whether one accepts Cage's program—in his own words, "a set of instruction for splicing together the recorded information"—as a score. In the same year, both Otto Luening and Vladimir Ussachevsky presented public concerts of tape music that were realized compositions, not merely "instructions."

In any case, Cage has pursued his notion that music consists of all possible sounds and has used electronic machinery to produce distinctly "unmusical" noises. He experimented with tape collages consisting of all sorts of miscellaneous "outside" noises that he gathered and then closely spliced onto a tape so that the resulting product sounds like a multivoiced singer sputtering a multiplicity of sounds. Biased toward aural experience without pattern—the "elimination of the will, of consciousness"—Cage finds electronic devices highly suited to his purpose. In his *Rosart Mix* (1965), he instructs the performers to put tape loops (junctures) selected from a pile of eighty-eight such loops onto twelve tape machines hooked into the amplification system. They make random substitutions in the course of the performance, and no one, not even Cage or the performers, can predict how the twelve will interact.

Cage has pioneered not only in "noise" but also in silence. When he wrote 4′ 33″, he opened a door to the New Music. This work was first performed in 1952. Pianist David Tudor approached the piano bench and sat—just sat still—for four minutes, thirty-three seconds. The "music" consisted of the coughs and creaks that arose from the audience and their seats during the "performance." In this piece Cage seemed to be endowing unintentional noise with the status of intentionally produced music and exploded the last connection with traditional definitions of "what music is." Since Cage could have no control over the aural accidents, he called this kind of music "indeterminate." Today, he considers the piece archaic because of its prearranged, or determinate, length.

Cage has explained that in his infamous 4′ 33″ he was seeking to demonstrate much more than a fun piece of neo-Dada. As a zone of tranquility is at the heart of a tempest, so silence lies at the center of sound storms—provided, that is, the listener makes the spiritual effort necessary to turn void into fullness. Cage seems to observe no distinction between music, noise, and silence. "Everything we do is music," he insists.

Unsurprisingly, no noise fascinates Cage more than chance noise, surprise noise. During a party one evening Cage winced when somebody put a Brahms symphony on a record player. Conventional music —indeed most conventional and traditional art—pains him. Midway through the first movement, however, the simultaneous ring of a telephone and the slam of a door cut across the Brahms sonorities. Cage turned with a smile to the person beside him. "Isn't that beautiful?"

Cage will certainly be remembered as one of the great innovators in music. No one, I think, pretends to "enjoy" Cage's electronic music; usually the listener gets the point of the deliberately insufferable din in a Cage piece within seconds, and declines to go on listening. But this very quality can make some observers view John Cage coolly; as Virgil Thomson wrote, "He prizes innovation above all other qualities—a weighting of the values which gives to all of his judgments an authoritarian, almost a commercial aspect, as of a one-way tunnel leading only to the gadget-fair." But his early ventures in electronic music, in chance music, in seeking Eastern bases for Western music— all of these have been profoundly influential.

Eric Salzman has well summed up Cage's accomplishment: *Of the important implications (often overlooked in all the fuss about "chance," "happenings," and the like) is the opening up of the natural external world as material for musical and artistic experience. This, as much as anything else, is the significance of Cage's infamous 4′ 33″ of silence or the almost equally notorious* Music for 12 Radios. *Finally, because of the philosophical and gestural ideas inherent in many of his activities (they are hardly "works" in the old sense), one can speak of a new theater inspired in part by his ideas and example. Such diverse manifestations as happenings, environments, participatory theater, mixed-*

and multi-media can trace many of their origins to the work, thought, and activity of John Cage.

EARLE BROWN

Earle Brown is one of the most interesting American avant-garde composers working today. His music bears a clear and intentional relationship to the plastic arts; Brown freely admits his debt to the ideas and mobile sculpture of Alexander Calder, as well as to the "action painting" of Jackson Pollock. He told an interviewer in 1963, "A composer of the future will try to bring about a total involvement of the listener's senses. In my own music I have aimed for Calder's mobility and changing forms, and Pollock's spontaneousness."

His scores are worked out graphically in their detail and predisposition, but Brown is fascinated with the principle of "a certain improvisation or mobility within a performance itself." Here one can clearly perceive the influence of the sculptures of Calder, whose mobiles consist of many parts moving freely in space, thus altering their relationships with one another from moment to moment. The musical analogy of Pollock's "action painting," created by the "action" of dripping paint onto a canvas, carries over in the performance of Brown's music to the freedom and improvisation accorded to the conductor, who cues the musicians as he sees fit. Brown insists that he is not trying to represent in sound any specific works of these visual artists. "I am not trying to make the listener hear a mobile or visualize a Pollock painting. I was inspired by the manner, the process of their way of working."

Translating Calder's "mobile" concept into musical terms, Brown applied the sculptor's ideas to a similarly free kind of musical score where the page-by-page details are notated and fixed, but where the sequence in which the notes are to be played may be varied. This concept, which has come to be known as "open-form" composition, was almost immediately adopted by several European musical avant-gardists. In 1956, Stockhausen composed his *Klavierstucke*, a series of brief segments for piano that could be constructed in various ways, depending on the performer's mood. But Brown had done almost precisely the same thing in 1953, with his *25 Pages*. Even earlier, in

1952, he had introduced controlled improvisation in a group of pieces called *Folio*.

Thus, as with the pioneering music of the Americans John Cage and Milton Babbitt, we have reached in music a phenomenon already familiar for a generation in painting: the exciting, new, avant-garde ideas come out of America and are eagerly copied by Europeans.

Earle Brown was born on December 26, 1926, in Lunenberg, Massachusetts. As an undergraduate, he first studied engineering in Boston and later studied and taught the highly organized composing technique of Joseph Schillinger. He barnstormed as a jazz trumpeter, but was becoming more and more interested in electronics. Working as a recording engineer and supervisor, he produced the "Contemporary Sound Series" for Time Records, a series of records today much prized by avant-garde collectors.

In 1967, he was awarded the W. Alton Jones Chair of composition at the Peabody Conservatory in Baltimore, although at that time his name was barely known to American music lovers. (Peabody eventually awarded him a Doctor of Music degree, *honoris causa*.) In Europe, Brown is regarded as something of a living legend and one of the most influential of modern composers, admired by such luminaries as Stockhausen and Boulez. In 1970 he accepted a year's residence in West Berlin as guest of the Berliner Kunstlerprogramm, managed by the Ford Foundation.

Brown's long and close association with John Cage goes back to the early fifties. At that time, together with Christian Wolff, Morton Feldman, and David Tudor, he joined Cage in "The Project of Music for Magnetic Tape" which Cage had organized. This was one of the very first experimental groups for electronic music in America.* Of Cage, Brown says, "John was the first musical mind I'd met that reflected some of the feelings I'd gotten from the work of Calder and Pollock—and those were more important to me than any musical influences I've ever known." He and Cage met in 1952 when Cage came through Denver, where Brown was teaching music privately. Cage was then on tour with Merce Cunningham, who was giving master classes in modern dance. Brown was invited to join the Cage-Cunningham circle in New York.

*See Chapter XI.

Brown was strongly influenced by Cage, the apostle of aleatory, or "chance," music. But today he no longer accepts Cage's belief that random aberrations in a performance are as valid artistically as the composed parts. Brown prefers a responsible, controlled, and more human improvisatory collaboration between composer and performer. "Mine is music by choice, not chance," he says. "My music enlarges the potential for musicians to take a more creative part in the music; yet I am not interested in everybody just doing his thing. I didn't compose by chance. I composed what I wanted to hear."

Understandably, Brown somewhat resents being almost inevitably linked, subordinately, with John Cage, who declines in recent pronouncements to impose controls on his compositions. "I'm not interested in noncontrol," Brown says. "We can all be noncontrolled, but that's not interesting."

Brown wants performer freedom within limits, but not chance music. "It's a subtle thing, misinterpreted many times, and I'm sick of it. Because chance music sounds more audacious, people put us all in the Cage bag." While Cage was tossing coins and consulting the *I-Ching* in order to let the content decide itself, in effect he also controlled the length of his pieces with a stopwatch. "I was doing the opposite," Brown says, "composing the content, writing out all the actual notes, and allowing the human element to operate by opening up the form."*

Of those heady days in the early 1950s when Cage, Feldman, and Brown were blazing new artistic paths in music, Brown has said, "Cage, Feldman and I did three distinct things—we never were a school in any sense. But we did have something in common in the 50s and it was that we looked *elsewhere* for ideas. A lot of composers stick their noses in the history of music and keep it there. They say, 'Webern did this, now what can I develop out of Webern.' They're not conscious of the thing going on in the world that is called art." But the Cage group looked at music as if it were a branch of art, or even a branch of life.

"The three of us—Cage, Feldman and I—were the bad boys of the American scene at that time. We were totally unacceptable to people like Milton Babbitt, Aaron Copland—that kind of American composer

*Interview in *The New York Times*, June 21, 1970.

—because we were influenced by other than musical events and ideas. Morty Feldman was influenced by a painter, Philip Guston, who was doing very gentle, delicate pastels with a palette knife. In music, Morty was a sort of imagist, a precursor of the minimal-art men. John, being about ten years older than we, was heavily influenced, I think, by Duchamp. And I was deeply impressed by Calder and Pollock."*

Brown also takes satisfaction from the fact that his startling ideas have caught on and have been extensively copied. "I worked with my stuff—open-form music and graphic notation—for years and nobody seemed to understand what was going on."

By the time he wrote his *Available Forms I* in 1961, however, the musical world had begun to watch him. As a result of what he, Cage, and Feldman did, Brown feels that "now there is a big difference in European music. More flexibility, more use of graph notation. The hard-core serialization concept is quite finished. People like Luigi Nono, who was originally critical of my ideas, have loosened up. Bruno Maderna has changed. So have Boulez and Stockhausen. You know, Stockhausen holds the position of being the most avant-garde European, but what is he doing? All the old Cage things. I love Stockhausen," Brown says, "but he's always waking up every morning and inventing the light-bulb."

Brown is convinced of the future of what he calls "open-form" music. His *Available Forms I*, which is scored for eighteen winds, string, and percussion players, is a Calderian example of what Brown calls "conceptual mobility." Each of its six pages contains five musical "events" which the instrumentalists play on specific orders from the conductor. To Brown, a Beethoven or Brahms symphony is "closed form"—that is, no options to choose materials are given to the conductor. In "open-form" music, in contrast, every note is precomposed (and rehearsed) and determined, yet the piece at hand can never sound the same way twice. "What I am actually doing when conducting," says Brown, "is creating a piece in the moment of performing it. I can feel it happening under my hands."

By his "open form" Brown also aims to involve the players more closely in the process of creation and to bridge the distance between

Ibid.

the work, the composer, the player, and the audience. In fact every score in "open form" is potentially many works, each of which is defined only at the moment of performance. Over the years Brown has become adept at regulating the degree of possible chance interference in the course of the work, and he composes material that lends itself well to relatively free assemblage in the performance and during rehearsal.

Earle Brown finds electronic sound "a fantastic medium" and yet he is too "interested in live people" to stay with it continually. His early electronic pieces were for tape alone, such as *Octet I and II* in the mid 1950s, for eight channels each and of indefinite length. *Light Music*, in 1961, included not only a full orchestra but lights as well—a move toward that "total involvement of the listener's senses." The recent *Times Five* combines flute, trombone, harp, violin, and cello in a spreading texture, with four tracks of tape whose sound begins rather brightly but darkens and deepens in color. The response of the "open-form" instruments to this fixed element comes across in a beguiling manner.

Brown is pleased that, for the first time in music's long history, Europeans respectfully listen to new American ideas in the art. Until recently, Europeans loved jazz and jazz musicians, but condescended toward "serious" American composers as being little more than provincial bumpkins.

"I've always been very much accepted in Europe," Brown says. "My music is unique to their ears. It's not like their music. Europeans don't want imitation European music by Americans, no matter how able it is. They've done that thing." Today the leading composers are eager to connect with a public, to loosen up, Earle Brown style.

I guess that's what Milton Babbitt means when he calls us the "the show-biz crowd," as he did in a New York *Times* interview last year. Milton irritates the hell out of me. I'm not fond of his attitude at all. It's as if he's speaking for modern music, but he's not. Just a certain group. It's like what Clive Barnes said about "Oh! Calcutta!" and pornography—Milton gives contemporary music a bad name.

"At one point in that interview Milton said there's his kind of really serious music and there's show-biz music. Well, if show-biz means you write music you like and it gets played at concerts and it does create a feeling between audiences and performers, that's okay with me."

What is Earle Brown's place in modern music? There is no one work of his to which one can point and say: this will endure. Brown's contribution has been in sponsoring, with Cage, a renewal of music, with his graph pieces and "Available Forms." He has shown us new ways of thinking about music, with his sketches, graph-symbols which notate only high, low, and middle registers and densities, and exist only in their mobility, while they are being made.

One can even say that Brown is not a composer at all, in our traditional sense; his projects can be more accurately termed stimuli to musical activity. By their very nature, they urge the creative participation of the performers, or conductor, who is invited to decide the order in which the sound events will take place. He has proposed an entirely new schema for musical performance, which consists of the composer, who devises the basic musical plan; the conductor, who decides when and in what order the sound events should occur; and players, who must play the notes as written, but not necessarily in time-conjunction with one another.

Earle Brown, like John Cage, presents us with a music that emulates the never-ending ambiguities, the "open ends," of nature itself. We have come a long way from our once-firm conviction that a composer must impose "order" on his material. The Western idea of the Will, of the artist's grimly wrought signature on his work of art, has eroded. Instead, we are approaching here a musical world based on the timeless ideas of the East; we are urged to be free from past and future, and to enter an autonomous Now.

MORTON SUBOTNICK

The first composers who began experimenting with electronic music in the 1950s are already referred to as belonging to the "classical" period of electronic music. We now have a flourishing new generation of composers, many of whom work with decidedly "liberated" ideas and are not at all tied to Webernian twelve-tone theory, as were many of their predecessors. Among the new men of today, none is more admired than the imaginative and skillful Morton Subotnick.

He is tied to no musical ideology, no musical style; in fact, he firmly believes that the musicians of the twentieth century have searched in vain for a common musical language. In the program notes to his own music, Subotnick wrote recently, "Each composer today individualizes his style, even changes that 'style' radically from one composition to another. If he adheres to a common language, it applies only to the group he has accepted (and been accepted by), and the group itself tends to remain in stylistic and aesthetic contrast to other groups."

Subotnick's remarks agree strikingly with Robert Jay Lifton's view of contemporary man as "Protean man"—named, of course, "after that intriguing figure of Greek mythology renowned for his shape-shifting." Lifton explains that he chose the term "in order to describe an emerging psychological style which I believe characteristic of much in contemporary life.... We may say then that young adults individually, and youth movements collectively, express most vividly the psychological themes of Protean man. But we may also say that Protean man's affinity for the young, his being metaphorically and psychologically young in spirit, has to do with his never-ceasing quest for imagery of rebirth. He seeks such imagery of rebirth from all sources, from ideas, techniques, religions ... and of course from special individuals of his own kind—that is, from fellow Protean voyagers—whom he sees as possessing that problematic gift of his namesake, the gift of prophecy..."*

Lifton's remarks sketch most admirably the musical ideas not only of Subotnick, but of his entire generation of composers, and help us understand their novel and varied musical thinking.

Morton Subotnick comments that one reason for the modern composer's "changing his style radically from one composition to another" is that "the twentieth-century composer is directly challenged—whether or not he accepts the challenge—by the historically accepted masters of his art. His intense awareness of the masters' styles and techniques as part of the living fiber of the society he lives in—an awareness unprecedented in previous centuries—compels him to adopt new positions. He must also be aware of the discrepancy between

*Robert Jay Lifton, *Boundaries: Psychological Man in Revolution* (New York: Random House, 1970), pp. 37–38.

the nature of his developing musical language (with its highly individualized form and content) and the traditional institutions this music functions within."

One hundred fifty years ago Franz Schubert uttered the despairing cry: "Who could ever hope to compose again after Beethoven?" This, Subotnick is saying, is the even more despairing cry of present-day composers, who have to follow not only Beethoven, but also Schubert himself, as well as Brahms, Wagner, Mahler, and the other towering figures of the last century. You can't compete with Beethoven in his own ball park.

Morton Subotnick was born on April 14, 1933, in Los Angeles. He earned his undergraduate degree in English Literature at the University of Denver, and got his Master of Arts in Composition from Mills College, where he studied with Leon Kirchner (who has written some impressive, Pulitzer prize-winning electronic music himself) and Darius Milhaud. While in California, Subotnick co-founded the Mills College Performing Group and the San Francisco Tape Music Center. At the same time he held posts as Assistant Professor of Music at Mills College, and Musical Director of Ann Halprin's Dancers' Workshop Company.

Like all of the composers considered here, Subotnick began as a composer for the conventional live-instrumental forms. (The day has not yet arrived when our embryonic composers spring at once to the synthesizer, bypassing traditional instruments entirely, but it is fast approaching.) He was proficient enough on the clarinet to be a member of the Denver Symphony while in that city, and later to play with the San Francisco Symphony. Before declaring himself in the electronic camp, Subotnick had written instrumental music that was quite well received: his *Serenade No. 1* (1960), an eight-minute piece for six performers, and his *Serenade No. 2* (1964) are both severely modern works employing daring innovations. (In the latter work, a clarinet is held in a French horn's bell as the players of both engage in an enormous crescendo.) His multi-media opus *Play! No. 1*, for woodwind quintet, piano, tape, and film, is also a startling piece. In this work, which to this listener-viewer seems to be a kind of musical theater of the absurd, the players gaze about, or sit motionless, or shout epithets, and are themselves interrupted at one point by a film of Subotnick himself back in San Francisco.

From an early age, Subotnick was immersed in the classics of literature as well as of music; his love of poetry is evident in the titles of his two famous works for electronic media. *Silver Apples of the Moon*, written in 1967, gets its title from a line of poetry by Yeats, while *The Wild Bull*, completed in 1968, was named after a poem by an anonymous Sumerian poet of around 1700 B.C. Subotnick remarks of it, "The state of mind which the poem evoked became intimately tangled with the state of mind my own composition was evoking in me. To title the work after the poem seemed natural." Certainly *The Wild Bull*, a strange, powerful lament with an extraordinarily wide range of sound, must be respected as serious romantic music.

Subotnick's interest in electronic music began early. While on the faculty at Mills College, he worked with an engineer, Donald Buchla, and another electronically oriented composer, Ramon Sender, to develop a superior electronic synthesizer that would perform the functions that Subotnick desired. "The three of us worked together for more than a year to develop an electronic music 'machine' that would satisfy our needs as composers," Subotnick says.

In the early 1960s Subotnick helped to assemble one of the first independent American studies, the San Francisco Tape Music Center. "We scrounged our equipment from fire sales and insurance auctions," he recalls. He now works with a transistorized modular unit built by Buchla at the tape center.

Subotnick is quite sold on the Buchla Synthesizer's potentialities: "The system generates sound and time configurations which are predetermined by the composer through a series of patches consisting of interconnecting various voltage control devices. It is possible to produce a predetermined sound event ... and it is also possible to produce sound events that are predetermined only in generalities.... This means that one can tell the machine what kind of event you want without deciding on the specific details of the event ... and listen ... and then make final decisions as to the details of the musical gesture. This gives the flexibility to score sections of the piece in the traditional sense ... and to mold other sections (from graphic and verbal notes) like a piece of sculpture."

Subotnick was appointed Musical Director of the Repertory Theater of New York's Lincoln Center during its first season, and in

1966 became associated with the Intermedia Program of the School of Arts at New York University. He has also written music for films, including some for the space-age opus, *2001*. He has served as director of Electronic Music at the Electric Circus in Greenwich Village and has presided over the "Electric Ear" series given there, which gave music lovers the unusual experience of fighting their way through panhandling hippies and bored-looking cops to sit on portable boxlike chairs in a large room and watch Morton Subotnick on stage, smoking cigarettes, occasionally fiddling with some of the knobs of the formidable array of electronic gear that surrounded him, while the sounds of his electronic compositions emerged from ceiling-mounted speakers. A highlight at the Electric Circus was an audio-visual affair conceived by Subotnick and the artist Anthony Martin, entitled *The Closer She Gets*. Proximity detectors were placed around the room, which later were activated by the dancers. On stage, one dancer launched into a kind of ceremonial Priapus worship, caressing and undulating around a looming, glowing rod. The closer she got, the less was left to the imagination.

Subotnick's chief success, significantly, is with works written directly on tape for performance in the home of the private listener rather than in the concert hall.* For example, his *Silver Apples of the Moon* and *The Wild Bull* were commissioned by Nonesuch Records in 1967 and 1968. A third piece, *Touch*, on the Columbia label, is regarded by many critics (including Eric Salzman) as the finest of the three works. Little wonder, then, that Subotnick, like Milton Babbitt and a host of other composers who have converted to the electronic

---

*Just how far from the staid concert hall Subotnick has moved is demonstrated by a recent article from Alan Rich's music column in *New York* magazine: "Creative Playthings, the new store on East 53rd Street next to Paley Park, contains as part of its—I guess you'd call it decor—an electronic score by Morton Sobotnick [sic] that is something of a creative plaything in itself. At intervals throughout the store there are panels with four push buttons, three green and a red, which customers young and old are free to push. Each button activates a tape loop: a rhythm track, a couple of melody tracks and a "sound-effects" track, all electronically produced. You push any or all of the buttons, rapidly or slowly, and *voilà!* you've created your own electronic composition. Each panel of buttons, furthermore, has its own set of loops, and Sobotnick plans to change them all for new loops from time to time."

medium, takes a harsh view of the present state of music and the meager reward that the concert hall offers the composer today.

Subotnick has written succinctly on this unhappy subject:

> *The fractionated nature of twentieth-century music has invalidated the concert hall as an effective institution for its presentation. An audience, before it can understand a new composition, must have time to adjust to the language of the particular style, whether it be a group or an individual style. The fact that there is so much music to be played (both past and present) and such a vast audience to reach, limits the number of times an audience can be exposed to new works. In such a situation, an audience has no opportunity to absorb the complexity of content in a new composition. Also, since the conductor knows that the audience is unfamiliar with the work he is presenting, he tends to devote too little time for its effective presentation. A few conductors are exceptions, and the gradual enlargement of this group is starting to change the dismal landscape a bit.*
>
> *Luckily, the concert hall is not the only available institution. The recording industry has the potential to satisfy the needs of twentieth-century music far better than the concert hall, even if the concert hall suddenly reformed. Generally, the extra time spent in preparation for a recording, and the editing done after taping, means that, more and more, recorded performances are accurate if not inspired. . . . It is my opinion that the recording, although it lacks the spontaneity of live performance, satisfies so many of the joint needs and desires of the audience and composer that it is as close to an ideal medium for new music as the parlor was for chamber music.*
>
> *The consequences of the record's becoming the primary medium for twentieth-century music are not altogether pleasant, but I have come to accept the drawbacks as well as the advantages and have for some time made no attempt to deal with the concert hall as an institution.* *

*Morton Subotnick, "Extending the Stuff Music is Made of," Music Educators Journal, November 1968.

Subotnick has been described as "the composer who writes music that even people like who usually hate electronic music." His work has wit and style and rhythm—so much rhythm, in fact, that this very quality has been termed by some critics "the Subotnick Beat." Nor does he hesitate to use traditional means of creating continuity—counterpoint and specific motifs, a sense of pulsation and repetitive order, all of which most composers of electronic music seem anxious to avoid as tainted echoes of "old-line" music.

His music is also endowed with electronic virtuosity: precise, even glittering compositions whose professionalism stands head and shoulders above most of the music of his electronic peers. What is more, Subotnick's music has personality, and personality is a very difficult quality to extract from an electronic synthesizer.

YANNIS XENAKIS

No avant-garde composer of today is more admired—or actually more *heard*—than the Greek Yannis Xenakis. His daring techniques mark him as a left-winger, even among today's "advanced" musicians; in Paris he is very much a culture hero; André Malraux and Claude Lévi-Strauss attend public discussions of his music and join the seething throngs of besweatered youngsters who attend his concerts. Paris conservatory students recently marched through the streets with placards that proclaimed, "Enough of Gounod. We want Xenakis!" Some of this enthusiasm, no doubt, is due to the fact that Xenakis, who fled Greece in 1947, has been sentenced to death *in absentia* by the present Greek regime for his guerrilla activities.

This enthusiasm is all the more remarkable when one considers that the music of Xenakis is difficult to grasp and heavily laden with mathematical and philosophical theories. Much of it, though, is very loud—his electronic work *Bohor* was the loudest piece to be heard at New York's Fillmore East—which may account for its being received by young people with the sort of ecstatic shouts usually reserved for the Rolling Stones.

Born of a wealthy Greek business family, Xenakis attended the Athens Institute of Technology during the war. Often the sounds of Xenakis' music—foghorn-thick brasses, squealing, creaking string glissandi—reflect the brutal memories of his youth.

"My wife, who worked in the French Resistance, says that all my music is about the War," Xenakis says. "It *was* a very intense part of my life, it's true. Listen. One night I heard a huge slogan-chanting crowd march on Constitution Square: suddenly, machine guns fired on it and the clear chorus broke into a thousand screams. Then there was an indescribable silence, a mistuned calm full of despair, death and dust.... I was left wondering what kind of music could ever express the totality of those changes in sound."

Left motherless at the age of six, he lived in Athens during the Italian and Greek occupations. In 1940, at the age of eighteen, he joined the Communist resistance during World War II. "The Communists were the only ones at the time trying to ease the suffering of the people," he later observed. He lost an eye and part of one cheek when he was struck by a shell fragment from a British tank in 1945. He was finally exiled from Greece by his own government. Though he fled Athens for Paris in 1947 and has since adopted French nationality, Xenakis' attachment to Greece still colors his whole life.

It was in Paris that he began the serious study of music with Arthur Honegger and Olivier Messiaen, the teacher of many now-prominent composers. During this period of musical apprenticeship, Xenakis earned his living by continuing his work in mathematics and architecture, part of the time in the architectural office of Le Corbusier. He collaborated with Le Corbusier on the Convent of La Tourette and on the famous Philips Pavilion at the Brussels World's Fair, for which Edgard Varèse, with the active support of Xenakis, wrote his celebrated *Poème électronique.** By this time Xenakis was already a composer in his own right; he had produced his notable *Pithoprakta* in 1956. A decade later he designed the Polytope of the French Pavilion at the Montreal Expo 67.

Xenakis deserves to be called a Renaissance man, not only for his appearance (he looks like a Ghirlandaio portrait come to life), but for his dizzying accomplishments. He is a polytechnician—engineer, mathematician, and architect—*par excellence* and a philosopher besides. All these attainments he puts to the service of his passion for

---

*For a chronicle of Xenakis' role as collaborator with Varèse and Le Corbusier in the *Poème electronique*, see Chapter VI.

music, which he claims is the "instrument man needs to surpass himself—the way to catharsis and ecstasy."

The young people who idolize him are probably unaware of Xenakis' lofty goal, which is nothing less than the marriage of twentieth-century music and science—an idea first proposed by Edgard Varèse, whom Xenakis reveres.

Xenakis believes that music cannot develop unless it encompasses the theories and techniques of modern science. "The two can no longer exist apart," he insists in his slow, preoccupied cadences. "Musicians are being forced into recognizing all kinds of technical advances. Their job now is to catch up with them and guide them. The new kind of music I am propounding is still in its infancy, but it has drawn tremendous strength from mathematical logic and the machine."

When pressed for further explanation, Xenakis resigns himself to reading out parts of his own manifesto, leaving his interviewer to flounder in Poisson's Law, the Kinetic Theory of Gases, and unending algebraic equations. "Even if people don't understand any of this," he says mildly, "it is useful for them to realize their ignorance: the laws I cite are incontestable treasures of human thought."

One of Xenakis' fundamental convictions brings him close to the thinking of Pythagoras: "Things are numbers, all things are provided with numbers, things are like numbers." He believes that mathematics, physics, and music should be as closely interrelated as they used to be in the days when they were all included within the broad embrace of philosophy. In our century, however, musical thinking has fallen far behind the advanced thinking in physics and mathematics.

Conservative musicians, encrusted in the veneration of the three B's—Bach, Beethoven, Brahms—view Xenakis and his theories with alarm and suspicion. What is more, he is also viewed with disfavor by many of the "academic avant garde"—to borrow Morton Feldman's phrase for the entrenched modernists for whom the cause of Schönberg and Webern are the true cause. Xenakis has explicitly disavowed the Schönberg serial system, despite the fact that he relies heavily on mathematics. (Ironically, his own theories about music are as complex, bewildering, and jargon-ridden as those of the followers of Schönberg and Webern.)

What makes Xenakis even more distasteful to many academicians is the fact that he is enough at ease with computers to employ them in calculating his compositions. Xenakis declares that the IBM 7090 computer, whose uses include NASA interplanetary control, has helped him to compose several works. Since Xenakis already had used calculus to resolve these compositions, he resorted to the computer simply as a means of speeding up the process. Ridiculed at first, this method has finally brought him world recognition. Perhaps with tongue in cheek, he recently submitted several computer-calculated compositions to a contest arranged by the International Federation for Information Processing in London and won first prize.

"It is time people realized that the music they're most used to, with its emphasis on feelings like joy or melancholy, is based on conventions that have become obsolete," he says. "What one must look for today are the dynamic and cosmic forces that surround those emotions."

The music of Xenakis, to a large degree, is an extension in sound of the calculus of probability, one of whose basic tenets is Bernoulli's law of large numbers. This law states, in effect, that the occurence of any chance event—the roll of a nine in dice, for example, or the random collision of stray molecules in the atmosphere—is more likely to conform to the given statistical odds with each successive attempt. "The explanation of the world and consequently of the sound phenomenon that surrounds us, or that may be created, required an enlargement of the causal principle, the basis of which is formed by the law of great numbers," he writes at the beginning of *Musiques Formelles* (published by Richard Masse, Paris). This law implies an evolution toward a stable condition, toward an end. He applies the word "stochastic" to his music, from the Greek *stochos*, meaning aim or goal.

To the casual music lover, who rather expects a composer to build his scores according to certain rules of harmony and counterpoint, Pythagorean formality and the concepts of Bernoulli may seem to be the last things on earth by which music may be composed. But to Xenakis this mathematical absolute has deep philosophical meaning and is a perfectly valid structure by which to be guided. He believes that it implies that the changing structure of events in life itself, as well as the sounds that man creates, may draw ultimately toward a state of stability, or *stochos*. Nothing demonstrates how far music (at least avant-garde music) has traveled in the last twenty years than Xenakis' own analysis of his *Pithoprakta*, a work composed in 1955–56 for nonelectronic instruments.

> Pithoprakta *is a confrontation of acoustical continuity and discontinuity (i.e., glissandos and pointillism of the string instruments, each of which has a separate part to play). This confrontation takes place within the framework of stochastic music, using the mathematics of probability.*
>
> *Predetermined surfaces, or volumes of sound, are constructed in continuous transformation. But this continuity takes discontinuity, or granularity, as its point of departure. Sufficient quantification is obtained by means of pizzicatos,* frappé col legno, *etc. The dense clouds of sound-atoms thus formed are spread across all registers in all nuances, thus giving our formation the appearance of continuous evolution, like the spirals of smoke from a cigarette or shifting cloud formations, etc. For purposes of certain definitions and control of these clouds, use is made of the law of large numbers: the normal curve of Gauss, of Maxwell, of Poisson, of continuous probabilities, etc. with the criteria of Pearson, Fisher, etc.*

So much for the composer's analysis. But how does one describe the effect of Xenakis' music? One's impression is of a "global acoustical event"—which is what the composer wants. (He also feels that it is immaterial whether or not a particular note is played, since in any case the ear cannot perceive it as a discrete entity.) One certainly feels that the composer is thinking of music in vast terms; as he says himself, "as masses evolving, erupting, succeeding one another, or vanishing. My elements are clouds of sound—like clouds of smoke—made up of an indefinite number of particles."

An excellent description of Xenakis' music has been caught by the dance and drama critic Clive Barnes, discussing Xenakis' score *Atrees*, which was used by the American choreographer Paul Taylor for a dance called *Private Domain* in 1969. Barnes wrote:

> *The music is a stochastic score by Yannis Xenakis. The sounds arise like random bubbles in an aquarium, proper, appropriate,*

yet without the normal structural justification we have come to expect from music. Xenakis treats music as a trampoline for his thoughts. Clumps of sound bounce upward with no normal—or rather traditional—structural relevance, and yet with an almost sculptural rightness. We are already used to seeing fireworks make fugitive architecture in an empty black air. Xenakis's music . . . of strange, structural insubstantiality, also seems to do something of that. *

Arthur Cohn has also tried to analyze Xenakis:

His sounds seemingly are ripped from the guts of electronic machines, but in fact they are usually produced by traditional instruments (though rarely played traditionally); the rhythms and lines seemingly are a razzle-dazzle of aleatoric processes, but in fact they are zealotically controlled and predetermined. In comparison with men like Berio, Maderna, Boulez, Messiaen, etc., Xenakis stands as Varèse did to such then-young advanced composers of the '20's as Copland, Sessions, and Cowell.

Xenakis is one of the rare composers who have been equally successful in writing for conventional instruments and electronic media. He moves with aplomb from one to the other. His reputation was based on such works as *Pithoprakta*, one of the first to be composed with big sliding, rapping, and plucking textures and densities. The subtle *Akrata*, written in 1964–65 and scored for sixteen wind instruments, is a strikingly structural piece with buildups of repeated and held notes spaced out in a Varèsean sonic architecture. The musical thought of Varèse—with its concepts of tone clusters and sound-density—is clearly perceived in the music of Xenakis.

Despite his formidably scientific approach, Xenakis' music bears his personal signature. During his composition called *Eonta* ("beings") three trombonists and two trumpeters march about the stage while a pianist flays wildly away at the keyboard. In *Terretektorh* (one of the coined Greek words that he uses to title his pieces), the musicians blow whistles, rattle maracas, clap wooden blocks, and crack small whips, besides coaxing unearthly sounds from conventional instruments. One of his most extraordinary compositions, *Strategie*, intro-

*New York Times, May 8, 1969.

duces mathematical game theory to the concert hall. Here, two full orchestras and two conductors literally duel for points on the same stage by improvising combinations in accordance with Xenakis' rules for the musical encounter.

He also has written some of our best electronic music, despite the fact that he has composed relatively little in the genre. His electronic *Bohor I, Orient-Occident III, Diamorphoses II,* and *Concrèt P-H II* (discussed in detail in the discography, Part Six) have not been surpassed by any composer working in the new medium.

If Xenakis has not actually composed many electronic pieces, he still remains one of the most important leaders and prophets of electronic music, and of New Music in general. The reason for his interest in the electronic medium is best summed up in his words written upon the death of Edgard Varèse: "Away with the scale, away with themes, away with melody, to the devil with so-called 'musical' music!"*

Xenakis is quite candid in expressing his opinions about other composers. For example, he is quite openly scornful about John Cage's "music of chance," which he has described as "a style and a mentality of mystico-romantic improvisation, which agitates ignorant souls." "I admire Cage very much, as a man," he says, "but what is 'chance'? If you think you are using chance in his way, you may simply be acting unrationally. The intuition of Cage is dangerous—instead of the start of a rational process, the first step may also be the last." Xenakis emphatically rejects the idea of intuitive and unreasoning randomness in composition and, by using formulas and such apparatus as the IBM 7090 computer, seeks to control his own music at every step. "It is my privilege to control my music, and my pleasure," he said. "That is my definition of an artist, or of a man: to control."

Thus Xenakis does not think much of Cage's (and Stockhausen's) chance music. "The forms known as 'mobile,' 'open,' 'aleatory,' 'graphic,' etc.—labels that are sometimes useful but have been abused —need not be taken into account. They express confusion—a confusion that has been felt only by the most disquieted composers. These forms are eddies at the edges of our Pythagorean-Parmenidean mental field, sometimes survivals of magic."

*In *Le Nouvel Observateur,* Paris, November 17, 1965.

Is a mathematical approach to music to be the salvation of the art in the last decades of the twentieth century? Xenakis says that he is quite aware of the dangers and problems in trying to bring about a music-science *rapprochement*, but he feels that "in the end, music must dominate mathematics—without that, it becomes either mathematics or nothing at all. You use mathematics only as a weapon, as a tool, not for itself."

The job of the next few generations, Xenakis believes, is to carry forward the integration of music with the sciences. "In these directions," he says, "they will have to be aided by computers and servomechanisms." To those who bridle at the idea of computer-composed music, he points out that computers are, after all, only tools, extensions of the human hand and the simple slide rule. Indeed, Xenakis eagerly awaits a new age of integration among the arts and the sciences. "We have decided that [music] must make up the lag in order to guide physics and mathematics again, as in the days of its Pythagorean birth. The arts of vision could likewise formalize themselves anew and conquer new domains parallel to those of their eldest daughter, geometry. The age of Scientific and Philosophical Arts has begun. From now on, the musician will have to be a manufacturer of Philosophical Theses and Total Architectures of combinations of structures (forms) and sonorous material."

Critics of Xenakis' music, and they are many, find much of it limited in its resources. They detest his penchant for string glissandi in his music for conventional instruments, and shrug off as pretentious babble his steady streams of edicts as to the relationship of the mathematical and philosophical theories on which he bases his "stochastic" music.

But whether the Music Establishment likes it or not, Yannis Xenakis seems to speak directly to young audiences in a language they want to hear. He has invented several of the compositional techniques that now constitute the *Lingua franca* of the avant garde. And, like few other contemporary composers, he succeeds with his music of strange, stalactite invention, his gushes and rushes of sound, his chilling, unworldly sonorities and architectural buildups into aural space. Within his ear-jarring, restricted emotional range, he is a modernist in the best sense of the word, reflecting a certain aspect and a certain vision of the world around us in our time. His music could have been written only in our time, and is perhaps marked by an individuality that transcends our time. It may endure. Like a laboratory scientist, Xenakis himself has no clear idea of where his musical experiments will take him—except to predict that his existing works, baffling as they may be to the ear, will seem rather tame beside "the infinite sounds" of the future.

And he has a sense of humor. When asked recently, "Who is doing the best work in electronic music right now?" his cheerful reply was: "The Bell Telephone Company."

LUCIANO BERIO

At the now-historic 1952 Luening-Ussachevsky concert of electronic music at the Museum of Modern Art in New York,* a young and unknown Italian composer, Luciano Berio, sat spellbound. This was the first public presentation of electronic music in this country, and the first that Berio had ever heard. Within two years he had co-founded the Studio Fonologia Musicale in Milan, one of the first European electronic music centers.

Today Berio is a prestigious composer, very much in vogue, and he moves confidently from electronic to live music, often combining the two in the same work. His most admired works are done in collage, a method he has developed more successfully than any other composer. Berio often takes musical "found objects" more or less intact and either transforms and transmogrifies them by electronic means or collages them with other musical materials until all the elements become a coherent and cohesive whole. His most famous work in this genre is his *Sinfonia*, commissioned for the 125th anniversary of the New York Philharmonic. In his program notes to one movement of the work, Berio says, "The references range from Bach, Schönberg, Debussy, Ravel, Strauss, Berlioz, Brahms, Berg, Hindemith, Beethoven, Wagner and Stravinsky to Boulez, Stockhausen, Globokar, Pousseur, Ives, myself and beyond. I would almost say that this section of *Sinfonia* is not so much composed as it is *assembled* to make the mutual transformation of the component parts."

Besides all this, the vocal text of the piece includes snatches and

*See Part III, Chapter XI, "The Scene in America in the 1950s."

fragments from the writings of Samuel Beckett, James Joyce, and Claude Lévi-Strauss among others, as well as "slogans written on the Sorbonne walls during the May, 1968, insurrection in Paris, at which I was present." Trying to cope with *Sinfonia* critically is no easy matter, as Harold Schonberg remarked in his review in *The New York Times*: "How to describe all this? Music of the absurd, perhaps, or a new kind of *Walpurgisnacht*. But it moves, and it has force, and it never lets the attention down. In a way this kind of composition is a synthesis, making use of many of the schools of music that have come up since World War II, including serialism, Dada, electronic music and a touch of aleatory. It marks the beginning of consolidation."

Perhaps Berio's collage method is the only way to confront all the bewildering messages that reach us in our technetronic age. The method is in vogue today in writing as well as in music. Donald Barthelme is the most successful practitioner of this style in fiction, and many believe that it is the valid style for our age, which is deluged daily with information input. In music, collage—the concentration and piling up of pure sound, orchestral sound, vocal sound, electronic sound, *all* sound—is a style that traces back to Edgard Varèse and John Cage, among others. Berio continues this tradition, and draws a parallel between the juxtaposition of various levels of sound in his scores and the multifarious nature of the sonic bombardment—jets, transistors, police sirens, and traffic—that reach urbanites every time they open a window in the mid twentieth century.

In his music, he also suggests a new kind of dramaturgy encompassing music, drama, word sounds, and, eventually, lighting and stage effects. Other composers have attempted this, but along the way they have lost the sound and the sense of music. In Berio's intensely affecting pieces, the music is paramount—and everything in them is a powerful statement of musical achievement.

"The most important development in music now is to integrate the new things to be heard in new environments," Berio says. "But I object to the term avant-garde, which is too often used in the United States. Anything I do of certain value will be experimental. This is really the only avant-garde aspect of my work."

Talking earnestly about music in his Italian-accented English, Berio is soft-spoken and mild-mannered, yet compellingly dynamic.

"The musician today," he observes, "is one of the few persons to allow himself the luxury of looking around with certain insights because music is the art that allows musicians and good listeners to become aware of the relations between things."

Although he is firmly rooted in Italian musical tradition, Luciano Berio is an internationalist in his interests, his activities, and his compositions. He was born October 24, 1925, in Oneglia (now Impernia), Italy. He heard chamber music in his family living room regularly from the time of his birth, and at the age of five he began to study harmony with his grandfather. Soon afterward, he learned to play on a grand piano. The family's musical heritage goes back for centuries; in 1782 one Steffano Berio, an ancestor, composed an oratorio. Luciano is the third generation of composers in his family, his father, and his father's father both having been church organists and composers. Young Luciano began his musical studies with his father and, like his father, completed his training at the Conservatory of Milan.

While carrying on his Conservatory studies, he was employed as coach and accompanist for the classes of two famous opera stars, Aureliano Pertile and Carmen Melis. Before graduating in 1950, Berio gained a wider practical experience as pianist-coach, conductor (and occasional timpanist) for a small touring opera company which played in northern Italian provincial cities and towns. The year after his graduation from the Conservatory, a Koussevitzky Foundation Fellowship enabled him to travel to the Berkshire Center at Tanglewood to study with his compatriot, Luigi Dallapiccola.

On his return to Italy, Berio joined the staff of Italian Radio, where in 1955 he established the Studio di Fonologia. The following year he launched a series of concerts of contemporary music that he called *Incontri Musicali* and edited a progressive music magazine of the same name. He has also served as conductor (chiefly of his own music) at La Scala in Milan, the Teatro le Fenice in Venice, and the Rome Opera, and he has conducted the Chicago Symphony. In 1965 Berio joined the faculty of the Juilliard School of Music in New York. Berio's appointment to the Juilliard staff confirmed a new and advanced approach to composition at the school, following as it did the addition of Elliot Carter to the faculty.

For many years Luciano Berio seemed a highly talented lightweight in a generation headed by the more aggressive and controversial figures of Boulez and Stockhausen. But in fact, over the last fifteen years he has produced a steady flow in impressive, large-scale works. They include chamber music for a great variety of instruments, orchestral works, vocal works for solo and chorus, theater pieces, and music for magnetic tape. In a period when Boulez' output has diminished to a trickle and Stockhausen has seemed increasingly willing to abdicate responsibility for the *content* as opposed to the basic *conception* of his scores, Berio's fertility and stature have grown apace. One reason for his continuing growth at a time when some of his generation seemed washed up on the rocks of experimentation is that he has retained strong links with the symphony orchestra without in any way compromising the exploratory side of his music.

Like many other composers, Berio welcomes the electronic media because they open up new domains of musical thought. Of his own efforts in this field he comments:

> *The products are not so important as the idea and research. I regard the experience of electronic music as very important precisely because rather than opening the door to the discovery of "new" sounds, it proved the possibility of a definite outcome of dualistic conceptions of musical materials, and gives the composer the practical means of integrating in musical thought a larger domain of sound phenomena viewed as segments of the sound continuum.*

The best way to understand the preceding nonstop lines is to listen to the piece *Visage*, with the voice of Cathy Berbarian (Berio's first wife), on Turnabout 34046S itself. The music is a Joycean celebration of the experience of sound—all sound—in its widest, all-encompassing range. Berio develops a clear, expressive, musical idea and gives us music that contains sound-action, sound-gesture, and sound-continuity.* In *Visage* Berio pits the human voice against electronic sound. The voice utters only one word: "parole," the Italian word meaning "words." There is nothing else but laughs, whispers,

---

*The perceptive Danel Henahan of *The New York Times* once wrote, "What Mr. Berio is after in many of his works, one realizes, is nothing less than a Joycean epiphany." I may add that Joyce is the ideal text for Berio because for Joyce the sensory moment is an end in itself. Also, like Varèse's early *Offrandes*, the work is a logical extension of Debussy's impressionism, rather than of Webernian serialism.

sobs, cries, and a kind of agonized pseudo-speech and song. The effect is shattering, and *Visage* remains one of the most important electronic works yet conceived.

Another superb work of Berio's is his *Thema: Omaggio a Joyce (Theme: Hommage to Joyce)* of 1958. This classic piece of *Musique concrète*, which also employs the extraordinary voice of Cathy Berbarian, explores new possibilities in sound, speech, and music. The only sound source used is the soloist's voice. The text is taken from the eleventh chapter of Joyce's *Ulysses*, a passage depicting Mr. Bloom's afternoon at the Ormond Bar in Dublin. The sound-play and Joycean effects—transformations of basic materials into complex sound and emotional events—that Berio achieves here are remarkable.

Electronic music has led Berio to a growing interest in what he terms "a kind of interdisciplinary approach" to various media. He has experimented with combinations of tape and light performance, co-ordinated with instruments and/or voices. He comments, "I am interested in those aspects of sound that are too often disregarded as nonmusical, that is, the richness of the human voice—the speaking voice. It is important to integrate this aspect of sound into the musical structure as it once was, the singing voice. The key to all this is Schönberg's *Pierrot Lunaire*, which explored the no-man's land between the speaking and singing voice for the first time."

Berio does not disparage the past, but he considers tonality to be worn out as a basis of contemporary composition: "In tonal music there were predetermined forms; now we invent form every time. In tonal music there was a hierarchy, with melody first, then harmony and finally rhythm taking their places. Now there are no such components—no melody as such.

"Tonality can still work, of course, for moments of escapism—when one wants to tickle oneself—like with jazz. But for serious art, absolutely NO!"

Politically, Berio candidly declares himself a leftist, and this has influenced his entire approach to music. He generally dresses in khaki work clothes, and he sympathizes with radical youth movements. He has written, "The literal reconstruction of the drama of the sonata form, which gave us so many classical masterpieces, leaves an impression of family theatricals. The audience, which is carried away by the events of that drama, knowing from the beginning that it will have a happy ending on a tonic chord, could very easily represent a society fundamentally oriented towards the acquisition of a swimming pool."*

Not surprising, therefore, are his harsh comments on American life and art. For example, in 1970 he told *The New York Times*:

> *There is a fetishism in America based solely on money. Rich people tend to reduce what should be a genuine cultural phenomenon into the preservation of an institution. People controlling opera here are really stupid. The good directors are few —you can count them on the fingers of one hand. And the whole of American musical life is controlled by the very rich. I just received a call from the conductor of the Oakland Symphony who will conduct my* Sinfonia *there in two weeks. He said that one of the orchestra's trustees offered a donation of $6,000 to the orchestra if it would just not perform my work. One of the reasons, I guess, is that it's new. Another may be my use of the name Martin Luther King in* Sinfonia.

Berio went on to say that even the creative aspects of American life are affected by the capitalistic idea:

> *The automobile industry views people as drivers. All men are viewed in relation to a product. So American music is overwhelmed by a special kind of commercial thinking in which things are separated, broken down, and viewed at incredibly short range. One group of composers attacks another in order to sell its own product. Such measuring according to an arbitrary scale implies that something has gone seriously wrong, that there is a lack of commitment to music. Musicians who participate in this kind of attack do not understand that history is moving them in spite of their intentions, that history is actually moving through them.*

Like most intellectuals who grew up under Mussolini's repressive regime, Berio became an active anti-rightist in early manhood:

*Luciano Berio, "Essay on Form," in *The Modern Composer and His World* (Toronto: University of Toronto Press, 1961).

It was not until 1945 that I first had the opportunity to see and hear the works of Schönberg, Webern, Hindemith, Bartok, and Milhaud. I was already nineteen years old! Of that crucial period let me simply say that among the many thoughts and emotions aroused in me by those encounters, one is still intact and alive within me today: anger—anger at the realization that Fascism had until that moment deprived me of knowledge of the most essential musical achievements of my own culture.

He is appalled that composers today seem to regard music as an isolated phenomenon, created in a vacuum for the "greater glory of musical systems." Never before, he says, "has the composer come so dangerously close to becoming an extraneous or merely decorative figure in his own society." For Berio what counts is man's civilized conscience. Some of his best theatrical works—*Laborintus, Circles, Passaggio, Opera*—are examples of music as a "social act."

Of course, his music by no means pleases all critics. *The New Yorker* magazine's Winthrop Sargeant wrote, apropos of Berio, "I am not sure about the aesthetic validity of this sort of thing. If the future of music is going to consist of salads tossed together with ingredients from the masterpieces of the past, it does not seem to me to be much of a future."

Despite such criticism, Berio continues his work and is gaining a growing audience by using the collage principle to cope with what he terms "the plurality of functions":

A composer's awareness of the plurality of functions of his own tools forms the basis for his responsibility just as, in everyday life, every man's responsibility begins with recognition of the multiplicity of human races, conditions, needs, and ideals. I would go so far as to say that any attempt to codify musical reality into a kind of imitation grammar (I refer mainly to the efforts associated with the Twelve-Tone System) is a brand of fetishism which shares with Fascism and racism the tendency to reduce live processes to immobile, labeled objects, the tendency to deal with formalities rather than substance. Claude Levi-Strauss describes (though to illustrate a different point) a captain at sea, his ship reduced to a frail raft without sails, who, by en-

*forcing a meticulous protocol on his crew, is able to distract them from the nostalgia for a safe harbor and from the desire for a destination.**

Luciano Berio, an outspoken leftist, an enemy of rigid musical systems, and the exponent of his own multi-tiered complex of sound in which composers of all periods and styles are subjected to and distilled through his own musical nature, has created for us a whole world of allusions that threatens to collapse about his and our ears. His work is a modern music in the spirit of the *commedia dell'arte.*

Berio conjures up an analogy of the *labyrinth* of emotional response. Whether it is everyday signals, such as headlines giving warning of holocaust, or a long musical quotation from Mahler, floating in and out of Berio's nightmarish stream of semiconsciousness, his music appears to communicate the knife edge of human existence, where feeling can at any time crumble into terror and neurosis.

During the Metropolitan Opera strike of 1968, Rudolf Bing presented a series of lectures on opera at the Juilliard School. At the end of one of the talks a man in the audience asked the subject of Mr. Bing's *next* lecture. "This one," he said, "was very disappointing, nothing but gossip and anecdotes, you treated the subject like a party joke." Startled by the insult, Bing demanded to know who the man was. "I'm a composer," the man said. A student in the back of the room rose and proudly proclaimed: "That's Luciano Berio!"

KARLHEINZ STOCKHAUSEN

In 1952 Karlheinz Stockhausen became the first man to make music of synthetic electronic sounds, and he rapidly emerged as a dominant figure of the European avant garde. Like John Cage, he is now a guru of the New Music; he was even celebrated on the cover of the Beatles' record *Sargeant Pepper,* and some of his electronic techniques were casually taken over by the Beatles and the Rolling Stones. He pours out a steady stream of sounds, as continuous and endlessly variable as life itself—which is usually his intention. He speaks of "expanded sense of time" and "sound-visions"; when he saw a sumo wrestling match in Japan, he enthused over "the prolonged

°The Christian Science Monitor, July 15, 1968.

preparation and then the quick violent act"; and he says, with boyish seriousness, that the same principle can be applied to his own acts of composition.

He is unquestionably our generation's musical bogeyman (although John Cage also has a good claim to that epithet) and his music is cordially hated by many listeners. Of course, the ability to arouse intense dislike may be a healthy symptom of creative potency; Berlioz, Wagner, and Schönberg, to mention a few enduring names at random, were despised by many of their contemporaries, who certainly would not have turned livid at the mention of their names if their music had been less arresting. Like them, Stockhausen seems to have the force to attract a loyal band of dedicated admirers—in fact, a larger band than that of any other avant-garde composer of today.

Of course the easy-to-hate syndrome does not in itself elevate Stockhausen into the pantheon of musical greats. His position in music history will more likely be that of a remarkable innovator; a restless, inquiring, brilliant intelligence that came along when music was at the end of a great line of development, and along with Cage, Boulez, Xenakis, and a few others, calmly proceeded to topple all our encrusted notions of what music is and to seek a new beginning.

"Stockhausen swims about in an enormous uncharted sea," Robert Morgan has written, "taking various routes of 'escape' as they present themselves to him. If we as listeners are apt to be conscious of the dangers of such a course, we should also keep in mind the enormous excitement it entails."

After the middle 1950s, the nature of avant-garde music in Europe underwent a drastic change. The radically new concept of a music that employs multiple, open, or chance forms and that conceives a new musical material based upon densities, textures, and colors captured the imagination of young composers. The development and acceptance of these ideas are largely due to Stockhausen, one of the most brilliant theorists music has ever known.

Even among those who admit his genius as a theoretician, the question of just how substantial a composer Stockhausen may or may not be is fiercely argued by many people who accept, or even welcome, other advanced composers. An international band of lively, fervent followers hail him as a sort of musical Messiah, come to rescue modern music and to lead us through the desert into a new artistic era; more listeners damn him as a self-publicizing charlatan, a clever fraud who has somehow captured the spotlight by endless lecturing and self-publicity.

Stockhausen seems resigned to his suspect place in modern music. He wrote recently: "It seems generically inherent in my musical development that what concerns most listeners at first contact with my music is not the music but the 'paraphernalia'—the 'spectacle,' to put it negatively. I don't quite know how to deal with this misunderstanding. I must put up with being labeled 'sensationalist,' 'out to create a shock,' even 'cabaret clown,' before understanding of the purely musical range of problems of tone-color composition sets in. Even when one no longer sees anything at all—in other words, when listening to loudspeakers—extra-musical associations possess many listeners."

Some serious composers, however, accept Stockhausen as a seminal force in modern music. America's Vladimir Ussachevsky and Milton Babbitt consider him one of the most inventive composers alive. Pierre Boulez says, "Stockhausen is the greatest living composer, and the only one whom I recognize as my peer."

Aggressively indifferent to criticism, and fond of hurling anathemas at composers dead and alive, Stockhausen continues to explore every corner of the aural landscape. He has completely done away with traditional musical forms, and his works are conceived in terms of carefully structured "moments" of time that follow no conventional rhythmic pattern.

Considering how recondite, even deliberately boring, his music sometimes becomes, it is amazing that Stockhausen attracts so many listeners who are willing to sit through his concerts. Like Xenakis, Stockhausen has the drawing power to sell out concert halls—quite an accomplishment these days when concerts of contemporary music have become, in one critic's words, "chaste little rites attended by the usual incestuous gatherings of critics, composers, publishers, and a handful of enthusiasts."

Peter Heyworth, the music critic of the London *Observer*, wrote recently of a performance of Stockhausen's *Gruppen* at London's Festival Hall, "If Bernstein and the Beatles had appeared simultaneously, the applause could hardly have been louder or more sustained. In the foyer, alongside the usual staid concert-going public in its Persian lambs and city suits, there was an astonishing gathering of young people. To judge by their clothes and hair, they seemed to have surfaced, as at some magical signal, from every hippie hole in London."

Perhaps it is Stockhausen's outrageous, nose-thumbing musical (or anti-musical) notions that attract young people. Consider his puzzling piece *Aus den Sieben Tagen,* whose score contains no notes but a series of what can only be described as meditative exercises. A group of instrumentalists improvise, while Stockhausen himself offers an electronic commentary that "reacts" to what the players provide.

His *Mikrophonie I* is an ear-jarring piece in which sounds resembling runaway trains, breaking glass, blasts of hot steam, foghorns, and whooshing jets flash, crash, and fade like movements in some psychedelic symphony. The effects are achieved by two men who rub, scratch, and bash a gong with sticks, stones, brushes, and mallets, while two other roving performers pick up the sounds with hand microphones and feed them into filters where other distortions are added.

Yet, for all the bizarre effects, Stockhausen's infuriating compositions have flashes of a kind of mad logic. His music is not, as many conclude on first hearing, the work of a prankster. He often composes twelve hours a day. "I want to be able to bring sounds from every surface area of the room," he says. "Why not loudspeakers on swings overhead, or a completely globular room with loudspeakers blanketing the walls and the listeners on a platform suspended in the center?"

From the foregoing remarks, one might easily conclude that Stockhausen celebrates chaos and random events in music, yet it certainly would be wrong to suppose that he is not also concerned with order. In fact, he is clearly obsessed by it, and it was his determination to serialize, not merely pitch in the manner of Schönberg, but every possible dimension of music, that first led him into the electronic studio simply because human players could not cope with the technical demands of his "Total Organization of Sonic Material." Indeed, the story goes that his piece, *Kontakte,* was itself originally devised for four percussion players, who, confronted by the problems posed, took to drink, so that Stockhausen was obliged to realize three parts by electronic means.

Karlheinz Stockhausen was born in Modrath, Germany, near Cologne, on August 22, 1928. Reared in that city under the trying conditions of World War II, he entered the Cologne Conservatory of Music after the war. When he had been there three years, the distinguished Swiss composer Frank Martin joined the faculty; under Martin's tutelage Stockhausen studied the twelve-tone system.

By 1952 he was in Paris studying with Olivier Messiaen, who had become mentor to virtually a whole generation of young European composers, as well as with Darius Milhaud. He became a visitor at the Club d'Essai, the famous experimental studio of *Musique concrète*, where Pierre Schaeffer and Pierre Henry were working.* At this studio Stockhausen produced an extensive series of tapes, chiefly for the purpose of analyzing problems of timbre.

He was attracted by the possibilities of electronic test equipment (at that time not yet in use for musical purposes) that was capable of producing simple, pure electronic sounds—"sine tones." He returned to Cologne, joined the group working with Herbert Eimert there, and developed his theories of a purely electronic approach to music, based upon the use of sound generators. His "sine tones," which are "pure" tones, not mechanically producible except electronically, have achieved a new importance for all composers.

It is now known that the musical tone is a far more complex entity than Greek, medieval, and Renaissance musicians ever dreamed it to be. In the eighteenth century, the French physicist Joseph Sauveur demonstrated that each vibrating string of an instrument generates not only one fundamental tone, but also a subsidiary series of faintly heard higher tones.** This is called "the harmonic series" in music, and prevents the listener from grasping the "pure" tone itself. (A pure sine-wave sound or "sinus tone" cannot be produced on traditional instruments, although the sound of a tuning fork or a note blown on a recorder approaches it.)

There is a basic theorem in acoustics that any tone, regardless

---

*See Chapters VIII and IX, "Musique concrète" and "The Cologne Studio."
**Though a deaf-mute from birth, Joseph Sauveur (1653–1716) studied and wrote about the science of sounds, which he was the first to call "acoustics."

of how complex it may be, is made up of a combination of "sine" or "sinusoidal" tones. And after World War II, the electrical generation of sound made it possible to produce a pure sine tone—a tone without any overtones. An ordinary alternating current will produce such a tone on a loudspeaker or on tape. This fact preoccupied Stockhausen and the other German investigators, who concerned themselves not with sound montages based on taped collections of natural sounds, as did the French, but rather with "pure" electronic music—*tape pieces created by sound generators alone.* This was the challenge that literally obsessed the German researchers.* By manipulating and combining sine tones in various ways, they sought to "control" the entire range of tones and sounds, and to produce any sound or combination of sounds the composer desired. Stockhausen, as we have seen, applied the principles of serial composition not only to pitch, but to rhythm and timbre, which was quite a dazzling intellectual accomplishment.

Stockhausen and his colleagues also concerned themselves with "the sound continuum." Strictly speaking, "pure" electronic music is based on the premise that a loudspeaker can be driven (activated) to produce sound by electromagnetic impulses. These impulses are derived from electronic generators, and range from simple sine waves to the random oscillation of all the audible frequencies, producing that primordial sound, "white noise." The pure electronic-music technique of the Cologne School enabled composers to explore the vast intermediate realm between noise and musical sound—including such phenomena as "colored noise," a filtered selection of frequencies within a given frequency band (as opposed to "white noise," which contains all such frequencies). Thus, the concept emerged among composers and researchers of a "continuum in the sphere of color or timbre," based on the frequency continuum and analogous to the color spectrum in painting.

In 1953 and 1954 new electronic works by Eimert and Stockhausen were recorded by the Deutsche Grammaphon Gesellschaft. Stockhausen's *Studie I*, composed in 1953, was the first European musical work to be based on sinus tones—pure musical sounds with-

---

*Otto Luening reminds me that Dr. Werner Meyer-Eppler really launched the German school of electronic music, and that Stockhausen went to Bonn University to study and consult with him.

out overtones. Timbres were assembled from the sinus tones by synthesis.

In 1954, Stockhausen surprised the musical world (at least the avant-garde musical world) with his *Composition No. 2*, in which, for perhaps the first time in Europe, all the musical parameters (dimensions) were achieved. Serialization of all the musical parameters in a piece would previously have been impossible because they are not precisely under the control of the performer. However, the use of sine waves made it possible. Stockhausen recognized the far-reaching significance of this as well as the fact that electronic music had opened the door to a "completely controlled," or, as Milton Babbitt prefers to say, a "totally organized" music.

Since then, in a well-publicized trail, Stockhausen has moved from total serialism to "open forms" and live-electronic combinations. His is a restless mind, and it has produced a seemingly endless stream of musical experimentation and novelties. Almost every new work of his presents an uneasy musical public with new notations, sonorities, degrees of indeterminacy, and modes of interaction between live and electronic elements. He also has delivered a steady outpour of lectures, program notes, and cultural polemics whose bulk is rapidly approaching that of the output of an earlier musical polemicist, Richard Wagner.

Stockhausen talks about ideas—music, physics, psychology, philosophy, electronics—with an engagement of mind that seems remarkably fresh and intense. When a notion strikes his interest, his eyes seem to generate electricity. A while ago, he came to Santa Barbara to give a tape-lecture on *Momente* and spoke of his concept of "moment form." This form is without beginning, middle, or end, and the large units of a work in moment form are theoretically interchangeable.

"It is a way of verticalizing time," he said. "If one thinks of time as a horizontal line, then 'moment form' can be said to expand the moment into a kind of eternity, to pulverize time. It is a way of perceiving time in depth." Because the entire emphasis of the "moment form" is on the here and now, Stockhausen regards it as the "lyric mode par excellence."

In contrast to many modern artists, who feel that their art is intuitive, its rightness *felt* rather than logically justified, Stockhausen claims to have had an exact idea of his purpose in each of his works and to be able to formulate it in words.

"For centuries we have dealt with intervals of pitch," he says, "but what about similar intervals, or proportions, of rhythm, volume, timbre, and other musical elements? We talk about an octave, which means the higher note has twice the vibrations of the lower, but what about an octave in volume, one level being double the other? Or a fourth of rhythm, or a major seventh of timbre?"

Perhaps because what he does can be understood logically and defended rationally, his music has been attacked for being cerebral, without appeal to the feelings. Asked recently if he thinks music should be immediately engaging, be fun, Stockhausen said yes, then reflected and qualified the answer: "But I wouldn't want people to respond only with the emotions. That would be wrong. No, I wouldn't want that."

He paused again and then added, "My music makes sense to me. I can't ever understand why it poses problems for others."

Perhaps, as always, a new generation of music lovers will come along (it may already be here) for whom Stockhausen's music will not pose problems. Whether or not his revolutionary ideas take hold, his reassessments have certainly shaken up all our concepts of music as a self-contained entity, with a fixed beginning, middle, and end.

Finally, a word must be said concerning Stockhausen's significant role in leading music of our time to an Eastern concept of music as "incantation" and away from the Western view of music as "incarnation." By what he calls his "circular" ideas, he has deliberately sought to release music from the imposition of will, and to seek out the play of the unconscious. "Beat" disappears completely from many of his works, which try instead to negate time. (The same applies to the loss of beat in the improvisations of such jazz musicians as Sonny Rollins and John Coltrane; with these jazz artists, the solo line becomes divided into fantastically rapid numerical rhythms that bring us close to an Eastern breakup of pitch sense.)

Stockhausen's music involves us in an aural universe in which there is no longer any dramatic sequence and in which the clear line between the objective reality of the external world and our subjective response to it has been eliminated. The old concept of progression—

of beginning, middle, and end—here become entirely meaningless; every "event" is coexistent with every other.

In much of the music of Stockhausen, one senses that we have been brought beyond the edge of chaos to disintegration. This in itself can be a rebirth, a religious act in the Eastern sense, a Revelation. The world of sound is a continuum, as Busoni observed many years ago, and the small world of our traditional concert music is but a fraction of a fraction of one ray from that music of the sun "which fills the heavenly Vault with Harmony."

PART FIVE

Music and Computers

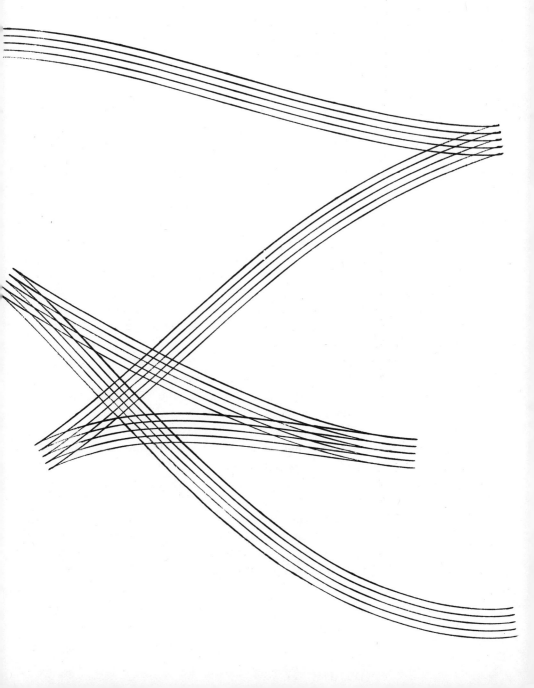

CHAPTER XIV

Pandora's Box

Mathematics is music for the mind
Music is mathematics for the soul.

Anon.

No human investigation can be called truly scientific if it does
not pass through mathematical methods of expression.

Leonardo da Vinci, On Painting, *1, 1*

That admirable Greek Pythagoras discovered that the basic musical harmonies depend on very simple numerical ratios in the dimensions of the instruments producing them (strings and pipes, for example). This discovery led him to interpret the world as a whole through numbers and served as the basis for the Pythagorean theory of numbers, the systematic study of which induced the intense Pythagorean devotion to mathematics and the subsequent development of this science by Greek thinkers.

Our contemporary composers, like the ancient Greeks, are fascinated by the relationship of tone to number, and their interest has been fanned by that remarkable invention, the computer. The potentialities the computer offers to the composer and the music scholar are dazzling. The computer can calculate, sort, and compare approximately a hundred million times faster than human beings can. And yet, although the computer seems little short of miraculous (or diabolical), it is useful to view it in the historical context of the other technological tools man has developed. Quite a few of the basic principles of the computer—the concept of a stored program, a system for encoding information, and electronic circuitry—have been used in the past. The unique characteristic of the computer is that it presents us with a *tool* that is an extension of man's *mind*.

Nevertheless, no aspect of music induces more confused thinking than electronic music, and no aspect of electronic music is more misunderstood—or resented—than the role of the computer. Antipathy toward the "machine music" of the electronic synthesizer is mild compared with the shuddering hostility aroused by discussion of the use of computers as a tool to aid composition and musical exploration. Probably much of this fierce opposition to computer research in music is due to our dread that these "supermachines" ultimately will make man obsolete. Man highly prizes his gifts of superior intelligence, and since tribal days he has feared any superior intelligence, such as that of a supernatural power. Today, we shudder at the notion of a machine intelligence superior to man's. In music this is doubly detested, because music is an art, and we are gloomily convinced that "computer music" means dehumanized music. We choose to forget such technological triumphs as the piano, the printed score, the symphony orchestra, and the phonograph record. No, we say, those are different: they forwarded the cause of music, but the computer in music seems like the end of music. We proudly insist that music is art, and the exclusive province of man and his "inspiration."

To a large extent, this attitude is based on superstitions which must be overcome. The computer is a fantastic tool that may lead us to utterly new worlds of sounds, and as such it should be welcomed. Nor is there cause to fear that the computer will make man obsolete; the human composer still will be needed. As Dr. Warren McCulloch remarks, "The brain is like a computing machine, but there is no computing machine like the brain."

In other words, the human brain and nervous system (not to mention artistic genius, whatever that may be) are still working in ways so fantastically complex that no conceivable machine, programmed by any techniques now known or imagined, can ever equal it. There are more than a trillion electrical connections among the neurons of the human animal, in whose nervous system there are also delicate and subtle chemical and thermal forces at work. To reproduce all these functions in a machine is now impossible, and may remain forever so—for which, perhaps, we may be thankful. So let us begin our examination of the computer in music by recognizing it as a *remarkable tool* of the 1970s, and in no sense a "competition" designed to bring on a Dr. Strangelove in the musical arts. After all, if it doesn't work out, we can always yank out its plug.

The Computer as "The Universal Instrument"

By the early 1960s, a new field had been added to the growing branches of electronic music: computer music. It seemed to be a way out of the composer's and researcher's frustration with the laboriously slow pace of composing on tape—mixing, splicing, re-recording, and so on. As the English composer Peter Zinovieff put it, "It seems preposterous that one should be expected to stick pieces of tape together and to collage simple recordings together by these techniques."

The introduction of computers into the art-science of music opened the door to a fantastic wonderland of musical automation. It now seems entirely possible that the computer can collaborate with the composer's brain, if the proper information initially is fed into the machine. There are two chief roles of computer experimentation in musical composition: to aid the composer in the construction of a score and to generate actual sounds.

As a musical experimenter, the computer is an endless source of fascination which, it has been predicted, may lead us to "radically different species of music based upon fundamentally new techniques of musical analysis." But can the computer eventually become "the universal musical instrument" some have foreseen it becoming? Many scientists believe this to be entirely possible, among them J. R. Pierce, who discusses this point in his article in the Appendix to this book.

Today there are many signs that the computer will indeed become the musical instrument of the future. The fact that its complexity will have a greater influence on composing than previous musical instruments have had can be a surprise only to those who have never seen the elementary connection between composing and instruments. The computer may also revolutionize our listening habits. A composer will program notes that a machine will translate into a tape containing electronic impulses, and a tape recorder can produce the specified musical sounds. During this composing technique absolutely no sounds are produced; only in performance can the music be heard. In this sense, the tape becomes the "score" of the piece and the playback machine (hooked up with amplifying equipment) becomes the performing instrument. Essentially, this means that hearing an entirely electronic piece in a concert hall is hardly different from hearing the same piece on the stereo at home. For performers of contemporary music, the concert hall may be obsolete by the end of the century.

Robert Moog and others are now working to combine synthesizers with computers so that a complex set of effects can be programmed and then reproduced instantly. Such a development would clear the way, perhaps within ten years, for a home-model synthesizer that people could sit down and play in their living rooms—if they can afford the price, estimated at $2000 for a portable system and $20,000 for a full-scale computer-controlled synthesizer.

Because of the specialized knowledge computer music still requires, work done in the field is just beginning to emerge. But Max Mathews of Bell Laboratories, who has been called "the father of computer music," sees an unlimited future. "Today the computer is something like the car in the twenties; it is fine to fool around with but you wouldn't want your wife and kids to use it. All this will change. Computers will be smaller, cheaper, more available. Compositional rules will be built into them. They will be used as performing instruments and become commonplace in the average American's home."

All this is still in the realm of the wild blue yonder. And yet, in the past ten years the speed and memory capacity of computers have increased more than tenfold, the concept of machine-aided coding has arisen, and the power of compiler languages has grown month by month. In the next several decades these trends will continue. Thus far, each advance in computer speed and capacity and each new insight into the functions of language has opened new doors, and this process will continue. Before this century is over, the decisive question will not be "Can machines create music?" but "What kind of computer-made music do we want to program, and is it worth the time and expense?"

The men doing computer work today do not presume to call themselves composers: they are researchers and experimenters. Their music is to be found in "laboratory notebooks" that often contain surprising results. The researcher is quite aware that his work is limited by his lack of skill and his lack of comprehension of how the computer may be harnessed to artistic purposes. Indeed, ever since the computer was developed, its usefulness to society has been restricted more by man's imagination than by the capability of the hardware. As researcher Lejaren Hiller puts it, "After all, a computer is really nothing more than a complex array of hardware. It can be tremendously useful hardware, however, but only if you know the limitations of logic, and how to ask sensible and precisely formulated questions. . . ." James Beauchamp, another researcher, observes, "We may now be at the threshold of the discovery of mathematical descriptions for 'beautiful tones,' as they are commonly termed in conventional music. All that is holding back the investigations is not criteria for what are 'beautiful tones,' but the fact that [researchers] as yet lack the information necessary to specify the sounds they imagine."

Of course, there are limitations on the part of the computer as well. As Gerald Strany remarked, "The computer is extraordinarily fast and extraordinarily accurate, but it is also exceedingly stupid and, therefore, it has to be told everything." What is more, it has no creative urge, no imagination, no emotion. All these vital forces of creativity are missing. What it *can* do is manipulate symbols, process information, obey complex instructions, and even learn by experience.

Interestingly, it can improvise by using random processes. It can select by testing patterns against criteria written into its program. It can survey and polish its own efforts by reference to higher-order criteria. All these steps are part of the normal creative process, and the machine can continue them until the constraints of its program are satisfied. Furthermore, the computer can draw on its superhuman resources of speed and endurance, which are important parts of the creative process. In a few hours it can search for, test, and accept or reject artistic and musical patterns that would occupy a man for a lifetime.

Perhaps this is not "creativity," but it is a fascinating business—and an impressive start indeed for this new branch of electronic music.

Will the computer take us anywhere worth going in music? No one can tell.* Over the years, computer equipment has become minia-

---

*Since the application of the computer to produce music directly does away with the performer, the next logical step, as the acoustical authority John Backus has laconically pointed out, is to let the computer also listen to its own music.

turized and infinitely flexible. The new technology clearly offers un-limited possibilities for sound. But if such sound is to be arranged in meaningful, perhaps even beautiful order, men of genius, as usual, will do the arranging. Composers will still have to select and reject and build edifices of sound in accordance with the dictates of their creative imaginations.

Today, technology is as much a god in music as in the rest of our lives, and whether we are ready for it or not, or like it or not, com-puter music is very much with us.

Some Problems of Computer Music

A computer must do what it is told to do, no more and no less. For this reason, instructions to computers must be clear and straight-forward. The machine can help the composer or researcher solve a complex problem, but only if the human being has first carefully broken the problem down into a number of tiny steps. As a result, the role of the human brain—the programmer—is still the key factor in computer work, and the composer or researcher must learn to talk to the computer with symbols it can grasp. Manipulating ideas by transforming and combining them in accordance with the logic of language is an act of human intelligence, and the same procedure must be followed in dealing with a computer if the machine is to be able to engage in an act of artificial intelligence.

The machine can be creative only in the narrow sense of imi-tation. (Some researchers predict that a way will be found to give a computer a "direction of purpose" and an "artistic unconscious," but this possibility is very much in the future and has no place in our present discussion.) The computer can compose anything—albeit in the comparatively simple situation of musical symbolism, and in an imitative fashion.

Still, from all signs and portents, the computer will obviate many of the staid aspects of music. There are estimated to be more than fifty computer projects already under way, involving everything from composition to score printing. The musicologist Allen Forte believes that computer analysis will lead eventually to "a metatheory of musical structure. But even thinking about that right now frightens me." Some advanced composers, such as James Tenney, believe that the day is not far off when developments of great sophistication will let the composer concentrate on the larger outlines of a piece while the computer fills in the details. To herald this brave new cultural world, the International Federation for Information Processing has launched competitions for music written by computer.

The greatest handicap at the moment is the expense—a commercial rate of $600 to $800 an hour for use of computer time. Another serious drawback is that composers do not know precisely—and therefore cannot tell the computer—what makes sound "interesting." But, as Professor J. K. Randall, who has written a *Variations for Violin and Computer* utilizing a refinement of the program developed by Max Mathews of Bell Laboratories, points out, "It's hard to listen to sound for what it is. If an event does not sound like anything you've ever heard before, then you're likely to call it electronic, or say it came from outer space."

A third handicap is that the computer composer cannot experiment with the computer as an instrument because he cannot play it in *real time*, as he plays the piano. Instead, he must wait patiently for hours, or even days, until his sound project can be completed and converted into sounds he can hear. This time lag can be maddening to the composer; in the words of one experimenter, "Imagine trying to learn the oboe in similar fashion. Every time you put it to your mouth, you must wait for eight hours to hear what you played." On the other hand, Hubert Howe, a researcher and composer of computer music, observes accurately enough that, "The delay before a composer hears his instrumental piece played is often much longer than the computer's delay."

The breakthrough will come when the machines are made more accommodating to the musician, not the reverse. For example, it is quite likely that input systems soon will be developed that are more gestural and musical than IBM cards, and the composer then will be able to draw closer to his new instrument, the computer.

If the music thus far produced by composers who seek the aid of the computer sometimes sounds like absurd fumblings, we must be patient and tolerant. Our young composers, so eager to study and unlock the rich treasure house of computer music—and all electronic synthesizers, for that matter—are primitives. They are tribesmen, discovering for the first time that a string stretched by a bow vibrates and makes sounds, some of them agreeable, and that a gourd or a hole in the ground can modulate sound.

We still have a long way to go, and the art of music still has many new paths to tread. As Edgard Varèse observed, today "the skyscraper is our symbol, not the pyramids of the Egyptians." In the same way, composers in our computerized age must be allowed to use the computer to express themselves and their times.

The Advantages of the Computer as Compared to the Synthesizer

With miraculous machines such as the RCA Synthesizer and smaller new machines such as the Moog, Arp, and Buchla systems now available, why are composers attracted to computers? Hubert Howe provides one answer: "Because you can do all kinds of things on the computer that you can't come close to with other systems."

To understand this, it is helpful to review what may be termed the technique of "orchestration" in electronic music—that is, the methods of putting the musical piece into a form that will make it come out on magnetic tape. This is an exhausting, discouraging business. To begin with, the composer must understand, in scientific terms, *the mathematical facts about every note in his piece.* He must know its duration in milliseconds, and he must know its pitch, amplitude (loudness), starting time, and "envelope" (the attack, sustaining, and decay pattern). He must be intimately familiar with the frequency and depth of any vibration or tremolo, and with the particular waveform and the manipulations and alterations required to produce the tone color he desires. (This all sounds mind-boggling, but think of what the conventional composer must know!)

The composer of electronic music has at his disposal a battery of devices that produce waveforms. The basic signal generators produce sine waves, white noise, and more complex waveforms called "squarewaves," "sawtooth waves," and so forth. The composer also works with a highly important modifying device called "envelope controls." The envelope deals with how sound begins and stops, and its characteristics in the time between. The attack is the most important moment in the lifespan of a given sound: it can be sharp, gentle, tremulous, and so on. The "decay," or ending of the tone, also can be manipulated so that it is abrupt, decisive, gradually fading away, and so on.

As yet, the composer preparing his equipment in the electronic studio has produced no sound. Only when all the characteristics of the desired sound have been programmed can the waveforms, still in the form of voltages, pass through an amplifier and loudspeaker so that they can be heard. And only when the composer is satisfied with his organization of sounds (on both the RCA and the smaller synthesizers), does he record the fragment of music on tape.

Now, the great attraction of computers is that they offer the composer the chance to eliminate entirely the process of complex and balky signal generating and processing equipment. In other words, the whole synthesizer is eliminated because a digital-to-analog computer, with the appropriate input, can produce and record sound directly. For example, the Nonesuch record entitled "Computer Music," released in 1970 and featuring music by Charles Dodge and two other composers, worked with a sound-synthesizer program that is a sophisticated outgrowth of a Bell Laboratory system called MUSIC IV. The composer introduces his musical ideas into a digital computer, and then the processed information is converted to analog form on another computer, which transforms the digital data directly into sound images on tape by recording continuous fluctuations in magnetism. By simulating his sounds in the program, this computer system does away with electronic sound generators such as filters, ring modulators, and even the latest synthesizing machines themselves. (And of course, no actual instruments are used.)

This is a fantastic scientific advancement, and this is why Milton Babbitt remarks, "The computer is the future. I don't work with it, so I can say that objectively." In the immediate future, Babbitt adds, the digital computer is certain to be teamed up with the new compact synthesizer, and when this happens, electronic music is likely to be shaken up once again. At present, composers in the computer field must deal with large digital computers, which store and release all the necessary information. But, the digital tape, as we have noted already, contains nothing but numbers, so that our composer-engineer-physicist must run it through a digital-to-analog converter in order to produce the playable tape. Inasmuch as there is no actual sound-generating equipment, the composer cannot test the sound of his music until the entire procedure has been completed. This a cumbersome business.

Computer Composition

Our music community has become infinitely more scientific-minded in the last twenty years, and the potentialities of the computer have fascinated our more far-out composers in white coats. Of course, there is no clear agreement as to how to exploit this remarkable and potentially revolutionary tool. Some composer-researchers are busy hooking up computers to synthesizers from which tape recordings can be produced; others, in particular Yannis Xenakis, develop their ideas with the aid of the computer and then assign the *performance* to live musicians or to the instruments of the sound studio.

Computers also have been employed to originate musical materials and to organize them. But rather than ask, "Can computers compose?" most composers who have experimented with computers have exploited them as *instruments of musical performance*, and/or to structure all the elements of their compositions—that is, tempo, timbre, rate and shape of attack and decay, register, and so on—to the same degree as the "traditional" composer controls pitch and rhythm in his score. The use of computers also has introduced a new element of flexibility into electronic music. Hitherto, an electronic composer's final tape was rigidly fixed and unalterable; the taped composition became the final form of the performance—precisely as a painter's canvas is his final form. In computer-aided composition, however, the work is coded onto computer cards. Thus, the composer can create different performances of his music on successive computer runs merely by changing a few cards. In short, the computer has in a sense reintroduced the distinction between composition and performance that the early composers of electronic music were so anxious to eliminate.

Into the Future: "To Reveal a New World of Sound"

There is only one condition in which we can imagine managers not needing subordinates, and masters not needing slaves. This condition would be that each [inanimate] instrument could do

> *its own work, at the word of command or by intelligent anticipa-*
> *tion, like the statues of Daedalus or the tripods made by*
> *Hephaestus, of which Homer relates that 'of their own motion*
> *they entered the conclave of Gods on Olympus; as if a shuttle*
> *should weave of itself, and a plectrum should do its own harp*
> *playing.'*

Aristotle, THE POLITICS, *ca.* 350 B.C.

Can the machine create art? Will it compete with the creative artist? Dr. Dennis Gabor, a leading computer theorist, says, "I sincerely hope that machines *will* never replace the creative artist, but in good conscience I cannot say that they never *could*."

Today, the computer is only a tool, far removed from the aesthetic and polemical battles that preoccupy composers and painters, but already we can perceive that the computer has achieved a radical extension in all art media and techniques. In the visual arts a great deal of truly exciting research has resulted in some absorbing work in the graphic arts. For example, Michael Noll of the Bell Telephone Laboratories made a provocative experiment. He analyzed a 1917 black-and-white, plus-and-minus picture by Mondrian, and produced a number of random computer graphics using the same number of horizontal and vertical bars placed within an identical overall area. Noll reported that 59 percent of all persons who were shown both the Mondrian and one of the computer versions preferred the latter; 72 percent of the viewers thought that the Mondrian was done by a computer.*

The reader may make of this what he will. It is certainly food for thought. The computer as budding artist is "culturally neutral"; it is not capable of making abstractions, and is devoid of the three prime forces behind creativity—imagination, intuition, and emotion. Nevertheless, computer art may quickly emerge as a new branch of art, as an extension of the age-old dialogue between the artist, his ideas, and his medium. The scope and diversity of what we call art will also most certainly be broadened by that formidable technological

---

*A fascinating book, *Cybernetic Serendipity* (New York: Frederick A. Praeger Inc., 1968), has many striking illustrations of computer graphics.

instrument, the computer. By launching a true collaboration of the artist and the scientist, the computer may usher in forms and concepts of art as yet undreamed of. Ironically, by opening up new realms of possibilities, the computer may, instead of threatening to deluge us with "cold, inhuman art," return to art some of its original sense of mystery.

And yet the question abides: will machines ever be able to produce worthwhile music? Will they write the equivalent of a Bach cantata in the twenty-first century? Can they be taught to organize the symbols of musical expression and thought into designs of intellectual creation?

We cannot answer with any certainty today. We can but speculate. The obstacles against such a development are enormous: it means simulating, with computer and program, the trillion workings of the human brain.

Nevertheless, in an age when machines have been built to take man to the moon and back, perhaps we should not be shocked at the idea that machines may be constructed to provide man with a new form of art. And it may be entirely new art, newer than we can even comprehend at present. After all, the computer undoubtedly will be programmed with far fewer preconditioned cultural restraints than the programmer himself lives with, consciously and unconsciously. Most computers have never heard of Beethoven or of the edicts of the Schönberg-Webern school. "He" is culturally free, even though he is the prisoner of his program. Given sufficient time to speed through the history of music, as well as the related arts, these remarkable machines may contribute to some startling innovations and breakthroughs.

Finally, the point cannot be stressed too much that the computer, for the artist, is a tool to be used by his own mind. It is not a superhuman automatic-writing machine; it has no sense of artistic purpose. The awareness of a task to be performed, or a work to be created, so striking in the human artist, is completely absent (as yet) in the computer.

Human intelligence, therefore, is still very much needed in the creation of music by computers. No matter how sophisticated the circuitry, the human brain is still necessary for the essential task of selecting or rejecting what the machine produces. In the words of Jasia Reichardt, "The possibilities inherent in the computer as a creative tool will do little to change those idioms of art which rely primarily on the dialogue between the artist, his ideas, and the canvas. They will, however, increase the scope of art and contribute to its diversity." In this context, and the words of Edgard Varèse should be borne in mind: "We should also remember that no machine is a wizard, as we are beginning to think, and we must not expect our electronic devices to compose for us. Good music and bad music will be composed by electronic means, just as good and bad music have been composed for instruments. The computing machine is a marvelous invention and seems almost superhuman. But in reality it is as limited as the mind of the individual who feeds it material."*

*Lecture at Yale University, 1962.

CHAPTER XV

Music and Numbers

MUSICIANS ALWAYS HAVE KNOWN THAT MUSIC AND MATHEMATICS were related; musical sounds can readily be translated into numerical terms, and the relationship between tones is numerical.

The computer itself is but the latest in an array of scientific hardware that has been used as a tool by musicians and musicologists alike. The notion of a stored program can be traced back to the various mechanical musical instruments that have appeared intermittently throughout the centuries. The basis of these machines was either a barrel or cylinder programmed by means of appropriately placed pegs or pins, or a punched paper tape, both of which performed certain mechanical actions when the barrel revolved by means of levers or jack-work.

The earliest device of this sort was the carillon, which is probably of Chinese origin, and was introduced into Europe during the Middle Ages. In the Netherlands of the fourteenth century, the belfries of large cathedrals possessed truly mechanized chimes, which depended for their operation upon a large revolving drum, provided with pegs, which activated the striking mechanism directly.*

The French also devised ingenious musicmaking mechanisms. For example, the carillon in the Abbey-Church of St. Catherine, near Rouen, was "programmed" to play the hymn "Conditor alme siderum."**

Mechanically driven organs appeared about 1500. These devices were activated by means of revolving drums programmed with appropriately placed cams. Salomon de Caus, a French engineer, was one of the first experimenters to deal with the theory of cylinders and their "pinning" (or programming, as we would say today). In 1644 de Caus wrote a treatise about a hydraulic engine that produced musical sounds when a water wheel was connected directly to a large revolving drum with pegs that activated a series of keys. The keys, in turn, opened valves that allowed air to flow from a wind-chest

*A. Wins, *L'horloge a travers les ages* (Paris, 1924).
**A. Ungerer, *L'horloge astronimique de la cathedrale de Strasbourg* (Paris, 1922).

through pneumatic tubes connected to corresponding organ pipes. De Caus also designed a hydraulic organ with pins placed in a "musical wheel" which depressed keys, causing air to be transmitted directly to the pipes. In his treatise, *New and Rare Inventions of Water Works*, de Caus illustrates, as an example of the pinning, the first six bars of Alessandro Striggio's madrigal "Che fera fed' al cielo" for performance by his hydraulically operated device.

After de Caus, a number of inventors and tinkerers designed contraptions that programmed cylinders for mechanical musical instruments. Robert Fludd, Athanius Kircher, and Johann Ungerer did outstanding work in this area. The revolving-barrel concept itself led inevitably to a steady stream of devices in the eighteenth century—musical clocks, barrel organs, music boxes, and so forth—all programmed by means of pegs inserted in revolving cylinders of one kind or another. One famous device was the music box (*musique à peigne*) of Louis Faure; this charming and enduring little machine combined for the first time a string-driven revolving cylinder, the pins of which activated a set of thin, comblike steel strips in a prescribed sequence. Sometimes a table or a mantel-piece was used as an auxiliary sounding board. Other mechanical musical instruments of the eighteenth century included Maelzel's "Panharmonikon," an animated machine orchestra of forty-two robot musicians. In 1775 an inventor named Engramelle spoke in his treatise *La Tonotechnie* of "noter les cylindres," and he actually invented a combination mechanical organ, dulcimer, carillon, and flute based upon this his theories.

The Nineteenth Century

The first attempts to develop a large mechanical computer were made by Charles Babbage (1792–1871). Babbage was obsessed with the idea of harnessing steam power to mechanical computation and of using such a computer for type-setting lengthy mathematical tables such as those used in navigation and astronomy. (Babbage hated music, by the way, particularly the noise of barrel organs, which, he claimed, interrupted his concentration.)

Babbage's first device, "The Difference Engine," was able in theory to compute by successive differences and to set type automatically, so that the output would be in the form of printed tables.

His "Analytical Engine" depended for its operation upon two sets of punched cards, containing nine positions and up to a dozen columns, to tell the machine what manipulations to perform at any stage in the successive calculations. Embodying the principles of what is now known as "programming," these instructions were maintained in the "store" of the device—an embryonic memory store. The set of operation cards programmed the engine to go through a sort of additions, subtractions, multiplications, and divisions in a prearranged sequence. Other "variable" cards stored the actual numbers to be acted upon by these operations. The real computation was performed in what was known as the "mill," a kind of primitive mechanical accumulator. The results were both printed on paper tape and punched on blank cards.

Thus, Babbage's "Analytical Engine" was in reality what we now call a symbol manipulator; a century before the electronic computer, it had both a stored program and a means for encoding information! Babbage anticipated virtually all of the basic concepts of modern electronic computer technology in his "Analytical Engine." This extremely complicated mechanical device was designed to store and manipulate numbers in much the same manner as present-day computers. The British government provided support for his work, but his plans were too extravagant and ambitious for the technology of his day and his engine was never completed.

Around 1840, the dashing Lady Ada Loveland, a fellow mathematician, speculated on the musical possibilities of Babbage's device. Her words were nothing less than prophetic: "The Engine's operating mechanism might act upon other things beside number, were objects found whose mutual fundamental relations could be expressed by those of the abstract science of operations, and which should be also susceptible of adaptations to the action of the operating notation and mechanism of the engine. Supposing, for instance, that the fundamental relations of pitched sound in the signs of harmony, and of musical composition were susceptible of such expression and adaptations, the engine might compose elaborate and scientific pieces of music of any degree of complexity or extent."*

Until the middle of the nineteenth century, the barrel organ and

*R. Taylor, *Scientific Memoirs* (London, 1843).

the music box were the only significant mechanical music-producing instruments. Various isolated "programmed" music devices appeared, but nothing very exciting came on the scene until the first pneumatic self-playing piano was produced in 1870. The piano played as a perforated sheet of paper moved over a reed chamber while air passed through holes that had been "programmed" into the paper and activated the keys.

A highly sophisticated "Pianola," invented by E. S. Votey in 1897, utilized a prepunched, perforated piano roll that moved over a capillary bridge. There were eighty-eight openings in the board, and when the holes in the roll coincided with one of the openings, air was transmitted into the apparatus, activating sets of bellows with their corresponding striking linkages. The fingers, or strikers, of the Pianola hovered directly, note for note, over the keyboard of the piano.

The next major breakthrough in the field of musical machines came with the invention of the phonograph, a momentous musical mechanism embodying storage of information for reproduction. The literature on Edison and the phonograph is too extensive to be discussed here, as is the history of the telegraph—both of which the reader is sufficiently familiar with. We should note, however, that the earliest experiments in electrical communication foreshadowed, in a primitive way, modern information theory. It was Samuel Morse who in 1832 developed the first successful device for transmitting information electrically. The telegraph drew long and short lines on a strip of paper, the sequences of which represented not the letters of a word, but their numerical equivalents as assigned in a dictionary, or code book.

The transformation of information into electrical form made for virtually instantaneous transmission of data from point to point and opened the possibility of coupling "engines" of one form or another for operating on this information without human assistance or intervention. The principles of encoding and decoding were in a primitive state at this time, of course, and the nearly endless possibilities of communication by electricity had been but barely sensed.

Some eighty years after Morse, J. M. Baudot developed a five-unit (or channel) code with two-condition signaling (each of the channels either punched or not punched), thus offering thirty-two character possibilities encompassing the entire alphabet.

Brilliant inventions followed rapidly. In 1859 David Hughes, a former professor of music, invented a typewriting telegraph, utilizing a piano-like keyboard to activate the mechanism. D. D. Parmelee had patented the first key-driven adding machine in 1850. By 1877 Dorr Felt had perfected a calculator with key-driven ratchet wheels.

In 1880 Alexander Graham Bell, who had long been interested in the study of sound reproduction, financed his own laboratory in Washington to promote research relating to sound and acoustics. Together with Charles Tainter, Bell devised and patented several mechanisms for transmitting and recording sound. In 1876, at the Philadelphia Centennial, Elisha Grey (another inventor of a telephone along with Bell) demonstrated his "Electromusical Piano," which was capable of transmitting musical tones over wires.

Hermann Helmholtz, one of the great German scientists of the nineteenth century, distinguished himself in physical science, mathematics, and in physiology; he also made important contributions to knowledge of the physiology of the ear and the perception of musical tone. His treatise, *On the Sensations of Tone as a Physiological Basis for the Theory of Music* (1875), became the basis of modern theories of consonance, tone-quality, and resultant tones.

The Twentieth Century

In 1906 Thaddeus Cahill introduced his "Dynamophone," which we have discussed in detail in Chapter V of this book. Yet despite all this and other remarkable inventions and demonstrations, there was still no solid breakthrough in understanding the *nature of sound, its measurement, and analysis.* This came with the introduction of the audion by Lee De Forest. The potentialities of this device as an amplifier and modulator were soon evident and led to revolutionary developments. In 1912 the vacuum tube was brought directly to the attention of the research laboratories of the Bell System, and its demonstration was to become a landmark in communications history. These laboratories soon launched a massive program of research involving a comprehensive analysis of the electrical qualities of speech and hearing in order to obtain better articulation over telephone lines.

This research started with an examination of the character of speech. A study of the organs of speech and hearing followed, then a study of music and sound in general. This led to the construction of devices to convert sound waves into electrical form and reconstitute them again into sound with a minimum of distortion. From the musical point of view, the most significant result of these efforts was the development of electrical, or "Orthophonic," recording in 1925 by J. P. Maxfield and H. C. Harrison.

A whole body of electronic musical instruments were developed as by-products of these experiments. Their design was based on the principle of vacuum-tube (audion) oscillators, planned or controlled by the researcher or performer, and combined with amplification and loudspeaker output. The most familiar of these electronic instruments is the "Electronic Organ" invented by Laurens Hammond, which employed a system of ninety-one rotary electromagnetic disc generators driven by a synchronous motor with associated gears and tone wheels. These tone wheels were shaped so as to generate sinusoidal currents in their associated coils. The wave forms thus produced could be synthesized into complex tones. The "Theremin" and the "Ondes Martenot" are other once-popular electronic musical instruments that made their appearance in the 1920s.

Sound Synthesis in the 1950s and 1960s

A great advance in sound synthesis came in 1955, when Harry Olson of RCA invented an "Electronic Music Synthesizer"—the progenitor of the famous and much-improved MARK II synthesizer at the Columbia-Princeton Electronic Music Center. In Olson's synthesizer, sawtooth waves, containing all possible harmonics, are filtered to remove the unwanted ones. The instructions, or program, are put into the machine by means of a keyboard that is roughly analogous to that of a typewriter and that punches the commands into a forty-channel paper tape fifteen inches wide, representing binary code numbers describing the desired musical sounds. The roll of paper (rather like a player-piano roll) in turn drives a series of tone generators to produce the actual sounds. These sounds may be the human voice, conventional instruments, or entirely new varieties and concepts of sound —"sounds as yet unheard."

In the 1950s, after the pioneering work of the *Musique concrète* group in Paris, the Cologne studio in Germany, and the Columbia-Princeton Center (all discussed in Part Three), there was an enormous interest in electronic music throughout the world. Forward-looking broadcasting stations in Europe set up experimental sound studios, and in America commercial scientific laboratories became interested in the field. More significantly, many universities established new sound studios, with a composer-engineer in charge. The presence of the computer on some campuses also was to be of enormous importance. Not only composers, but also enthusiastic engineers, physicists, and technologists experimented with the computer as a tool to create any desired sound by means of a sequence of digital numerical samples representing the amplitude of that wave of successive points. This, together with the computer's ability to work out statistical routines, led to several path-breaking experiments in computer music. In one type of experiment, the apparatus "composes" music, selecting notes according to mathematical rule or numerical sequence (probability), or any other system the composer wants to try. In a second type of experiment, the computer "plays" music, and in this case the waves of the notes themselves (including frequency, duration, and intensity) are expressed mathematically as a sequence of numbers and are converted by an analog device into oscillations that drive a loudspeaker.

The Illiac Suite

In 1955 Lejaren Hiller and Leonard Isaacson began a series of experiments in computer-composed music at the University of Illinois. By 1956 they had accumulated enough computer output to assemble the now-famous *Illiac Suite for String Quartet*, which was later published as a score by the Theodore Presser Company.

Hiller and Isaacson were seeking to evaluate a broad range of compositional techniques in terms of their practicality for computer programming. They demonstrated that the computer either could generate musical scores by conventional means or could deliver an output governed by probability distributions. In the *Illiac Suite* the computer stored in its memory a numerically coded chromatic scale with a range of about two and a half octaves. The machine selected notes at random, rejecting them if they violated the established rules of the period of music within which it had been instructed to compose. Thus it produced sequences of letters and numbers that were stored on the machine's "memory" until a short melody was derived. This music was then transcribed by hand into conventional musical notation quite appropriate for human performance. Because of the admittedly insufficient characteristics of the rules, the *Illiac Suite* was, the researchers themselves concluded, very little like the music it was supposedly based on.*

Illiac and "Chance" Music

The Illiac experiment was novel in that it involved a program for composing music by the deliberate introduction of *chance* in computer programs, although this chance element was still subjected to rules.** Music by chance has intrigued composers at least since the time of Bach. In the eighteenth century, many dice compositions were created as parlor games. "Puzzle canons," in which the solver had to "realize" the second voice, were also a popular musical game. Mozart, it is fairly certain, composed sets of alternative measures of music, in which, by means of tossing dice to determine the sequence of musical measures, a nonmusical person could "compose" a variety of "do-it-yourself" pieces. The *Illiac Suite* emphasized, in a signal fashion, the interest of some contemporary composers (especially John Cage and his many disciples) in music of chance—that is, music determined by random means or casually by number play. (Needless to say, many contemporary composers firmly reject all "chance" speculations in music.)

As we have seen, the computer used by Hiller and Jacobson was instructed to select musical notes *at random*, fast and furiously; then it subjected the ensuing sequences of notes to several tests, based on established rules of composition. Thus, in a (much misunderstood) sense, the computer as used here has "created" music—even though,

*See Lejaren Hiller, "Computer Music," *Scientific American*, CCI (1959). Also, Hiller and Beauchamp, "Research in Music With Electronics," *Science*, CL (1965); Hiller and Isaacson, *Experimental Music* (New York: McGraw-Hill Book Company, 1959).

**Six years before Hiller and Isaacson began their experiments with Illiac, John Pierce and M. E. Shannon of Bell Laboratories composed elementary statistical or "chance" music, based upon a repertory of permissible root chords in the key of C. Several pieces were thus composed by throwing three specially made dice, and by employing a table of random numbers.

of course, it has done so within the limits of the program established by the human brain that controls it. In other words, the "machine-as-artist" has no creative urge. It can improvise by means of random processes; it can select by testing resultant patterns against criteria written into its program; and it can polish the output by reference to higher-order criteria. What is more, the machine can draw on its superhuman resources of speed and endurance, and within a few hours seek out, test, reject, and accept artistic patterns that a man could not sift through in a lifetime.*

Bell Laboratories Computer Work

In 1957 Max V. Mathews, a Ph.D. in electrical engineering and the Director of the Behavioral Research Department of Bell Laboratories, happened to attend a concert of Schönberg's twelve-tone works. Fascinated and intellectually aroused, Mathews was sufficiently curious to sketch out a system that would generate such "mathematically controlled" sounds on the computer. After years of research, and work with several separate processes, he achieved his goal. We have seen how one of the driving urges of the pioneering Cologne Studio group in the 1950s (Eimert, Stockhausen, et al.) was to extend, through electronics, the tone-building ideas of Schönberg and Webern, and with Mathews' work the long shadow of Schönberg is felt once more upon electronic music—although Mathews' system has no specific musical relation to Schönberg.

Max Mathews, J. R. Pierce, and their associates at the Bell Laboratories began generating music by computer in 1958. (Bell Labs, of course, had been doing important work in acoustical research for many decades, particularly under Dr. Harvey Fletcher.) In the process they found a quite new application for the computer in connection with music, apart from analysis or production of musical scores. They used it directly in the *production of musical sounds*. They were led to this development by the use of the digital computer at the Bell Laboratories as a means for simulating the performance of complex speech-processing devices such as vocoders. In such stimula-

*The composer Hubert Howe comments laconically on this, "Yes, but that's why humans can't go about it the same way!"

tion, a speech act is reduced to a numerical description, which is then processed by the computer as the original speech wave would be processed by the device simulated. The computer produces a sequence of numbers that represent the output of the device, and this sequence of numbers is recorded on magnetic tape and then converted into sound.

It is easy to go from this use of the computer to the idea of having the computer produce by prescribed rule a sequence of numbers to be converted into the corresponding sound. This is what Mathews and his associates did. Further refinements of the Bell system of computer sound production were subsequently carried out at Princeton University, where the entire program was rewritten by Godfrey Winham and Hubert Howe.

Several large-scale university-sponsored projects now dealt with the unique problem of musical input. A special vocabulary had to be constructed to represent within the computer the multidimensional aspects of each note, including the dimensions of pitch, duration, timbre, and register. Obviously, this problem of "defining a musical sound to the computer" is enormous and crucially important, and outstanding work has been done on it by several groups.

The computer also has supplied some developments for the field of musicology and music research, and it is extremely useful as a tool for traditional harmonic analysis. By enabling the scholar to accomplish in a short span of time the labor that otherwise would have demanded his entire lifetime, the computer has much to offer music outside of the field of computer composition. The first use of machine methods for the handling and analysis of large masses of quantitative musical data was made by Bertrand Bronson in his comparative study of British-American folksongs, which appeared in 1949. Other innovating and successful programs include Harry Lincoln's project of developing a thematic index of sixteenth-century Italian music.

PART SIX

Electronic Music on Records

CHAPTER XVI

Reviews of Selected Recordings

As ELECTRONIC MUSIC IS ALMOST ALWAYS COMPOSED TO BE HEARD on a phonograph, we are especially interested in recordings of this branch of music.

In this chapter, "Reviews of Selected Recordings," a number of works of electronic music that are of musical or historical importance are discussed in detail.

The next chapter consists of Peter Frank's admirable catalogue of just about every recording of electronic music, including many titles now deleted.

MILTON BABBITT, *Composition for Synthesizer* (1964). Columbia MS 6566, "Columbia-Princeton Electronic Music Center." Also, works by Arel, Davidovsky, El-Dabh, Luening, and Ussachevsky.

A purely electronic composition created entirely on the RCA synthesizer. The great flexibility of pitch succession that electronic sources permit is utilized with imaginative musical effect. As an orchestrator, Babbitt carries the tradition of Berlioz, Rimsky-Korsakov, and Stravinsky to the next dimension—with mid twentieth-century electronic tools.

MILTON BABBITT, *Ensembles for Synthesizer*. Columbia MS 7051.

This is hardly accessible music, but the rewards are many for the listener who has the patience to play it over a few times until he begins to blink and feel his way through Milton Babbitt's closed world of "total organization." Babbitt has often said that "nothing becomes old as quickly as a new sound"—the curse that haunts so many composers of electronic music who contribute nothing to our ears except new technological gimmickry. Babbitt gives us musical substance to chew on; this is sternly intellectualized music, subtle, rich, organic, and artistic. The *Ensembles for Synthesizer* is really a prismatic gathering together of tiny pitched notes into a commanding whole. At the farthest possible point from an aural electronic orgy, it makes a convincing case for the use of electronic music by the imaginative composer. Like all of Babbitt's music, it is structured by the organization of musical elements in every dimension of texture and form. This is important art of our time.

MILTON BABBITT, *Philomel*, for soprano, recorded soprano, and synthesized sound. Also, Fred Lerdahl, *Wake*. Bethany Beardsley, soprano; members of Boston Symphony Chamber Players, David Epstein, cond. Deutsche Grammophon 0654083.

At last we have a recording of what is perhaps Milton Babbitt's most important work (and certainly his most enjoyable), his 1963 setting of John Hollander's poem, "Philomel." The piece was commissioned by Bethany Beardsley, under a Ford Foundation grant.

As in his earlier setting of Dylan Thomas's "Vision and Prayer," Babbitt employs the sound and ambience of a human voice woven into the synthesized electronic sounds produced by the RCA synthesizer at the Columbia-Princeton Electronic Music Center. The result is a rewarding presentation of Babbitt's rich and complex twelve-tone style. No open form, chance, or indeterminacy here; Babbitt's works are rigidly controlled and (in the tape part) organized tightly down to the last detail.

In the classical myth, Philomel was a woman who was ravished, had her tongue taken out, and was then turned into a nightingale. This, I assume from the poem, is meant to be an image of the modern poet in this sad world—the poet who finds his voice out of pain and darkness. The electronic part includes the voice of soprano Beardsley transformed into myriad shapes and sounds—sometimes almost like birdsong, sometimes pluralized into whole choruses. This is crystalline music, notable for its lyric and dramatic power, and the striking interplay between the electronic and live music. Like few of the other compositions in twelve-tone music which seek to organize all musical elements into every dimension, this one evokes an emotional response.

A special bow to the admirable Miss Beardsley, whose phenomenal voice contributes so much to the success of *Philomel*, and to the Acoustical Research Contemporary Music Project and Deutsche Grammophon, who co-sponsored this album.

Fred Lerdahl's *Wake* is an intense, nonelectronic treatment of the Anna Livia Plurabelle episode from James Joyce's *Finnegans Wake*.

LUCIANO BERIO, *Differences*; BRUNO MADERNA, *Seranata No. 2*; *Luigi*

Nono, Poliphonica; Monodia; Ritmiea. Works for Chamber orchestra conducted by Maderna and Berio. Mainstream 5004.

> Berio's *Differences* makes use of multi-channel tape and five instruments—flute, clarinet, harp, viola, and cello. It is a good example of live music with electronic "extension." The effect on the listener is purely kaleidoscopic; we hazily listen to constantly dissolving and reforming patterns, much as we would gaze at the constantly changing patterns of the rain on a window pane.
>
> A good analysis of what Berio is up to here is provided in the liner notes by the well-known composer Henri Pousseur: "More or less elaborate sound materials, played by all instruments, are recorded to provide the substance of the accompanying tape, where they appear either in their original form or more-or-less altered by electro-acoustical means. In this recorded version the tape sounds are placed to the left and right of the 'living' instrumentalists, and also at the center behind them to give a recorded 'optical illusion.' The work's form and elaboration of the rich possibilities implied by such a complex 'instrument' brings to life, in its happy alternations of humor and gravity, garrulity and discretion, tenderness and virility, a modern music in the spirit of *Comedia del arte.*"
>
> The other two works on the record are good examples of avant-garde music for chamber orchestra, composed in the 1950s by two famous Italian exponents of "The New Music."

LUCIANO BERIO, *Circles* (after poetry by e e cummings). Cathy Berbarian, voice; François Pierre, harp; Jean Pierre Drouet, percussion I; Boris de Vinogradev, percussion II. Also, SYLVANO BUSSOTTI, *Frammento.* Cathy Berbarian, voice; Luciano Berio, piano. JOHN CAGE, *Aria With Fontana Mix.* Cathy Berbarian, voice; magnetic tape. Time 58003

> *Circles* (1960), inspired by the American lower-case poet e e cummings, is similar in effect to Berio's *Homage to Joyce.* Cummings was of course out to "open up" the English language much as Joyce did, and proves an excellent subject for Berio's subtle musical treatment of word-sounds, word-images, and word-sound-emotions, rather than of the poetry's meter or significance. *Circles* uses no conductor; the singer acts as a coordinator at various times.

KARL-BIRGER BLOMDAHL, Suite from the opera *Aniara.* Orchestra of the

REVIEWS OF SELECTED RECORDINGS

Vienna Volkoper, Werner Janssen, conductor. Electronic and Concrete effects by Swedish Radio. Columbia MS 7176.

> Blomdahl, who died in 1968, achieved a highly sophisticated blending of conventional and electronic sounds in this opera *Aniara*. Somewhat resembling the film *2001*, *Aniara* is a story of a man at the mercy of an electronic brain. The plot is also concerned with a voyage through space in the year 2038.

> It is interesting to know that Blomdahl was highly skeptical of the possibilities of electronic music, except as special, "unworldly" sound-effects. He told a conference of composers in Toronto in 1960, "As I see it, the electronic means are still in such a primitive state of development that they cannot be successfully used independently for pure musical purposes."

JOHN CAGE, *Indeterminancy*. John Cage reading; David Tudor, music, plus electronic effects. Folkways FT 3704.

> This superb album is gravely billed as "New aspects of form in instrumental and electronic music," but it is nothing more than some ninety short anecdotes read by Cage, with sporadic piano and electronic noodlings. According to the composer, "the continuity of the stories was not planned . . . my intention in putting the stories together in an unplanned way is to suggest that all things, sounds, stories, *are* related."

> In any case, Cage's voice is hypnotic, the stories are marvelous, and what the occasional electronic blips add to the record I cannot tell you. Don't miss this album, if only for Cage's uncanny readings.

JOHN CAGE, *Fontana Mix-Feed*. See under: "Max Neuhaus, *Electronics and Percussion: Five Realizations.*"

JOHN CAGE and LEJAREN HILLER, *Hpschd* for Harpsichords and Computer-Generated Tape Sounds. Nonesuch H 71224.

> This ear-torturing mess, complete with pontifical liner notes, must surely be Cage's most successful put-on in a career that has been rich in Dadaesque absurdities that critics treated solemnly.

> *Hpschd* is computerese for "Harpsichord"; in computer transmission six letters are the limit. Cage presented this four-and-a-half-hour piece (cut down here to one side of a disc) at the University of Illinois in

1969. The work is scored for one electronic harpsichord, six conventional harpsichords, eight movie projectors, fifty-two tape recorders, and sixty-four slide projectors. The program for this eye-and-ear boggling kinetic phantasmagoria was fed into a computer, and the recorded excerpt comes complete with a "printout" by which the listener can join the fun himself by twirling the knobs of his stereo rig. In sum, a god-awful racket, not to be taken seriously even if you like Zen.

JOHN CAGE, *Variations IV, Volume 2.* Everest 3230.

Variations IV runs about six hours and is being released on records in forty-five minute chunks. As usual with Cage, Stockhausen, Berio *et al.*, it is not the music's intrinsic value but the innovating *ideas* behind it that stimulate our interest. In these *Variations*, Cage seeks a collage effect, a musical counterpart to the "combine paintings" of Cage's close friend Robert Rauschenberg. The painter flung together pillows, rags, tattered posters, color plates of Goya and Rembrandt, old neckties, etc., worked them over brilliantly with bright paint, and produced some of the most sensational art of his period. Cage here is working along the same lines.

Of course the problem with applying the collage technique aurally is that a chaotic hash of sound appalls and distresses us and can be almost painful to endure—whereas you can stand before the same idea worked out visually in a painting, smile with amusement, and walk away after a minute or two. Cage uses recorded sounds of an opening at a Los Angeles art gallery, traffic sounds, a recorded French lesson, as well as stretches of Chopin, Beethoven, and other hallowed composers collaged into the electronically transmuted mix.

Is the result of value? I cannot tell. But perhaps Alfred Frankenstein is right: "One thing Cage may be pointing out here is the degree to which the celebrated music of the past has become part of the sonic garbage with which we are all surrounded today. If so, he likes the garbage; and he makes a fine case for it, in all its aspects, in this most remarkable work."

CHARLES DODGE, *Earth's Magnetic Field.* Nonesuch H 71250.

Labeled as "Realizations in Computed Electronic Sound," this computerized work claims to be a succession of sounds bearing some sort of relationship to electromagnetic events that took place between the earth and the sun in the year 1961. I haven't the faintest idea what all that is about, but the sounds produced here are simple, diatonic, and often intriguing. This is one of the best examples of computer music we have as yet. Charles Dodge has studied with Otto Luening and Vladimir Ussachevsky, among others, and at the present time is director of a research project in computer sound synthesis at the Columbia University Computer Center.

MARIO DAVIDOVSKY, *Three Synchronisms for Instruments and Electronic Sounds, No. 1 for Flute* (1963). CRI S 204.

A sensitive integration of the electronic medium and the flute by the Pulitzer prize-winner in music for 1971. The problems of coordinating a live performance with a constant-speed tape recorder are resolved in a completely musical conception.

One is aware of a special quality of intensity in the music of Davidovsky (b. 1934), a native of Argentina who first came to the United States in 1958 to study with Aaron Copland at Tanglewood. Davidovsky, who is not exclusively an electronic composer, came to the Columbia-Princeton Center, where he is now an associate director, when he took up permanent United States residency in 1960.

His music succeeds with grace and inventiveness in his stated purpose: to introduce the electronic part "as an extension of the other instrument, rather than opposing it." Concerning the *Three Synchronisms* here, Mr. Davidovsky writes, "They belong to a series of short pieces wherein conventional instruments are used in conjunction with electronic sounds. The attempt has been made to preserve the typical characteristics of the conventional instruments and of the electronic medium respectively—yet to achieve integration of both into a coherent musical texture."

TOD DOCKSTADER, and JAMES REICHERT, *Omniphony I.* Owl Records ORLP 11.

Orchestral sounds—many of them expanded through electronic means —combine with electronic sounds in a five-movement work of remarkable variety and power.

TOD DOCKSTADER, *Quartermass* (1964). Owl Records ORLP 8.

Dockstader is a sound engineer, a musical lone wolf, and one of the most technically expert composers at work in the new medium. If the result is not as esoteric as some music employing electronic media, it is more accessible to the unschooled ear. Elements of melody, form, and rhythm are evident, and the sound sources—from a penny balloon to a slammed door—are prosaic materials amazingly transformed.

JACOB DRUCKMAN, *Animus I for trombone and tape* (1966). Also, works by Berio and Ilhan Mimaroglu. Turnabout TV 34177.

Man and tape machine compete in concerto style. The trombone material is imitated by tape. In the first dialogue, the performer is overwhelmed by rapidly moving tape sounds. The trombone enters the dialogue again with more determination but the tape again imitates, then drives him from the stage. In the third section, the tape exhausts itself, the trombonist returns, and the two end in a draw.

HALIM EL-DABH, *Leiyla and the Poet* (1962). Also, works by Arel, Babbitt, Davidovsky, Luening, and Ussachevsky. Columbia MS 6566, "Columbia-Princeton Electronic Music Center."

Voice effects manipulated electronically conjure up a realistic world of a madman and a poet who attempt to persuade Leiyla to follow different paths. *Leiyla and the Poet* uses purely electronic sounds sparingly but obtains most of its effects by applying the tape manipulation technique of speed transposition, and electronic reverberation, to the instrumental and vocal materials prepared and recorded by the composer.

El-Dabh, born in Egypt, is United-States educated and has been a member of the Columbia-Princeton Electronic Music Center that has nurtured so many interesting composers.

Electronic Music from the University of Toronto. Works by Hugh Le Caine, Myron Schaeffer, Arnold Walter, Harvey Olmick, Robert Aitkin, Val Stephen, J. D. Robb, Jean Ivey, and Victor Grauer. Folkways 3436 (mono only).

This 1955 album is not a very original one by our present-day standards, but it was certainly exciting when first released. Today it sounds as though the experimenters were simply playing around, and the end result is a too-familiar list of electronic clichés—decaying repeats, garbled speech, shattering effects, and so forth. But there is one remarkable standout: Hugh Le Caine's *Dripsody*, which is based upon the single sound of the fall of a drop of water. Le Caine is highly ingenious in his manipulations, and the piece reminds one of the best efforts of the *Musique concrète* school of Paris in the early 1950s. All of the works on this record are products of the Toronto Studio.

DONALD ERB, *Reconnaissance; In No Strange Land.* Stuart Dempster (trombone); Bertram Turetzky (double bass); Bonnie Douglas (violin); Rand Forbes (double bass); Ralph Grierson (piano); Kenneth Watson (percussion); Michael Tilson Thomas (Moog Synthesizer); Leonard Stein (Moog polyphonic instrument); Donald Erb cond. Nonesuch H 71223.

Erb was originally a jazz trumpeter, yet apart from a few passages of *In No Strange Land*, there is little indication of that background to be heard here. Tone color is Erb's strong point; there is little shape or direction to these pieces.

This record was one of the first to bring together conventional instruments and new devices that are able to reproduce many of the effects of an electronic studio during actual performance. This technique was copied by many composers who were seeking to create "live electronic sound," as the rock musicians do. Both pieces here use conventional instruments and electronic sounds—a fascinating gambit that is attracting young composers more and more. The electronic material is treated as an intriguing extension of tone-color possibilities when these are combined with traditional instruments. *Reconnaissance* utilizes a Moog Synthesizer and a Moog keyboard instrument, which are not at all the same thing. (This distinction has led to endless confusion among audiences who watch performers "playing on a Moog" and believe that synthesized sound is being achieved.)

For *In No Strange Land*, tape tracks were realized at the Moog Studios in Trumansburg, N.Y., and instrumental tracks were realized in La Jolla, California. Here again the technical exploration of tone-color possibilities seems more successful than the musical results. The recording was another in the series commissioned by Nonesuch Records.

As a footnote to the formidable complexities of realizing electronic music, it should be noted that for *In No Strange Land* the composer required three assistants to help him move the plugs and switches of the Moog's control panels.

KENNETH GABURO, *Electronic Music. Antiphony III (Pearl-white moments).*

Antiphony IV (Poised). Exit Music I. Exit Music II (with New Music Choral Ensemble, Members of the Illinois University Contemporary Chamber Players conducted by Kenneth Gaburo). Nonesuch H 71199.

Kenneth Gaburo's two *Antiphony* works are interesting examples of the combination of electronic music with live performance. This music was conceived as a concerto for voices, and the interplay between live performers and sounds on tape is thoroughly explored. For this recording, the sixteen singers were divided into four groups (sopranos, altos, tenors, and basses), and spatially distanced from each other as well as from the loudspeakers that carried the pretaped material. The electronic taped sections are of three kinds: a simulation of live sounds; transformations (or rather transmogrifications) of these sounds beyond the capacities of human performers; and imaginative synthesized sound. The result resembles clever musical pop art at times, but there are many evocative and poetic passages.

The two *Exit Music* pieces, which serve as filler, are amusing and inconsequential electronic trifles.

PIERRE HENRY, *Le Voyage* (from the *Tibetan Book of the Dead*). Limelight LS 86049.

Le Voyage is a superb work, very long and very provocative in many respects. Henry conjures up extra-musical states instead of bombarding us with ponderous musico-mathematical theories. *Le Voyage* uses purely electronic material, and yet it suggests a relation to the *Musique concrète*, which confined itself largely to the treatment of natural and instrumental tones and noises. The electronic material is treated to recall distorted natural sounds, such as breathing or gears meshing.

Le Voyage attempts to depict in sounds the miraculous cycle of the Wheel of Life, which moves from death through reincarnation, as described by the *Tibetan Book of the Dead*. Breath is the symbol of life, and the hearer is acutely aware of the movement of air, particularly in the first and final sections of the piece. This is a gripping effect, achieved in part through the synthesis of filtered bands of "white noise."

Le Voyage is programmatic music, but not in the literal sense; rather, it is a fantastic attempt at music that may be termed "total environment." Time flows, recedes, unites, as sketched in the ancient Oriental writing.

Pierre Henry (born in 1927), was a pupil of Nadia Boulanger and Olivier Messiaen. He was one of the influential members of the *Musique concrète* group in Paris, a confrère of Pierre Schaeffer. In 1958, Henry left the group to set up his own Studio Apsome.

LEJAREN HILLER, *An Avalanche for Pitchman, Prima Donna, Player Piano, Percussionist, and Prerecorded Playback* (text by Frank Parman) (1968); *Nightmare Music from "Time of the Heathen" for Tape Alone* (1961); *Suite for Two Pianos and Tape* (1966); *Computer Music for Percussion and Tape* (1968). Royal MacDonald (pitchman); Norma Marder (prima donna); Robert Rosen (percussion); George Ritscher (audio technician); Roger Shields (piano); Neely Bruce (piano); G. Allan O'Connor (percussion). Heliodor Stereo 2549 006.

Lejaren Hiller has a large reputation in the New Music for his success in producing music by means of electronic digital computers. He was co-composer, or rather co-engineer (with Leonard Isaacson), of the *Illiac Suite* (see Chapter XV). He is also the co-author of a *Computer Cantata*, composed with Robert Baker.

In all four pieces on the present record, there are some moments that hold our interest, yet no one piece, to my ears, can be called successful. Hiller here is much concerned with combining the styles of "pure" electronic music with *Musique concrète*. The resulting stylistic mingling is not impressive.

The best piece here is *Nightmare Suite*, part of a score written for a film. Childrens' cries are superimposed on thunderish electronic sounds. The work contains a very good climax, à la Rossini, with sounds that leap higher and higher while the speed rate gallops faster and faster.

Also of interest is *Avalanche for Pitchman*, a campy fun piece which is constructed of prerecorded work from six people, including (who else?) John Cage. Percussion and player piano effects have been overlaid, and it is all a rather amusing parody of American "pitch-man" culture.

LEON KIRCHNER, *String Quartet No. 3 for Strings and Electronic Tape*. Also, Weinberg, *String Quartet No. 2*. Beaux-Arts Quartet. Columbia MS 7284.

Kirchner's study for live musicians collaborating with synchronized sound (from a Buchla) won the Pulitzer Prize in 1967. As in all music that combines traditional and electronic synthesized sound, what holds us here is chiefly the contrast of the live and synthesized sonorities. The musical appeal of Kirchner's piece is strong, and he has certainly shown us that, with high technical proficiency, much can be done in the new and challenging form of live-cum-tape material. In fact, Kirchner's aim here, if I am not mistaken, is to prove that an acceptable continuity between traditional and electronic music can be maintained, and with a gain of drama and tension.

In the ever-growing repertory of tape plus instrumental music, Morton Subotnick and Jacob Druckman, in particular, have made worthy explorations; now Leon Kirchner has achieved a highly satisfying commingling and blending of string instruments and taped sounds —so much so that the electronic materials often seem a "fifth member" of the string quartet. In other words, the possibilities of the string-quartet form, as used here, are emphatically broadened in expressiveness and imagination, and this is a real advance.

Kirchner, a musical conservative, feels it is the artist's responsibility "to get to know all the media," but he quips that he went electronic "because everybody else had given it up for dead." Kirchner, who is *not* an electronic composer, was initiated into the mysteries of the "Buchla Box" by Morton Subotnick, produced his tape portion in three days, and carried off a Pulitzer Prize on his first "electronic try." "With the old equipment it would have taken a year," he comments. Thus the old order changeth.

The Weinberg quartet, on the reverse side, is a nonelectronic, totally structured work that is devoted chiefly to rhythmic explorations and may be described as a total rhythmic experience.

OTTO LUENING, *Synthesis for Orchestra and Electronic Sound.* Also, works by McPhee and R. Legger. CRI 219.

Luening is really creating something here; the fact that he chooses, in this instance, some electronic means is of secondary import. The electronic sections are treated in the concerto-contrast tradition, with the orchestra providing the dramatic statements while the electronic medium provides the lyrical. Eventually both elements combine in a broadly expressive composition.

OTTO LUENING and VLADIMIR USSACHEVSKY, *Concerted Piece for Tape Recorder and Orchestra.* Oslo Philharmonic Orchestra, Jose Serebrier, conductor. CRI 227 USD.

> The *Concerted Piece* was composed in 1960 on commission by Leonard Bernstein and the New York Philharmonic. The music bears some resemblance to a movement from a classical concerto, with the tape recorder in the role of soloist or concertino. The first part, composed by Luening, ends with the cadenza for taped sounds alone. The second part, by Ussachevsky, makes considerable use of antiphonal interplay between orchestra and tape.

OTTO LUENING and VLADIMIR USSACHEVSKY, *A Poem in Cycles and Bells.* Also, works by Bergsma and Ussachevsky. CRI 112.

> This work was commissioned by conductor Alfred Wallenstein, who, in 1954, requested a private hearing of the entire repertoire of tape music composed both jointly and separately by Luening and Ussachevsky. He then suggested that two solo tape pieces, Luening's *Fantasy in Space* and Ussachevsky's *Sonic Contours*, could be changed and expanded into a single composition for tape recorder and symphony orchestra. The composers were immediately interested and worked on the project through the summer of 1954. *A Poem in Cycles* resulted.
>
> Following the opening for orchestra, the singable material is repeated by tape recorder with the flute as a sound source. Complex variations and transformations are accompanied by orchestra. The lyrical theme is restated by celesta, harp, English horn, glockenspiel, and cello. The second section contains a modal theme treated in canonic imitation with sounds that resemble a Balinese gamelan orchestra. Bell effects, both low and metallic and high and tinkling, create a maze of echoes. So exotic are the beauties created that even those most resistant to the idea of electronic music will find their resolution weakened. A real meeting of East and West.

OTTO LUENING and VLADIMIR USSACHEVSKY, *Tape Music.* Desto DC 6466. (The following review was written by Jon Appleton for the *Contemporary Music Newsletter*, 1970. Reprinted by permission.)

> Although only twenty years have passed since Vladimir Ussachevsky and Otto Luening made the American debut into the field of electronic

music, this recording of the historic 1952 concert at the Museum of Modern Art truly sounds like history. If you listen to Side II first, you hear early 20th-Century-Scandinavian music in the person of Otto Luening.* His two pieces, *Lyric Scene* and *Legend*, the first for flute and strings and the second for oboe and strings, are lovely, sunny works. They explore no new territory but this is obviously not their aim. *Lyric Scene* is a variation set in a new-classic vein; its formal outline is beautifully conceived and executed.

But this review is meant to be about tape music and specifically about some early pieces by Luening and Ussachevsky which appear on Side I. After hearing the Luening pieces mentioned above, the listener will be aware of the magnitude of the departure from tradition made by these two composers in the early 1950s. Today our ears are filled with the result of sophisticated electronic music equipment developed over the past ten years, and it is difficult for one who has not tried to make music with two tape recorders to appreciate the significance of these works.

Is this meant as an apology? No. *Sonic Contours, Low Speed*, and *Incantation* are fine pieces exploring a limited composition objective with startling precision. *Fantasy in Space* wears less well because of the tiresome repetition of modal fragments. *Invention in Twelve Notes* has a "flute filagree" which if detached from the repetitious ostinato would be more interesting. Part of the fault lies with the limitations of "feedback"—something not recognized at the time of composition.

OTTO LUENING and VLADIMIR USSACHEVSKY, *Rhapsodic Variations for Tape Recorder and Orchestra.* Also, works by Ibert and Read. Louisville 545–5.

An aesthetic use of electronic sounds, this music is musical first, experimental second. For a detailed discussion of the *Rhapsodic Variations*, see the biographical article on Otto Luening in this book.

SALVATORE MARTIRANO, *L's GA for Gassed-Masked Politico, Helium Bomb and Two Channel Tape.* Polydor 24–5001.

This tour de force by Martirano was one of the outstanding successes of the recent Electric Ear series of programs at New York's Electric

*Otto Luening is of Scandinavian descent, but he was born in Wisconsin.

217

REVIEWS OF SELECTED RECORDINGS

Circus. At that time a lively "gassed-masked" narrator and a vivid film were included as elements of the performance, and the recording suffers somewhat from the absence of the additional visual impacts. Nevertheless, this is absorbing, highly imaginative electronic music.

L's GA begins with the simulation of a deafening helium-bomb explosion. Then the narrator recites Lincoln's Gettysburg Address (L's GA)—with insane distortions and exaggerations. Sometimes. it all sounds like Hitler in a hash dream, sometimes it's as simple as a child's scream. The total effect is switched-on Kafka. Special note should be made of Michael Holloway's effective recitations.

ILHAN MIMAROGLU, *Bowery Bum* (1964). Also, works by Avni, Carlos, and Lewin-Richter. Turnabout TV 34004S, "Electronic Music."

The *Visual Study No. 3* is after a drawing by Jean Dubuffet. Just as the artist limited himself to India ink, the composer draws all his sound substance from a rubber band. By amplification, filtering, speed variation, and superimposition, he has created a composition that vividly interprets a painting.

MAX NEUHAUS, *Electronics and Percussion: Five Realizations*. Earle Brown, *Four Systems*. Morton Feldman, *The King of Denmark*. Sylvano Bussotti, *Coeur pour batteur*. Karlheinz Stockhausen, *Zyklus*. John Cage, *Fontana Mix-Feed*. Max Neuhaus, percussion. Columbia MS 7139.

This fascinating disc is a good example of just how dizzy experimental music in the seventies has become, and how the boundary between live and electronic music grows less fixed from year to year. "Realizations" in the title here refers to Neuhaus' contribution to the music, which is far more than the usual percussionist's "performance"; in all of these pieces of our uncertain age, the shape of the work is in varying degrees left up to the performer's disposition. The term "electronics" here is used in a liberal sense, and comes down to the fact that Neuhaus incorporates electronic resources into the performances. Neuhaus has also, as part of his "realization," extended the live sounds by means of electronics. For example, the amplified cymbals in the Earle Brown "realization" have characteristics bordering on those of electronic white noise.

The unifying theme of all the works on this record (all by luminaries of the New Music) is that the responsibility for deciding the nature of the piece is left almost entirely up to the performer, who "realizes" the final form. Thus, Earle Brown's *Four Systems* is made up of merely a group of vertical and horizontal lines of various lengths and widths (very pretty to look at); the performer is allowed freedom of choice to interpret this as he pleases. (In fact, there could be *any* number of performers, playing any number of instruments.) The choice of "Four Amplified Cymbals" was made by Neuhaus, not Brown. The performer remarks on the notes, "Rather than a strict interpretation of Brown's patterns, during the 'live' performance, I allowed my eye to pick out various combinations that seem interesting or relevant to that particular moment in the piece."

The result is not exactly music that rivets the listener. Rather, it is machine-age sounds with softened edges. But the free-form idea seems to be taking hold more and more among composers, and will lead, it is to be hoped, to something more artistically enjoyable.

The Bussotti "realization" amplifies "inadvertent" vocal grunts as well as curious sounds produced by Neuhaus' body in motion. Perhaps this is the environmental music of the future.

Feldman's (nonelectronic) piece is a pensive aural landscape with soft bell-like timbres. The work is played entirely with the fingers, and many of these soft effects, as Neuhaus remarks, are audible only in a recording—hence another valid concept of "electronic" application to a score.

Stockhausen's (nonelectronic) *Zyklus* has been greeted by the faithful as a small masterpiece. In this work, a certain amount of freedom is alloted to the performer, but within a firmly prescribed framework. Perhaps that is why it sounds more firmly structured and directed than the other "loose" works on this record. Since Stockhausen's score is in the form of a spiral, it may be read either "forward" or "backward" and can be begun at any point. The piece is over when the performer returns to his starting point. Neuhaus' version is strong, and one of the best of the many versions of this apparently durable composition.

The piece by John Cage uses charts originally prepared for an electronic tape piece. The present version consists of feedback produced by the device of attaching microphones to various percussion instruments in front of loudspeakers. For this listener, the version of

Fontana-Mix on tape in combination with Cage's *Aria* (sung by Cathy Berbarian on Time Records) is certainly more effective. As almost always has been the case until now, electronic music comes off best when mixed with other means—a dramatic voice, for example, or stage dancing.

PAUL BEAVER and BERNARD KRAUSE, *The Nonesuch Guide to Electronic Music.* Nonesuch HC 73018.

This album is less a guide to electronic music than a useful compendium of sounds that may be produced through various techniques of electronic synthesis. Most of the space on the two discs is devoted to demonstration samples of the basic signal generators used in electronic studios, and of the many modulation and filtering techniques that can be applied to such signals.

What is exasperating, however, is that the recorded examples are not clearly coordinated with the syllabus in the accompanying booklet. Trying to find out just what is going on in a particular band involves one in a bewildering procedure of skipping around in the booklet. Even then the listener cannot be quite sure of what he is listening to. Besides, there is no spoken narration preceding the samples, although this sort of demonstration cries out for such a clarifying accompaniment.

In sum, this set will have to do until a better "Guide" comes along. A harmless composition called "Peace Three" is included at the beginning of the set and is repeated at the end. Also included are a glossary and the score for "Peace Three," as well as the sixteen-page booklet discussing the basic principles of sound synthesis, which, besides the drawback already mentioned, devotes too much space to the authors' notions of electronic notation.

ARNE NORDHEIM, *Epitaffio for Orchestra and Tape.* Also, *Response I* for 2 percussions and tape. Limelight LS 86061.

Arne Nordheim is a resourceful Norwegian composer, and both pieces here explore tape-cum-live music possibilities. *Response I* (1966), for two percussion groups and tape, presents some forceful ideas with the percussionists' immediate response to the pretaped portions of sound, partly guided by graph notations.

Epitaffio is for large orchestra and tape, with the taped material consisting of electronically altered and extended dialogues between flageolets and vocalists. The most successful effect of this piece is the composer's contrasting use of tone color and contrasting effects of low and high, light and dark, and so on.

HENRI POUSSEUR, *Rimes pour differentes sources sonores* (1959). Also, works by Brown, Maderna, Penderecki, and Stockhausen. Victrola VICS-1239, "The New Music."

As the title implies, this two-movement composition combines taped electronic sounds with live instruments. In the second section, complex contrasts of timbre evolve toward simplicity.

HENRI POUSSEUR, *Scambi or Echanges* (1958). Also, works by Boucourechliev, Eisnert, Henry, Kagel, and Lig. Limelight LS 86048, "Panorama Electronique."

At first halting and abrupt, the sound material builds into a flowing contrapuntal surge of power, then returns to its duel with silence.

HENRI POUSSEUR, *Trois visages de Liege (Three Faces of Liege*, 1961). Also, works by Babbitt and Cage. Columbia MS 7051.

Three movements, "The Air and Water," "Voices of the Village," and "Forges," lend a programmatic content that brings the music into relevant focus for the listener. The second movement utilizes people of the city speaking the names of their streets and institutions. The effect is quite gripping most of the time.

MEL POWELL, *Events for Tape Recorder; Improvisation; Second Electronic Setting; Two Prayer Setting.* Also, works by Ussachevsky and Luening-Ussachevsky. CRI 227.

Mel Powell, once better known as a sideman of the Benny Goodman band, is Director of the Electronic Music Studio at Yale. His music is characterized by a delicate lyricism and a passion for clarity. The most interesting piece here is the dramatic *Events* (1963), which uses three prerecorded voices reading Hart Crane's "Legend" and electronically generated sounds. Voices and sounds are overlapped into a poem-collage. The return and repeats of isolated phrases and words create a number of subsidiary meanings and associations, thus "interpreting" the poem.

STEVE REICH, *Violin Phase; It's Gonna Rain.* Paul Zukovsky (violin); Brother Walter (preacher). Columbia Stereo MS 7265.

This is a maddening, sometimes fascinating disc, reminiscent of Terry Riley's equally maddening *In C*. Steve Reich (born 1936) studied with Milhaud and Berio and is a prominent young avant-garde musical innovator and explorer. Here he subjects small bits of sound to a kind of magnification in time, to allow us to hear things that ordinarily escape us—rather as a microscope enlarges tiny fragments and reveals hidden beauties that we could not otherwise behold.

Violin Phase is a repetition of ten notes played by Paul Zukovsky on his Stradivarius. Via tape recorder, this motif is transformed into a phase-manipulation study, with the violinist gradually speeding up his tempo against the original melody. The effect of twenty minutes of this is sheer ennui and frustration—which of course may be just what the composer intended, as "music of boredom." Reich remarks, in the liner notes for *Violin Phase*, "... a human being plays against several pre-recorded tapes of himself. In two sections of the piece the performer gives a sort of auditory "chalk talk" by simply playing one of the pre-existent inner voices in the tape a bit louder and then gradually fading out, leaving the listener momentarily more aware of that particular figure. The choice of these figures (there are many of them) is largely up to the performer."

It's Gonna Rain is a similarly harrowing and exhausting out-of-focus étude of a sidewalk preacher yelling "It's gonna rain." There are two separate versions here, both of which employ the device of gradually shifting phase relations between two or more identical repeating figures. According to the composer, "This process determines both the note-to-note (sound-to-sound) detail and the over-all form as well. ... The voice belongs to a young black Pentecostal preacher who called himself Brother Walter. I recorded him along with the pigeons one Sunday afternoon in Union Square in downtown San Francisco. Later, at home, I started playing with tape loops of his voice and, by accident, discovered the process of letting two identical loops go gradually in and out of phase with each other."

ANDREW RUDIN, *Tragoedia in Four Movements for Electronic Music Synthesizer*. Nonesuch H-71198.

This was the second of a series of electronic works commissioned by Nonesuch (the first being Subotnick's controversial *Silver Apples of the Moon*). Andrew Rudin, at the time of this release, was director of the Philadelphia Musical Academy Electronic Music Center, and this piece was produced there on a Moog Synthesizer. *Tragoedia* is "pure" electronic music, in that it contains no "live" sounds. The sole materials used are white noise and sine, triangle, rectangular, and sawtooth waveforms produced on the Moog.

One interesting aspect of this piece is Rudin's attempt to write with traditional musical procedures of form in mind. For example, the first movement contains five sections of about equal length; the first four of these sections follow a basically uncomplicated crescendo pattern, each time with greater intricacy.

Rudin also introduces ominous electronic tympani thuds, brass climaxes, and so on, in what would seem to be an attempt to unite a large-scale, four-movement electronic music symphony. Not a success, to my ears, but an interesting attempt that most other electronic composers have deliberately avoided.

ERIC SALZMAN, *The Nude Paper Sermon* (Tropes for Actor, Renaissance Consort, Chorus, and Electronics). Stacy Keach (actor); The Nonesuch Consort; Members of the New York Motet Singers conducted by Joshua Rifkin. Nonesuch Stereo H–71231.

Eric Salzman (born 1933) is perhaps our most perceptive critic of contemporary music. As a composer he offers us here what can be termed a paradigm of the ideas and ideals of so many young composers at work today.

The work is composed to texts by the American poets John Ashbery and Steven Wade. Using the medium of the phonograph record in new ways, combining actor, voices, old instruments, and tape in a cheerful eclecticism, *The Nude Paper Sermon* seeks to unite the worlds of Renaissance music, electronics, pop, politics, poetry—all the experiences of modern man in his electronic global village—to create a multi-layer sound drama. As far as mixing verbal and musical imagery, Salzman, on his own terms, succeeds. He tells us that the droning voice of the actor (Stacy Keach declaiming a mishmash of poems, speeches, and "found sounds") is intended to suggest "that endless language stream of all those who use words to manipulate others."

Perhaps Mr. Salzman wants to make a new style out of chaos, as John Cage often seems to be trying to do. Or perhaps he embraces chaos, curious to find out what can be learned from it. We are presented with sound effects consisting of contrasting speech vocal solos, choral episodes, parts for wind instruments, soprano, counter-tenor, gamba, lute, and so forth, including even "Madrigal singing with electronic graffiti." Do not search for explanations, let alone comprehension, of this music. In the composer's own words, "By and large, printed texts would be beside the point; spoken language—heard and overheard, comprehensible and incomprehensible, clear, elusive, simple, complex, logical, mystifying—is the subject matter here."

In sum, this is work that strives to achieve Zen no-mindedness. Following his own somewhat grim and prolix formula, the composer for 44 minutes and 53 seconds allows us only snatches and clues of musical slogans, as it were, and never an entirely completed musical impression. It is all carefully calculated, very shrewdly done. But to what expressive purpose or statement, besides the possible statement that there can no longer be any coherent statement, I cannot hear or tell.

The electronic sounds were realized by the composer at the Columbia-Princeton Electronic Music Center. The work was composed in "tracks" and recorded and mixed through a collaboration among composer Eric Salzman, conductor Joshua Rifkin, and producer-engineer Peter K. Siegel.

KARLHEINZ STOCKHAUSEN, *Gesang der Jünglinge (Songs of the Youths)*. Deutsche Grammophon DGG 138811.

This haunting work has been hailed as one of the rare masterpieces of electronic music, and with good reason. The composer has combined sung sounds and electronically produced ones. Only at certain points do the sung sounds become comprehensible words; often they are merely "Sound Values." Whenever speech *does* emerge in a clear form, it is to praise God, utilizing the text of Daniel 3, "Song of the Men in the Fiery Furnaces." I have seen nothing written relating this material to the death-furnaces of the Nazi concentration camps, but for this listener, at least, the reference is unmistakable.

The score calls for five groups of loudspeakers which surround the audience; according to Stockhausen, who loves claiming "firsts": "This work is the first to use the direction of the sounds and their movement in space as aspects of the form."

A chilling, impressive work.

KARLHEINZ STOCKHAUSEN, *Kontakte* for electronic sounds, piano and percussion. Refrain for three performers. Aloys Kontarsky (piano, percussion, and woodblocks), Christoph Caskel (percussion, vibraharp, and bells), Karlheinz Stockhausen (celesta, cymbales antiques). Candide 31022.

> Stockhausen has written two versions of *Kontakte*. There is a Deutsche Grammophon version (DGG 138811) of electronic instruments alone; the Candide disc here contains the version for piano and percussion in dialogue with electronic sounds.
>
> *Kontakte*, in either form, is one of Stockhausen's more satisfying pieces, even though few admirers will claim to understand it. The "contacts," it would appear, are between electronic reproductions of sounds and electronic sounds in their own right. I prefer this version with instruments, which allows more sheer diversity and inventiveness of sound. The composer himself seems to think highly of *Kontakte*, for he quotes it in several later works—*Prozession*, for example.

KARLHEINZ STOCKHAUSEN, *Mikrophonie I* for tamtam, two microphones, two filters and potentiometers. Aloys Kontarsky, Fred Alings (tamtam), Johannes Fritsch, Harald Boje (microphones), Karlheinz Stockhausen, Hugh Davies, Jaap Spek (filters and potentiometers). *Mikrophonie II* for choir, Hammond organ and ring modulators. Members of the West German Radio Chorus and the Cologne Studio Choir for New Music. Alfons Kontarsky (Hammond organ), Johannes Fritsch (timer); conducted by Herbert Schernus. Columbia MS 7355.

> To review this record according to any known aesthetic criterion is impossible. I can only describe, for those who care, some details concerning this maddening and exhausting pair of works by Germany's *Wunderkind* composer. This is a solemnly proclaimed "official" work of Stockhausen, with the composer himself in charge of the activities.
>
> *Mikrophonie II* can only be described as a turned-on musical extravaganza. Live, electronic, and electronically treated live sounds are dealt with in a spirited and deliberately chaotic manner. Some of the effects are diverting, but chaos rules—which of course may be precisely what Stockhausen intended.
>
> *Mikrophonie I* is played as follows: two people "excite" a tamtam with various materials and in various ways (rubbing, scratching, etc.); each is picked up by a directional microphone which is held nearer or further away from the source of sound, or moved about by

another person. And in turn, the sound from each channel is manipulated by someone operating an electronic filter and a potentiometer, thus further affecting timbre and pitch.

All this is done according to a very complicated chart of instructions. The result? An exasperating succession of noises, which often sounds like dogs and cats, though towards the end human voices cut in. In *Mikrophonie II*, mercifully, some musical element (plus a Hammond organ now and then) can be heard. The sounds of groups of four singers are introduced.

KARLHEINZ STOCKHAUSEN, *Opus 1970*. Aloys Kontarsky, piano; Johannes G. Fritsch, electric viola; Harald Boje, electronium; Rolf Gehlhaar, tamtam; Karlheinz Stockhausen, sound direction. Deutsche Grammophon 139461.

This long work (almost an hour) is Stockhausen's homage to Beethoven on his two hundredth birthday. Stockhausen in this piece has given each player fragments from works of Beethoven, prepared in a method that gives the fragments the characteristics of short-wave transmissions. Each of the tapes is different; each can be heard only when the player opens a loudspeaker control. The result is an improvisation on transformed Beethoven fragments which have themselves been transformed by Stockhausen in the tape process. All the music played is picked up by a microphone and further manipulated electronically, with the composer (Stockhausen, not Beethoven) at the controls, and passed through loudspeakers as part of the "live" performance.

Does it work? What is it? Numbing boredom is the net result, unless one is ready to accept the idea (popular in other arts these days), that boredom itself is a meaningful value, and may even be a legitimate artistic aim. In any case, there is no use listening to this piece as one listens to traditional music. According to Stockhausen enthusiasts (and they are many), you must yield, learn to listen "slowly" and let his "sound world" wash over you.

KARLHEINZ STOCKHAUSEN, *Prozession*, for tamtam, viola, elektronium, piano filters and potentiometers. Alfred Alings, Rolf Gehlhaar (tamtam), Johannes G. Fritsch (viola), Harald Boje (elektronium), Aloys Kontarsky (piano), Karlheinz Stockhausen (filters and potentiometers). Candide 31001.

In *Prozession* the musical process is indicated in the score by methods similar to those used by Stockhausen in his *Mikrophonie* pieces. The musical events are not given detailed notation; they are variations on phrases and sections from the composer's own earlier works. Technically, at least, the result is a brilliant display of live electronic engineering. There are many moments of vivid sound-imagination.

The pianist plays references to Stockhausen's *Klavierstuke* and *Kontakte*; the violist to *Gesang der Jünglinge* and *Momente*, the elektronium player to *Sole* and *Telemusik*. The composer himself plays the potentiometers and filters. The score indicates for each player the degree of change with which he should react—either to what he himself has just played, or to what another instrumentalist has just performed. The result, according to Stockhausen, is that an "aural tradition" is established of the collected works of Karlheinz Stockhausen.

It sounds crazy, but the net result is more than simply a string of aural effects. *Prozession* leaves one with an impression of a canvas shaped with discipline and purpose, even though it certainly is not "enjoyable." Which is perfectly okay with Herr Stockhausen.

KARLHEINZ STOCKHAUSEN, *Solo für Melodie-Instrument mit Ruckkopplung* (*Solo for Melodic Instrument and Playback System*). Also, Berio, *Sequence V*; Globoker, *Discours II*; Alsona, *Consequenza*. Deutsche Grammophon DGG 137005.

This disc is a good example of the contemporary composer's near obsession with the practically unlimited potential of the collaboration of instruments and electronic sound. In this rather maddening piece, a trombonist plays into a microphone. His performance is recorded and transmitted to him over loudspeakers after a time lag, superimposed and distorted by the composer, who is seated at the electronic control panel. The soloist then is required to react to his own sounds as they are played.

The listener is not clearly aware of what is going on in this weird mirror-play hocus-pocus, but the method is then reversed, in this version, and one hears Stockhausen's tape commenting on the live performance.

Musical values for this listener are zero here: this disc is for those who care for cabalistic instrumental-electronic gimmick manipulation.

KARLHEINZ STOCKHAUSEN, *Zyklus*. See under: Max Neuhaus, *Electronics and Percussion: Five Realizations*.

MORTON SUBOTNICK, *Silver Apples of the Moon*. Nonesuch H–71174.

> *Silver Apples* was perhaps the first piece of electronic music to be found palatable by people who detest electronic music. This work was commissioned by Nonesuch, and it is a beauty. Subotnick has accomplished that rare thing: he has created electronic music that is not wearisome, predictable, and unattractive. He has taste in sounds, and an impeccable ear for selecting and balancing his sounds. One feels that here is a formally organized piece, in the traditional sense of the term, and not merely a random stringing together of pretty and unpretty electronic sounds. The piece runs thirty-one minutes—a very long duration span for electronic music in its present state. According to Subotnick, the title, a line from a poem by Yeats, was chosen because it aptly reflects the unifying idea of the composition, heard in its pure form at the end of Part Two. Side Two is by far the more interesting, and contains a controlled crescendo at the peak, and a skipping, white-noise pattern with tremendous rhythm that will remind some listeners of a weird, electronic *Bolero*.
>
> As the liner notes proclaim rather breathlessly, "This album represents a signal event in the related history of music and the phonograph: for the first time an original, full-scale composition has been created expressly for the record medium." The piece, like all of Subotnick's electronic works, was created on the modular electronic system built by Donald Buchla of the San Francisco Tape Music Center.

MORTON SUBOTNICK, *The Wild Bull*. Electronic Synthesizer. Nonesuch H–71208.

> This recording is a successor to Subotnick's *Silver Apples of the Moon*, which Nonesuch commissioned in 1967, and which was an unprecedented success in the electronic medium. *The Wild Bull* is just as striking—in some ways, more so. Subotnick has emerged as a composer who moves about the synthesizer with a virtuoso assurance.
>
> The leitmotif of *Silver Apples* was bright, appealing bell-like tones; that of *The Wild Bull* is great primitive horns—the horns of the death-god. (The album's title is based on a three-thousand-year-old

Sumerian poem, and was chosen by Subotnick after he wrote the piece.)

The technical accomplishments of this work are many, and worth discussing. Subotnick works with the Buchla system synthesizer, which has a sequencer device at its center that can be directed to produce complex, automatic patterns and rhythms. (Subotnick also employed this sequencer although in a less pronounced manner, in *Silver Apples.*) In *The Wild Bull* he does not hesitate to utilize rock-music electronic techniques: vibrato circuits, spring-reverberation sound (Hammond "echo"), and rapid, regenerative-filter sweeps. All this brings us to the fascinating thesis that the nature of the Buchla machine-beast itself decidedly influenced the sound of the music. *The Wild Bull* is graced with a sense of orchestral spread and depth, and an unusually wide range of "voices"—not the usual predictable beeps and shrill siren wails of electronic music. And—most remarkable— *The Wild Bull* is blessed with a "worldly" sound: for once we are out of the studio, away from synthesizers and programmers. This is studio-liberated electronic music of a quality few composers since Edgard Varèse have achieved.

MORTON SUBOTNICK, *Touch*. Created on the Buchla Electronic Music System. Columbia MS 7316.

This is Subotnick's third recording following his much acclaimed *Silver Apples of the Moon* and *The Wild Bull.* Like its predecessors, *Touch* holds the listener with a sense of dramatic narrative and exposition. There is also a strong sense of rhythm present; shuttling rhythms appear and disappear, and can be recognized when reintroduced. Subotnick is fond of gigantic climaxes, and he piles them on here, contrasted with deep silences.

There is wit in all of Subotnick's music and this piece is no exception. His clean, crisp compositional lines seem to glitter with precision. For sheer technical, electronic dazzle (which is sometimes *too* slick), Subotnick has no superior today.

Why is it called *Touch?* The composer offers no explanation, but a good guess would be because this piece was realized on a Buchla sound synthesizer, which does not have the keyboard arrangement usually attached to the Moog; rather, touch-sensitive plates are used as the composer's input control touch technique manipulating device.

For this listener, *Touch* is more effectively constructed than its predecessors. Its sections are more self-sustaining; the dark-and-bright contrasts more striking (with its alternation of gamelan-like percussive sounds and long drawn-out timbres), and the buildups are stronger. There is even a sense of harmonic and melodic flow.

TORU TAKEMITSU, *Coral Island for Soprano and Orchestra; Water Music for Magnetic Tape; Vocalism Ai (Love) for Magnetic Tape*. Mutesumi Masuda (soprano), Yomiuri Nippon Symphony Orchestra, Hiroshi Wakasugi cond. RCA Victrola VICS 1334.

Toru Takemitsu (born 1930) is a remarkably talented Japanese composer who uses avant-garde Western musical techniques and is considered one of the best composers in the Orient today. Of the pieces on this disc, all but *Coral Island* (1962) were composed for magnetic tape.

The most interesting work presented here is the surrealistic item called *Vocalism Ai*. The jacket notes describe the work as a "72-hour tape montage of *ai*" over and over in different pronunciations, with various intonations and speeds. This is a dramatic number, on the bizarre side.

Water Music (1960) is longer, but far less compelling. All sound elements are sounds of drops of water, changed and given rhythm by the composer's manipulations. This is the same notion Hugh Le Caine used in *Dripsody* (Folkways 3436), but far less successfully carried out.

Coral Island is the most ambitious work here, and is set for soprano and orchestra. An intensely dramatic work, it appears to be written in a Japanese-inflected twelve-tone style. Takemitsu is a highly skillful orchestrator, but this listener prefers his excursions into tape music.

BERTRAM TURETZKY, *The New World of Sound*. Erickson, *Ricercar à 3*. Pleskow, *Three Bagatelles With Contrabass*. Childs, *Mr. T. His Fancy*; Diemente, *Quartet*. Lombardo, *Nocturne for Contrabass Alone*. Felciano, *Spectra*. Bertram Turetzky (contrabass); Nancy Turetzky (flute); Henry Larsen (clarinet); Tele Lesbines (percussion). Ars Nova/Ars. Antiqua AN 1001.

This album is largely concerned with the exploitation of novel timbral effects, made possible by the formidable virtuosity of contrabassist Bertram Turetzky, who has commissioned over one hundred pieces for his once-neglected instrument. Of special interest on this disc is Robert Erickson's *Ricercar à 3*, a tour de force for three basses—two of which have been prerecorded and are presented to us performed on tape. The composer introduces Eastern influences, microtonal inflections, and odd percussive sounds which are produced by striking the wood of the double bass. "The total double-bass" could be an apt subtitle for this work.

VLADIMIR USSACHEVSKY, *A Piece for Tape Recorder.* Also, works by Bergsma and Luening. CRI 112.

This successful piece from 1955 is an excellent introduction to electronic music. The composer invites "a variety of subjective interpretations" from each listener, "according to his own taste and imagination."

VLADIMIR USSACHEVSKY, *Of Wood and Brass.* Also, works by Luening and Powell. CRI 227.

This 1965 piece demonstrates what can be done by manipulating conventional instrumental sound sources. The composer attempts "to remove the final sound materials as far as possible from the quality of the original instrumental sounds." The title is derived from the materials used in composing the work.

VLADIMIR USSACHEVSKY, *Creation-Prologue* (1962). Also, works by Arel, Babbitt, Davidovsky, El-Dabh, and Luening. Columbia MS 6566, "Columbia-Princeton Electronic Music Center."

Four full choruses, antiphonally treated, are electronically manipulated for maximum interpretation of the text. An electronic accompaniment, for this listener, suggests torch-lit bridges in a cavernous, mother-earth conception.

VLADIMIR USSACHEVSKY, *Wireless Fantasy.* Also, works by Luening and Powell. CRI 227.

In this work the age of "wireless" communication—that is, early radio —is interpreted in a nostalgic concoction of sounds. Written to honor Lee De Forest, whose inventions led to the development of radio broadcasting, the composition includes such now-seldom-heard sounds as code signals produced on old spark-generators, as well as a fragment from Wagner's opera *Parsifal*, "as a result of Mr. Ussachevsky's learning that Lee De Forest used this work as the first ever to be broadcast anywhere."

EDGARD VARÈSE, *Poème électronique*. Columbia MS 6146.

> Created for the Philips Radio Corporation's pavilion at the Brussels Exposition, this classic of modern music, as well as most of the other works by Varèse, is discussed at length in the Chapter II of Part Two in this book.

Voice of the Computer. Pieces by M. V. Mathews, Jean-Claude Risset, James Tenney, J. R. Pierce, R. N. Shepard, and Wayne Slawson. Decca DL 71080.

> This record contains experimental pieces by some of the leading figures in computer music. The most interesting is the *Eight-Tone Canon* by J. R. Pierce. Most musical sounds (aside from those produced by some percussion instruments) are made up of overtones, which are harmonic frequencies. By using the computer, however, one can produce tones with overtones at any frequencies. In this way one can achieve additional control over the way in which the various tones of a chord blend together. Such control has been used by Dr. Pierce in his *Eight-Tone Canon* to cause the texture to develop gradually from a very thin sound at the beginning, to a thick sound in the middle, to a thin timbre at the end.

RUTH WHITE, *Flowers of Evil*. An electronic setting of the poems of Charles Baudelaire, composed and realized by Ruth White. Limelight LS 86066.

> *Flowers of Evil* is an impressive example of the possibilities of electronic music "set" to poetry. The composer used her own voice as the generator of the original sounds to be altered or "dehumanized." Changes of timbres were achieved by filters. Tape speed changes were used to control pitch. Choruses were created by combining slight delays with multiple track recordings. Sound waves and white noise have been injected into the shape of some words, thus changing the quality of their sound but not the flow of their delivery. Altogether, this is an absorbing performance, although some purists may prefer their Baudelaire straight.

CHARLES WUORINEN, *Time's Encomium.* Synthesized and processed synthesized sound. Nonesuch H 71225.

This much-praised disk has the distinction of being the first work of electronic music to win the Pulitzer Prize in music (1968), and deserves to be discussed at length. Wuorinen has achieved a near breakthrough: he has written electronic music that absorbs the listener (no mean feat for a thirty-minute piece) and that is impressed at all times with the stamp of an original and authoritative musical personality. This authoritativeness—taken for granted in superior music written for conventional instruments—is remarkable because so much of electronic music still sounds lamentably indistinguishable from the next composer's dehumanized bleeps and sirenlike glissandi. A true artistic personality is at work here, and you hear it.

This work was produced, over the course of more than a year (from January 1968 to January 1969), on the RCA synthesizer at the Columbia-Princeton Center. From the evidence of this recording, Wuorinen ranks as one of the few composers who have succeeded in mastering the secrets of that notoriously complex leviathan. The RCA synthesizer produces only notes of definite pitch (the twelve tempered notes of the octave) and Wuorinen uses more or less the notes of the chromatic scale. As a result, there is a distinct twelve-tone tinge to his piece.

Time's Encomium is totally, even rigidly controlled. There is none of the improvisation or indeterminacy of the John Cage school here. Time is all; segments of time measured by the clock, instead of by metric pulse. The work as a whole, in Wuorinen's words, "consists of a core of synthesized music, most of which appears in Part One, surrounded and interlaced with analog-studio transformations of that music. The synthesized can always be identified by its clarity of pitch and the familiar, almost instrumental sounds of its constituent events. The process almost always contains reverberation. Thus, metaphorically, the listener stands in the midst of this synthesized music, which presents itself to him with maximum clarity, and stretching away from him, becoming more and more blurred in detail, the various transformations—from the slightly altered to the unrecognizable.

This is a solid work, with a solid sense of order. Wuorinen is one of the new breed of young composers who move with ease and assurance from compositions for live performers to electronic works; in *Time's Encomium* he has delivered a satisfying, provocative example of what electronic music can be in the hands of a capable and thoroughly musical composer.

Wuorinen remarks that he has made an effort to bring to the electronic medium a sense of human involvement and freedom—"the inflection" of a "live" performance. He has succeeded. One senses the composer's hand, his personal participation, a human involvement.

Interestingly, *Time's Encomium* sounds exactly right for home listening from an electronic box—the phonograph. Thus the circle is satisfyingly completed: music ordered for performance by the phonograph and designed for hearing at home rather than in the concert hall.

A special salute is due to Nonesuch Recordings, which are rapidly becoming the Count Esterhazy of contemporary music. This work was written as a commission specifically for the Nonesuch series of electronic music.

YANNIS XENAKIS, *Concrèt P-H II; Diamorphoses II; Orient-Occident III; Bohor I.* Nonesuch H 71246.

Although he is enormously influential among composers of electronic music, Xenakis has written comparatively little music in this medium himself. Curiously, like composer Gyorgy Ligeti, he creates such bizarre effects with his ingenious orchestration for live instruments that people often believe that it is electronic music they are hearing.

The works on this disc were all composed in the late 1950s and early 1960s. *Concrèt P-H II* (the numeral after each piece refers to the specific version of the piece we are hearing—Xenakis sometimes does several), a work dating from 1958, was written for performance at the Philips Pavilion at the Brussels Fair of that year. This famous pavilion was the site of Edgard Varèse's great triumph of electronic music, the *Poème électronique.*

Xenakis at that time (see section on Xenakis in Part Four) was the dauntless associate of Le Corbusier, who had designed the spectacle of the pavilion, with Xenakis as collaborator on the architecture. Xenakis was also of great aid to Varèse in keeping at bay the conservative directors of Philips, who were aghast at Varèse's music. Just then beginning to emerge as an experimental composer himself, Xenakis contributed *Concrèt P-H* to the pavilion's program. The piece was intended to prepare the public psychologically for the futuristic ambiance that was waiting for them inside. Four hundred loudspeakers lined the interior of the shell in a spectacular stereophonic effect. Xenakis took advantage of these "sonic scintillations" for his own work. The architecture was based entirely on nondevelopable ruler surfaces, or "hyperbolic paraboloids"—*paraboloides hyperboliques*—hence the title "P-H."

Xenakis says that he tries to suggest in his music the roughness of the concrete and its coefficient of internal friction, which is echoed in the timbre of the sonic scintillations, as well as the common emanation, or swarm of sound, from architecture and music. The composer also describes the music as "lines of sound moving on complex paths from point to point in space, like needles darting from everywhere."

Nonesuch bills this disc as "Electronic-Acoustical Music" and "a more advanced form of *Musique concrète*," but it is purely *Musique concrète*—the splicing of innumerable little pieces of tape containing sounds drawn from many sources, which are then assembled and manipulated on tape by the composer—and does not need this pretentious apellation.

Xenakis loves to write dense notes about the awesomely recondite mathematical computations he has made for the bulk of his music. But what we have here is first-rate *Musique concrète*, constructed in the manner of the period, with the composer shaping his sounds in space, much as a sculptor sculpts his clay or marble. Xenakis unabashedly seeks to infuse his music with mysticism and poetry.

Diamorphoses II, composed a year earlier (the present version was rewritten in 1958), is devoted to the emotional effect of what Xenakis himself calls "ugly sounds"—crashing railroad cars, jet planes, earthquake sounds—all the aural ugliness and horror of our noise-polluted age. The work is composed in four parts, and each section modulates slowly into the next, with the dividing line between them not always clearly distinguishable. Somewhere in the middle of the piece one can detect the high-pitched percussive sound of the tiny sheep bell worn by animals in the pastures of Greece, recalling, for some, the arcadian paradise that has been aurally lost to us. This is an effective piece, and will remind some listeners of an electronically souped-up version of Antheil's *Ballet mécanique*, Honegger's *Pacific 321*, and other this-is-the-ugly-noise-of-our-ugly-civilization successes of the 1920s and thirties.

Orient-Occident III, a much more sophisticated work, was created in 1959–1960. This is a successful piece, and perhaps may be, as James Brody hails it on the liner notes of the record, "Along with *Gesang der Jünglinge* of Stockhausen and the *Poème électronique* of Varèse, one of the classics of the first decade of European electronic music . . . and a milestone in the use of new materials to create powerful structures."

The work is particularly striking for Xenakis' successful utilization of what seems to be his primary technique: gradual transformation within a cloud of events, a technique he applies with equal skill to his instrumental music.

Orient-Occident was written for a UNESCO film that depicted a museum tour, comparing objects and sculpture of various world cultures and showing the interaction between the art of Europe, Asia, and Africa since antiquity. This is an attractive theme for a composer of today who believes in "one world culture, one music," and Xenakis has made the most of it. Different transitions and changes are constantly employed, as the sounds flow in a virtual study of overlapping, superimposition, sudden shift, cross-fading, and so on. Xenakis uses many ingenious techniques here, such as a cello bow drawn over cardboard boxes, gongs, and metal rods. The result is a work of eery and slowly varying sounds. The final section contains some otherworldly (or perhaps insectlike) cries, which are ionosphere signals transformed into sound. At one point the composer also introduces an excerpt, much slowed down, from his own orchestral work *Pithoprakta*.

Xenakis deals with "mass structures"—that is, individual particles subordinated to phenomena consisting of many particles moving together and assuming a larger shape. According to Brody's liner notes, "Xenakis's concept of mass structure was rooted in the profound impact and impressions of the powerful forces of rebellion, insurgency, and conflict which he received during his participation in the Greek resistance to Nazi occupation." He adds, "Poetic natural events, too—such as crickets at night, swarms of locusts, rain, and hailstorms—exhibited this character of mass structure, which, Xenakis felt, had to be introduced into music."

All this sounds a bit much, but Brody assures us that "A poetic description of these influences is given in the first chapter of Xenakis's book, *Musique Formalles* (Paris, 1963), to be released in translation by the Indiana University Press."

Orient-Occident III is certainly a very effective tone-color piece and one of the most listenable and absorbing works in the electronic medium so far composed.

The last and most important work on this strong program, *Bohar I* (1962), occupies all of side one and is intended for a ballet choreography. (The composer's own stunning design for stage backdrops appears on the record cover.) *Bohor* has been acclaimed by most critics. Alfred Frankenstein writes, "Put this work alongside [Debussy's] *Pelléas* [et Mélisande], the *Sacre* [*du Printemps*, by Stravinsky], *Pierrot Lunaire* [by Schönberg]: it's one of the scores whereby the music of our century will be measured." Whether Frankenstein's heady enthusiasm is warranted or not, *Bohor* is certainly an arresting achievement. The work seems to be profound—which of course cannot be said about the majority of electronic pieces. It was composed in 1962 at the studios of the *Groupe des recherches musicales* of the French Radio (O.R.T.F.), and is dedicated to Pierre Schaeffer, the innovator of *Musique concrète*.

The piece was realized on eight channels, here mixed to two. For those who dote on the fanciful appellations that composers blithely give their creations, *Bohor* was the name of a brave knight of the Round Table. According to Xenakis, whose prose is even more dense than his music, the work is "monistic with internal plurality, converging and contracting finally into the piercing angle of the end."

In its cosmic sound and dimensions, and in its concept of a single, evolving, musical substance, the music itself curiously resembles the superb *I of IV* by the gifted American composer of electronic music, Pauline Oliveros, although the latter piece is produced by sine waves and their transformations, rather than by the *Musique concrète* techniques used by Xenakis. (According to the record jacket notes, the sound sources for *Bohor* were nothing more (nor less) than various Oriental bracelets and other jewelry, and a Laotian mouth organ.)

The remarkable acceptance of Xenakis' scores by lovers of New Music is discussed in Part Four. It also should be noted that in May 1965 a Xenakis Festival was held in Paris, where, in October 1968, *Bohor* was performed on "Xenakis Day" during the city's International Contemporary Music Week. The audience was quite broken up by the sensational ending of *Bohor*, with its enormous, surgingly high sound level that can shatter your phonograph. People were screaming, standing and cheering. According to the composer's estimate, "Seventy percent of the audience loved it, and the rest hated it."

Electronic Pop Music

WALTER CARLOS, *Switched-On Bach*. Sinfonia from Cantata No. 29; Two-Part Inventions: in F; in B flat; in D minor; Jesu, Joy of Man's Desiring; Well-Tempered Clavier, Bk. 1: Preludes and Fugues: No. 2, in C minor; No. 7, in E flat; Chorale Prelude, Wachet auf; Brandenburg Concerto No. 3, in G. Walter Carlos, synthesizer, with the assistance of Benjamin Folkman. Columbia MS 7194.

Switched-On Bach, released late in 1968, quickly became the most hailed and the most damned record of electronic music ever made. It is also, by a wide margin, the most popular electronic disc yet produced—over a million dollars in sales were chalked up by Columbia on this one. It is one of the most discussed records of recent times; everyone, including Glenn Gould, saw fit to write a thinkpiece on *Switched-On Bach*. *Life* gave it a column, and Walter Carlos appeared on the Today Show to explain the mysteries of the Moog to the millions.

The music consists of a program of well-known short Bach pieces as rendered by an electronic synthesizer, the Moog. (This record also can claim to have made *Moog* a familiar word among people who are far removed from electronic music.) The electronic reconstruction by Carlos is fiendishly clever, and endlessly fascinating. One reason it startled everyone so much was that in it Carlos triumphantly revealed that electronic instruments had reached a sophistication few people suspected they had attained. The Moog, of course, is capable of infinite shadings of timbre, and Carlos has taken full advantage of this characteristic to shape phrases—much the way a Segovia shapes them by conjuring up tone colors on his guitar. The Moog also proved itself superbly able to bring out Bach's lines and planes (particularly in the Brandenburg), even for many listeners who had barely realized they were there. Against the Moog's immaculate performance, orchestral versions sound, at first hearing, uncomfortably thick and unclear.

Carlos has not hesitated to introduce some wry humor here. In the second movement of the Brandenburg, for example, at a place where improvisation seems to be indicated, he comes up with some weird electronic effects, sounds that seem to resemble bird twitterings, water gushing over stones, glissando swipes, and so on. Whether all this is permissible or enjoyable depends on how you feel about the inviolability of Johann Sebastian Bach. Glenn Gould objected to another aspect: "There are, nevertheless, moments of rather questionable taste—the predictable and Mantovani-ish Siren-sound with which the main tune in *Jesu, Joy of Man's Desiring*, salutes those commuter serenades your favorite Good Music Station spins to bring Dad safely down the freeway at 5:15 P.M."

These lapses aside, Carlos is unflaggingly musical, and keeps everything within the spirit, if not the letter, of Baroque laws of improvisation. If one can overlook the great whooshes of sound, aquatic burblings, and what seem to be Chinese wood blocks and ominous beeps for science fiction movies, one is immediately aware how remarkably the synthesizer separates the complex strands of Bach's polyphony.

The most valid complaint against *Switched-On Bach*, I believe, is that it gives people an entirely wrong idea of what electronic music is all about. It is about original, creative music; it is not about Mickey Mouse, amazingly lifelike Baroque trumpet and oboe sounds, or electronic evocations of the Baroque organ, no matter how ingeniously the job is done. Nevertheless, *Switched-On Bach* incontestably put electronic music on the map for the general public—for better or worse.

WALTER CARLOS, *The Well-Tempered Synthesizer*. Selections from Bach, Monteverdi, Scarlatti, and Handel. Columbia MS 7268.

Billed by Columbia as the "Sensational Follow-Up to *Switched-On*

Bach," this album is far less satisfying and has sold far less well than its illustrious predecessor. Perhaps we got the point in the first album. It's all here again—simulated oboe tones with a soft, controlled vibrato, tidal waves of eighteenth-century sixteenth notes, and grandiose transcriptional effects that remind one uncomfortably of Stokowski's notorious Bach transcriptions. But Stokowski, nevertheless, introduced Bach to millions of the other generation who would not otherwise have dreamed of listening to him, and perhaps Walter Carlos will have the same effect on the switched-on kids.

The Moog Strikes Bach. Bach, *Toccata and Fugue in D minor,* S. 565; Mozart, *Eine kleine Nachtmusik,* K. 525; *Sonata for Piano, in A,* K. 331; *Turkish March;* Chopin, *Etude in G flat,* Op. 10, No. 5; Rachmaninoff, *Vocalise,* Op. 34, No. 14; Prokofiev, *Prelude, Op. 12, No. 7;* Wurman, *Thirteen Variations on a Theme of Paganini.* Hans Wurman, synthesizer. RCA Red Seal LSC 3125.

Those expecting another *Switched-On Bach* from this record will be disappointed. The transcriber-performer on this disc, Hans Wurman, simply lacks the dazzling ingenuity of Walter Carlos, who realized the famous electronic Bach disc. The overall effect here is of Mozart *et al.* played on a weird mammoth organ, with endless stops and variety. The result is yawning dullness. In fact, this record only makes us appreciate more just how effective Walter Carlos was with *Switched-On Bach.*

THE BEATLES, *Magical Mystery Tour.* Capital SMAL 2835.

Several cuts on this album use tape-sound in a vivid and successful manner. In *I Am the Walrus* a complex all-at-once radio-tuning cacaphony, laden with snatches of voice fragments and unidentifiable sounds, wraps up the piece. In *Blue Jay Way,* as well as in *Flying,* backward vocal and instrumental tape passages are employed.

THE BEATLES, *Sgt. Pepper's Lonely Hearts Club Band.* Capitol MAS-2653.

In this famous album, recorded voices in the background cascade in a rolling sea of sound. In *A Day in the Life,* the listener is spun out electronically into a turned-on fantasy world.

PERREY AND KINGSLEY, *Kaleidoscopic Vibrations,* Vanguard VSD-79264.

Pure fake, pure bubblegum music. Arrangements of standard pop tunes and a few originals for electronic sounds plus percussion. A much more interesting recording by these composers is *In Sound From Way Out*, Vanguard 7922.

JIMI HENDRIX, *The Jimi Hendrix Experience*. Reprise 6261.

Interwoven with a heavy rhythmic chord style are intriguing electronic sounds, especially on side two, *Third Stone from the Sun*. On this cut, backward-tape rhythm and half-speed voices are employed.

PINK FLOYD, *Ummagumma*. Capitol STBB388.

A stunning accomplishment by a superb British rock group, this record contains an outpouring of highly imaginative electronic effects superimposed on the live music sections. The result, to my ears, is by far the most successful use of electronic possibilities by any pop group thus far. At one point a voice yells something that sounds like, "Do ya dig it, Edgard Varèse?" Varèse would have dug it. Don't miss this one.

Ceremony. An electronic Mass, written by Pierre Henry and Gary Wright; rock music performed by Spooky Tooth; electronic music by Pierre Henry.

This piece is one of the best of the religious rock efforts much in vogue these days, with expert and tasteful electronic treatments by that French veteran of electronic music, Pierre Henry, who goes all the way back to the giddy days of *Musique concrète* studios in Paris in the 1950s.

The United States of America. Columbia CS 9614.

This record was the first to be promoted as "Electronic Rock." The album lists "electric harpsichord, electric drum, electric bass, and electric guitar," as well as electric violin and "electronic music." It all sounds electronically turned on, but unfortunately it is just another gimmicky pop record. Burbles and glissandi abound, all predictable, but the music itself never takes off.

The record opens and closes with a wide-open, sock-it-to-me Production Number that is a sound collage of everything you have ever heard, but the whole thing just doesn't jell, let alone come off. Electronic tinsel, despite all the pretentious circuitry.

PAUL BEAVER and BERNARD KRAUSE, *In a Wild Sanctuary*. Warner Brothers stereo WB-1850.

Beaver and Krause created the pioneering album, *The Nonesuch Guide to Electronic Music*. What they offer us here is a harmless mishmash of *Musique concrète*, blues piano, rock sounds, and other-worldly sounds on a Moog Synthesizer. This album seems to be trying (unsuccessfully), to cash in on the present vogue for flashy, semi-spooky electronic music that has hit the "background-music" market.

GEORGE HARRISON, *Under the Mersey Wall; No Time or Space*. Apple ST 3358 stereo.

Harrison is, of course, an illustrious Beatle, and has been experimenting for some time with electronic possibilities (*Revolution Nine* by the Beatles remains one of the landmarks of electronic music). Of the two products offered here, the first was made in England; the other in California, with the assistance of Bernard Krause, the co-author (and co-composer) or the *Nonesuch Guide to Electronic Music* album.

Nothing exactly eventful is to be heard on this disc; most prevalent are the predictable droning effects which so many rock musicians utilize to suggest drugs and space-tripping.

MICHAEL CZAJKOWSKI, *People the Sky*. Cardinal VCS 10069.

Judging by the effect aimed for by the groovy album cover, this would seem to be way-out psychedelic rock; instead, it turns out to be very soundly constructed electronic music by a solidly trained musician who was a student of Persichetti, Sessions, and Berio. The score was created on the Buchla modular electronic music system, and realized at the Composers' Workshop at the New York University School of Arts Intermedia Program.

Environments. Volume One: *The Psychologically Ultimate Seashore; Optimum Aviary*. Atlantic 66001, or from Syntonic Research, Inc., 663 Fifth Avenue, NYC 10022.

A fast-selling underground record, this is a kind of anti-noise-pollution musical nirvana. Or, more precisely, *Environments* is a multispeed record that creates the surf sound on one side and the twitterings of thirty-two kinds of birds on the other. It can be played, with wildly differing effects, at 16 1/2, 45, or 33 1/3 rpm. The company claims, "*Environments* is an aid in everything from speed-reading to love-making—even turning on." It also observes that ninety percent of its purchasers are single people. In any case, it's fun, and tranquilizing.

Environments, Volume Two: *Tintinnabulation; Dawn at New Hope, Penn.* Atlantic SD 66002.

More "contemplative sound." *Tintinnabulation*, which is solemnly billed as a "thought enhancer," uses bell sounds as a sound source. Like Volume One, it can also be played at any speed, in full stereo. Producer Irv Teibel says, "Imagine five different bells, each as big as an average room, which are sounded very, very softly and reverberate for minutes afterwards. The sound seems to float in the air, slowly moving around the room as a physical presence." Peace. Like Volume One, this recording was calculated on an IBM 360.

CHAPTER XVII

A Partial Discography of Electronic Music on Recordings by Peter Frank

The following symbols have been used in the preparation of this discography:
*The work is for electronic sound with live *accompaniment*
**Non-electronic work available on record to bring the composer's discography up to date
†Recording uses a live electronic instrument, usually the Theremin or Ondes Martenot; taped electronic sounds are not present; only records produced in the United States are listed (1) licensed for public performance by BMI (2) licensed for public performance by others (3) performing rights status in the United States unascertainable as of June 1, 1970.
Where the information was available the publisher is also listed.

AITKEN, ROBERT
Noesis (1) Folkways FM 33436
Alpha Film Music

ALMURO, ANDRE
Phonolite I and II (3) Mouladji/
Festival
EMZ 13514 (mono)
Structure rouge (3) Mouladji/
Festival
EMS 13510 (mono)

AMM
*Improvisation (3) Mainstream
MS 5002

ANHALT, ISTVAN
Composition #3 (1960) (1)
Composition #4 (1962) (1) Allied

Record 17
Berandol Music

APPEL, KAREL
Musique barbare (3) Philips (Neth.)
99954 DL (mono)

AREL, BULENT
Electronic Music #1 (1)
Fragment (1)
Music for Sacred Service: Prelude
and Postlude (1) Orpheum SN-3
Purist Ent. Ltd.
Stereo Electronic Music #1 (1)
Columbia MS 6566
ACA

ARTHUYS, PHILIPPE
Boite a musique (3) Ducretet-

Thomson
DUC 8 (mono)
Et l'enfant resta seul (3) Disques
Lumen LDI-511 (45 rpm, mono)
Le crabe qui jouait avec la mer (3)
Boite a musique BAM LD 070 (mono)

ASHLEY, ROBERT
*Untitled Mixes (1) ESP Disk 1009
*Wolfman (1) ESP Disk 1009; Source
1 (included in "Source" magazine #4)
Unpublished

ASUAR, JOSE VINCENTE
Preludia "La Noche" 1 (3) Jornadas
de Musica Experimental JME ME
1-2 (mono)

AUSTIN, LARRY
*Accidents (1) Source 2 (included in
"Source" magazine #4)
Composer Performer Edition

AVNI, TZVI
Vocalise (3) Turnabout TV 34004S

BABBITT, MILTON
Composition for Synthesizer (1)
Columbia MS 6566
Ensembles for Synthesizer (1)
Columbia MS 7051
*Philomel (1)
Co-written with John Hollander,
Acoustic Research Record
**All Set (1) Columbia C2S 831
**Compositions for four instruments
(1)
**Composition for viola and piano (1)
CRI 138 (mono)
Associated Music Publishers, Inc.

**Du (3) Son-Nova S-1
**Partitions (2) RCA Victor LSC
7042

BADINGS, HENK
*Armageddon (1) Point Park College
KP 101 (mono)
C. F. Peters Corp.
*Capriccio for violin and two sound
tracks (3)
Genese (3)
Evolutions (3) Limelight 86055
Kain et Abel (3) Philips (Neth.)
400036 AE (45 rpm, mono)
*Pittsburgh Concerto (3) American
Wind Symphony SR 4S-3263
**Louisville Symphony (#7) (3)
Louisville 56-6 (mono)
**Sonata #2 for 2 violins (3)
**Contrasts (3) Washington
University
TS-XM 913/4 (mono)

BARRAQUE, JEAN
Etude (3) Barcley 89005 (mono)

BAYLE, FRANCOIS
Andromede (3)
Titan (3) Musique pour l'image
MPI/LP-105 (mono)
Lignes et points (3)
L'archipel (3)
Espaces inhavitables (3) Philips (Fr.)
836895 DSY
L'oiseau chanteur (3) Candide CE
31025, Philips (Fr.) 836895 DSY
*Pluriel (3) Philips (Fr.) 836894 DSY
Vapeur (3) Boite a musique BAM
5072

BEAVER, PAUL, and KRAUSE, BERNARD L.
Nonesuch Guide to Electronic Music (2)
Peace Three (2) Nonesuch HC 73018

BEECROFT, NORMA
*From Dreams of Brass (3)
RCA Canada CCS 1008

BEHRMAN, DAVID
Wave Train (3) Source 1 (included in "Source" magazine #4)

BERIO, LUCIANO
*Differences (1) Mainstream MS 5004; Time S8002
Momenti (1) Limelight LS 86047
Mutazioni (3) RAI (Fonit) included in "Elettronica" magazine #3) (mono)
Perspectives (1) Compagnia generale del Disco ESZ-3
Visage (1) Turnabout TV 34046S
**Circles (3) Mainstream MS 5005; Time S8003; Wergo WER 60021
**Rounds (1)
Rounds with Voice (1) Wergo WER 60028
**Sequenza I (1) Mainstream MS 5014; Time S8008; Wergo WER 60021
**Sequenza III (1) Wergo WER 60021
**Sequenza IV (1) Candide CE 31015
**Sequenza V (1) Deutsche Grammophon DGG 137005; Wergo WER 60021

**Serenade I (3) RCA Victrola VICS 1313
**Sinfonia (1) Columbia MS 7268
Universal Edition/Theodore Presser

BERK, ERNEST
Extracts from works (3) Conroy International Film Library (mono)

BLACHER, BORIS
Elektronische Impulse (1) Wergo WER 60017
Bote & Bock

BLOMDAHL, KARL-BIRGER
*Aniara (1) Columbia M2S 902
*Aniara Suite (1) Columbia MS 7176
Schott/Belwin-Mills Publishing Corp.

BOISSELET, PAUL
*Le robot (3) Societe Francaise de productions phonetiques 30006
*Symphonie Jaune (3)
*†Symphonie rouge (3) Societe Francaise de productions phonographiques 30007

BONDON, JACQUES
†Kaleidoscope (3) Musical Heritage Society MHS 988

BOUCOURECHLIEV, ANDRE
Texte I (3) Limelight LS 86048
Texte II (3) Boite a musique BAM LD 071 (mono)

BOULEZ, PIERRE
Etude II (sur sept sons) (3) Barclay 89005 (mono)

BOZIC, DARIJAN
*Kriki (3) Desto DC 6474-77

BRESS, HYMAN
*Fantasy (1) Folkways FM 3355
(mono)
Alpha Film Music

BRISCOE, DESMOND
Electronic Sound Picture (3)
His Master's Voice CLP 3531
(45 rpm, mono)

BROWN, EARLE
*Four Systems—Four amplified
cymbals (1) Columbia MS 7139
*Times Five (1) Boite a musique
BAM 5072
**Nine Rare Bits (1) Wergo WER
60028 Unpublished
**Available Forms I (1) RCA
Victrola VICS 1239
**Music for violin, cello and piano (1)
**Music for cello and piano (1)
Hodograph (1) Mainstream
MS 5013; Time S8007
Associated Music Publishers, Inc.

BRUN, HERBERT
Futility (3) Heliodor HS 25047
Klange Unterwegs (3)
Anepigraphe (3) Amadeo AVRS 5006
(mono)

BRUYMEL, TOM
Collage Resonance II (3)
Reflexen (3)
Relief (3) Europese Fonoclub
EFC 2501 (mono)

BRYANT, ALLEN
*Pitch Out (1) Source 2 (included
in "Source" magazine #4)
Composer Performer Edition

BUSSOTTI, SYLVANO
*Coeur pour batteur—Positively Yes
(1) Columbia MS 7139
Universal Edition/Theodore Presser

CAGE, JOHN
*Aria with Fontana Mix (2)
Mainstream MS 5005; Time S8003
Fontana Mix (2) Turnabout
TV 34046S
Fontana Mix-Feed (2) Columbia
MS 7139; Mass Art M-133
(4 different performances, mono)
Cartridge Music (2) Mainstream
MS5015; Time S8009
*HPSCHD (with Lejaren Hiller) (2)
Nonesuch H-71224
*Indeterminacy (2) Folkways
FT 3704 (mono)
*Solos for Voice 2 (2)
Odyssey 32160156
*Variations II (2) Columbia
MS 7051; Jornadas de Musica
Experimental JME ME 1-2 (2
versions, mono)
Variations IV (2) part I: Everest 3132
part II: Everest 3230
Williams Mix (2) Avakian JCS-1
*Atlas Eclipticalis (2)
*†Winter Music and Cartridge Music
(2) Deutsche Grammophon
DGG 137 009
**Amores (2) Time S8000
**Concerto for prepared piano and
orchestra (2) Nonesuch H-71202;
Avakian JCS-1
**Dance (2) Folkways FX 6160
(mono)
**Sonata for clarinet (2) Advance

FGR-4 (mono)
**Sonatas and interludes for prepared
piano (2) CRI 199 (mono);
Avakian JCS-1
**Variations I (2) Wergo WER 60033
**Variations III (2) Deutsche
Grammophon DGG 139442

CANTON, EDGARDO
Voix inoues (3) Jornadas de Musica
Experimental JME ME 1-2 (mono)

CARLOS, WALTER
*Variations for flute and electronic
sound (2)
*Dialogues for piano and electronic
sound (2) Turnabout TV 34004S

CARSON, PHILIPPE
Turmac (3) Boite a musique
BAM 5072

CASTIGLIONI, NICCOLO
Divertimento (3) Compagnia
generale del Disco ESZ-3

CHARPENTIER, JACQUES
*†Lalita (3) Musical Heritage Society
MHS 821

CHEYNE, JY-VAN
*Three Chapters of Lao-Tze's Tao
Teh Ching (3) Jade JLP 1001 (mono)

CLEMENTI, ALDO
Collage II (3) Compagnia generale
del Disco ESZ-3

CONSTANT, MARIUS
*Le joueur de flute (3) Philips (Fr.)
A76. 050R (mono); Radiodiffusion-
Television Francaise (mono)

CUNNINGHAM, JAMES
Tic-Toc Fugue (2) Dunwich D-159
(45 rpm, mono)

CZAJKOWSKI, MICHAEL
People the Sky (1) Vanguard
VCS 10069
Ryerson Music Publishers, Inc.

DAVIDOVSKY, MARIO
Electronic Study #1 (1) Columbia
MS 6566
Unpublished
Study #2 (1) Orpheus SN-3
Purist Ent. Ltd.
*Three Synchronisms for solo
instruments and electronics (1)
CRI SD204
McGinnis and Marx

DESSAU, PAUL
*Lukullus (Ausschnitt von 3 für
Subharcord) (3) Eterna 820423-4
(mono)

DOBROLOWSKI, ANDRZEJ
Muzyka na tasme magnetofonowa #1
(3) Muza Warsaw Fest 211 (mono)
*Muzyka na tasme magnetofonowa i
oboj solo (3) Muza Warsaw Fest 244
(mono)

DOCKSTADER, TOD
Apocalypse (2) Owl ORLP-6;
Owl ORLP-7 (2 fragments)
Drone (2)
Water Music (2) Owl ORLP-7
Eight Electronic Pieces (1) Folkways
FM 3434 (mono)
Groton Music, Inc.
Luna Park (2)

Traveling Music (2) Owl ORLP-6
Omniphony I (with James Reichert)
(2) Owl ORLP-11
Quatermass (2) Owl ORLP-8

DONATONI, FRANCO
Quartetto III (3) Compagnia generale
del Disco ESZ-3

DRUCKMAN, JACOB
*Animus I (2) Turnabout TV 34177

DUCKWORTH, WILLIAM E.
Gambit (2) Capra 1201

DUFRENE, FRANCOIS, and
BARONNET, JEAN
U 47 (3) Limelight LS 86047

EATON, JOHN
Prelude to "Myshkin" (2)
Piece for solo Syn-Ket #3 (2)
*Song for R.P.B. (2) Decca 710154
Soliloquy for Syn-Ket (2)
Duet for Syn-Ket and Moog
Synthesizer (2)
*Thoughts on Rilke (2) Decca 710165

ECHARTE, PEDRO
Treno (3) Jornadas de Musica
Experimental JME ME 1-2 (mono)

EGER, JOSEPH
*Classical Heads (1) Probe
CPLP 4516
Crossover Music Co.

EIMERT, HERBERT
Elektronische Musik (lecture) (1)
Variante einer Variationen von
Anton Webern (1)

Zu Ehren von Igor Stravinsky (1)
Wergo WER 60006 (mono)
Epitaph für Aikichi Kuboyama (1)
Sechs Studien (1) Wergo WER 60014
Etude uber Tongemische (1)
Funf Stucke (1)
Glockenspiel (1) Deutsche
Grammophon DGG LP 16132 or
17242 LPE (mono)
Selection I (1) Limelight LS 86048
Universal Edition/Theodore Presser

EL-DABH, HALIM
Leiyla and the Poet (1)
Columbia MS 6566
Symphonies in sonic vibrations—
Spectrum #1 (1) Folkways FX 6160
(mono)
C. F. Peters Corp.

ENGLERT, GIUSEPPE
*Vagans animula (3) Deutsche
Grammophon DGG 139442

EPSTEIN, BRUNO
Essay III (3)
Essay IV (3) Paravan Synton 57357-8
(45 rpm, mono)

ERB, DONALD
*Reconnaissance (1)
*In No Strange Land (1) Nonesuch
H-71223
Unpublished

ERICKSON, ROBERT
*Ricercar a 3 (1) Ars Nova An 1001
ACA

FASSETT, JAMES
Symphony of the Birds (1) Ficker

FR 1002 (mono)
James Fassett Pub.

FERRARI, LUC
*Compose-Composite (3) Philips
(Fr.) 836894 DSY
Etude aux sons tendus (3)
Etude aux accidents (3) Boite a
musique BAM LD 070 (mono)
Tautologos I (1) Boite a musique
BAM 5072; Gravesaner Blatter
EP ML 48
Tautologos II (3) Boite a musique
BAM LD 070 (mono)
Tete et queue de dragon (3) Candide
31025; Philips (Eur.) 835487 AY
Visage V (3) Limelight LS 86047

FONGAARD, BJOERN
Homo Sapiens for tape (3)
EMI CSDS-1088

GABURO, KENNETH
Exit Music I: The Wasting of
Lucrecetzia (2)
Exit Music II: Fat Millie's Lament (2)
*Antiphony III: (Pearl-white
moments) (2)
*Antiphony IV: (Poised) (2)
Nonesuch H-71199
Lemon Drops (2)
For Harry (2) Heliodor HS 25047

GASLINI, GIORGIO
Corri, nella miniera si odono voci (3)
Voce del Padrone QELP 8086 (mono)

GASSMANN, REMI, and
SALA, OSKAR
Electronics (1) Westminster

WST 14143
E. B. Marks Music Corp.

GERHARD, ROBERTO
*Collages (Symphony #3) (2)
Angel S36558
Mills Music, Inc.
Excerpts from "DNA in Reflection"
(3) Southern Library of Recorded
Music MQ 760 (45 rpm, mono)

GLOBOKAR, VINKO
*Discours II (3) Deutsche
Grammophon DGG 137005

GRAINER, RON
Giants of Steam (3) Decca (Eng.)
STO 8536 (45 rpm)

GRAUER, VICTOR
Inferno (1) Folkways FM 33436
Alpha Film Music

GRUBER, HEINZ KARL
Konjugationen (3) Serenus Sep 2000
(mono)

GUTTMAN, NEWMAN
Pitch Variations (3) Decca DL 79103;
Bell 122227 (mono)

HAMBRAEUS, BENGT
*Constellations II (3) Limelight
LS 86052
Tetragon (3)
*Rota II (3) Riks LP-75

HAMM, CHARLES
*Canto (3) Heliodor HS 25047

HAMPTON, CALVIN
*Catch-Up (1)

*†Triple Play (1) Odyssey 32160162
C. F. Peters Corp.

HELIER
*Labyrinth for cello and tape (3)
Orion 7021

HELLERMANN, WILLIAM
Ariel (1) Turnabout TV 34301
ACA

HENRY, PIERRE
Apocalypse de Jean (3) Philips (Fr.)
837923/25
Tam-Tam III (3)
Batterie fugace (3)
Musique sans titre (3) Ducretet-
Thomson DUC 8 (mono)
Cinq histoires etranges (3)
Musique et Modernite (2 extracts),
extracts from Adrienne Mesurat
and Pochette surprise (3)
Radiodiffusion-Television Francaise
(mono)
Entite (3) Limelight LS 86048
*La mariage de la feuille et du cliche
(cantata by Milhaud) (3) Vega
DR 30 SL (mono)
La reine verte (3) Unidisc
STE 30 3005
L'Evangile selon St. Jean (interludes)
(3) Unidisc PM 30 Jn 01-07 (mono)
L'Evangile selon St. Luc (interludes)
(3) Unidisc PM 30 Lc 09-17 (mono)
L'Evangile selon St. Marc (interludes)
(3) Unidisc PM 30 Mc 27-33 (mono)
L'Evangile selon St. Matthieu
(interludes) (3) Unidisc PM 30 Mt

19-25 (mono)
Le voile d'Orphee (1953 version,
2 extracts) (3) Supraphon DV 6221
(mono)
L'Homme du XXIe Siecle
(background music) (3) Unidisc
EX 33 145 (45 rpm, mono)
Le Martyre de Polycarpe et Ignace
d'Antioche (background music) (3)
Unidisc UD 25 123 (mono)
L'occident est bleu—L'an 56 (for
poems by Claude Pascal) (3)
Discolivre (mono)
Ma faim et vous (background music)
(3) Unidisc EX 33 195 (45 rpm,
mono)
Malefices (3) Philips (Eur.) 432762
BE (45 rpm, mono)
*Mass for Today (3)
The Green Queen (3) Limelight
LS 86065
Orphee (3) Philips (Eur.) 835484 LY
Saint-Exupery (background music)
(3) Unidisc UD 25 103 M (mono)
Spatiodynamismes I and II (3)
Edition du Griffon (incl. in book,
Nicholas Schoffer, 45 rpm, mono)
Tam-Tam IV (3)
Astrologie (3)
Antiphonie (3)
Vocalises (3) Ducretet-Thomson
DUC 9 (mono)
Variations for a Door and a Sigh (3)
Limelight LS 86059

HILLER, LEJAREN
*Computer Cantata (with Robert

Baker) (2) Heliodor HS 25053
*Machine Music (2) Heliodor
HS 25047
Peroration (Electronic Study #7)
(2) Jornadas de Musica Experimental
JME ME 1-2 (mono)
*Avalanche (2)
*Suite for two pianos and tape (2)
*Computer Music for tape and
percussion (2) Heliodor 2549006

ICHIYANAGI, TOSHI
*Extended Voices (1) Odyssey
32160156
*Life Music (1) Nippon Victor
SJV 1501
*Music for Strings #2 (1) Toshiba
3ER 188 (mono)
Music for Tinguely (1) Minami
Gallery (incl. in catalogue of 1963
Tinguely exhibition, 45 rpm, mono)
Situation (1) Nippon Victor SJU 1515
C. F. Peters Corp.

ISHII, MAKI
Hamon-Ripples (3) Nippon Victor
SJU 1515
Kyoo (3) Nippon Victor SJX 1004

IVEY, JEAN EICHELBERGER
Pinball (2) Folkways FM 33436

JACOBS, HENRY
Chan (1)
Logos (1)
Rhythm Study #8 (1)
Electronic Kabuki Mambo (1)
Folkways FSS 6301

Sonata for Loudspeakers (1)
Folkways FX 6160 (mono); Folkways
FS 3861 (full version, mono)
Tape Loops (1)
Rhythms (1) Folkways FX 6160
(mono)
Alpha Film Music

JANSON, ALFRED
*Canon (3) Limelight LS 86061

JOHNSTON, BEN
*Casta Bertram (2) Nonesuch
H-71237

KAGEL, MAURICIO
*Phantasie for organ with obbligati
(1)
Deutsche Grammophon DGG 137003
Transicion I (1) Limelight LS 86048
*Transicion II (1) Mainstream
MS 5003 or Time S 8001
**Improvisation ajoutee (3) Odyssey
32160158; Wergo WER 60033
**Match for 3 players (1)
Music for Renaissance instruments
(1)
Deutsche Grammophon DGG 137006
Universal Edition/Theodore Presser

KIRCHNER, LEON
*String quartet #3 (1) Columbia
MS 7284
Associated Music Publishers, Inc.

KOENIG, GOTTFRIED MICHAEL
Klangfiguren II (3) Deutsche
Grammophon DGG LP 16134
or 17243 LPE (mono)

KOMOROUS, RUDOLF
Nahrobek Malevicuv (1) Supraphon
DV 6221 (mono)
Universal Edition/Theodore Presser

KOTONSKI, WLODZIMIERZ
Etiuda (3) Muza Warsaw Fest 200
(mono)
Mikrostruktury (3) Muza Warsaw
Fest 211 (mono)

KRENEK, ERNST
Quintona (1) Jornadas de Musica
Experimental JME ME 1-2 (mono)
Ernst Krenek (S. P.)
Pfingstatorium—Spiritus Intelligentiae,
Sanctus (1) Deutsche Grammophon
DGG LP 16134 or 17244 LPE
(mono)
Unpublished

KUBICZEK, WALTER
*Ein Stadtbummel, Fox für
Subharcord und Tanzorchester (3)
Eterna 720205 (mono)

KURTH, ADDY
Der faule Zauberer (3) Eterna 720205
(mono)

KYROU, MIREILLE
Etude I (3) Philips (Eur.) 835487 AY

LANDOWSKI, MARCEL
*†Concerto for Ondes Martenot (3)
Musical Heritage Society MHS 988

LANZA, ALCIDES
*Plectros II (3) Jornadas de Musica
Experimental JME ME 1-2 (mono)

LE CAINE, HUGH
Dripsody (1) Folkways FM 33436
Alpha Film Music

LEWIN, DAVID
Study #1 (3) Decca DL 79103;
Bell 122227 (mono)
Study #2 (3) Decca DL 79103

LEWIN-RICHTER, ANDRES
Study #1 (3) Turnabout TV 34004S

LIGETI, GYORGY
Artikulation (1) Limelight LS 86048
Schott/Belwin-Mills Publishing Corp.
**Atmospheres (1) Columbia MS
6733 or Columbia MS 7176; Wergo
WER 60022 or MGM S-1E13ST
Universal Edition/Theodore Presser
**Aventures (1)
Nouvelles Aventures (1) Candide
CE 31009; Wergo WER 60022
**Concert for cello and orchestra (1)
Wergo WER 60036
**Etude #1, "Harmonies" (3)
Candide CE 31009; Deutsche
Grammophon DGG 137003
**Lux Aeterna (1) Deutsche
Grammophon DGG 137004;
Wergo WER 60026;
MGM S-1E13ST; Columbia
MS 7176
**Volumina (1) Candide CE 31009;
Deutsche Grammophon
DGG 137003; Wergo WER 60022
C. F. Peters Corp.

LINDBLAD, RUNE
Satellite (3) Paravan Synton 57357-8
(45 rpm, mono)

LONGFELLOW, GORDON
Notes on a History of the World,
Part 3 (1) 350-2 (1) Folkways
FSS 6301
Alpha Film Music

LOUGHBROUGH, WILLIAM
For the Big Horn (1) Folkways
FSS 6301
Alpha Film Music

LUCIER, ALVIN
*North American Time Capsule:
1967 (1) Odyssey 32160156
Berandol Music

LUENING, OTTO
*Gargoyles (1) Columbia MS 6566
*Synthesis for orchestra and electronic
sound (1) CRI 219 USD
**Fantasia for organ (1) CRI 219
USD
**Lyric Scene (1) Desto DC 6466
Fantasy in Space (1) Desto DC 6466;
Folkways FX 6160 (mono)
**Prelude to Hymn Tune (1)
Desto DC 6429
C. F. Peters Corp.
Legend (1) Desto DC 6466
**Symphonic Fantasy (1)
**Kentucky Rondo (1) CRI 103
(mono)
**Two Symphonic Interludes (1)
Desto DC 6429
Low Speed (1)
Invention in twelve tones (1)
Moonflight (1) Desto DC 6466
Highgate Press

LUENING, OTTO, and
USSACHEVSKY, VLADIMIR
*Carlsbad Caverns, Music from Wide
Wide World (1) RCA Victor
Suite from King Lear (1) CRI 112
(mono)
ACA/BMI Writer
Incantation (1) Desto DC 6466
Highgate Press
*Concerted Piece (1) CRI 228 USD
*Poem in Cycles and Bells (1) CRI
112 (mono)
*Rhapsodic Variations for tape
recorder and orchestra (1)
Louisville 545-5 (mono)
C. F. Peters Corp.

LUNDSTEN, RALPH
Energy for Biological Computer (3)
Suite for electronic tape (3)
Odeon E 061-34052

LUNDSTEN, RALPH, and
NILSSON, LEO
Kalejdoskop (3)
Aloha Arita (3) Sveriges Radio LPD 1

MAAS, GUNTER
Etude XIIa (3)
Etude XIIIa (3)
Komposition XI (3)
Komposition XII (3) Die Junge
Galerie 7 PAL 2917-8 (included in
book *Bilder und Klangbilder*) (45
rpm, mono)
Komposition III (3) Lempertz
Galerie (45 rpm, mono)

MACHE, FRANCOIS-BERNARD
Prelude (3) Philips (Eur.) 835487 AY

Soleil rugueux (3) Gravesaner Blatter EP ML 48
*Synergies (3) Philips (Fr.) 836894 DSY
Terre de feu (3) Boite a musique BAM 5072; Candide CE 31025 (2nd version)
Volumes (3) Boite a musique BAM LD 071 (mono)

MacINNIS, DONALD
*Collide-a-Scope (2)
Golden Crest S-4085

MADERNA, BRUNO
Continuo (3) Limelight LS 86047
Musica su due dimensioni (II) (3) Compagnia generale del Disco ESZ-3
Notturno (3) RAI (Fonit) (included in "Elettronica" magazine #3) (mono)
**Concerto for oboe and chamber orchestra (3) RCA Victrola VICS 1312
**Honeyreves (3) Mainstream MS 5014; Time S8008
**Hyperion 3 (3) Wergo WER 60029
**Serenata #2 (3) Mainstream MS 5004; Time S8002

MAGNE, MICHEL
Carillon dans l'eau bouillante (3)
Concertino triple (3)
Larmes en sol pleureur (3)
Memoire d'un trou (3)
Meta-mecanique saccadee (3)
Self-Service (3) Paris 313001 (mono)

MALEC, IVO
Dahovi (3) Candide 31025

Reflets (3) Boite a musique BAM 5072
*Tutti (3) Philips (Fr.) 836894 DSY

MALOVEC, JOZEF
Orthogenisis (3) Turnabout TV 34301
Vyhybka (3) Supraphon DV 6221 (mono)

MARIN, ROGER
Natural Pipes (1) Folkways FX 6160 (mono)
Alpha Film Music

MARTIRANO, SALVATORE
*L's GA (2) Polydor 24-5001
*Underworld (2) Heliodor HS 25047

MATHEWS, MAX V.
Bicycle Built for Two (3)
The Second Law (3)
May Carol (3)
Joy to the World (3) Decca 79103
Cyclic Study (3)
Masquerades (3)
Pergolesi Development (3)
Substitution Study (3) Gravesaner Blatter EP ML 372 (45 rpm, mono)
Numerology (3) Decca 79103, Bell 122227 (mono)
Three against Four (3) Bell 122227 (mono)

MAXFIELD, RICHARD
Night Music (1) Odyssey 32160160
Pastoral Symphony (1)
Bacchanale (1)
Amazing Grace (1)
Piano Concert for David Tudor (1) Advance FGR-8
Unpublished

MAYUZUMI, TOSHIRO
Campanology (1) Nippon Victor
SJU 1515
Mandare (3) Nippon Victor SJX 1004
1964 Tokyo Olympics Music (1)
King SKK 122
**Bacchanale (1)
**Phonologie Symphonique (1)
Angel S36577
**Mandala Symphony (1) Odyssey
32160152
**Nirvana Symphonia (1) Mainstream
MS 5006; Time S8004
**Piece for prepared piano and
strings (1) Louisville S-636
**Prelude for string quartet (1)
Deutsche Grammophon
DGG 137001
**Samsara (1) Louisville S-666
C. F. Peters Corp.

MAYUZUMI, TOSHIRO, and
MOROI, MAKOTO
Variations sur 7 (1) Nippon Victor
SJU 1515; Universal Recording
(Tokyo ALP 1009) (mono)
C. F. Peters Corp.

MAZUREK, BOHDEN
Bozzetti (3) Turnabout TV 34301

MELLNAS, ARNE
Intensity 5/6 for tape (3)
EMICSDS-1088

MERCURE, PIERRE
Tetachromie (1) Columbia MS 6763
Unpublished

MESSIAEN, OLIVIER
*†Turangalila Symphony (3) RCA
Victor LSC 7051
*†Trois petites liturgies dans la
presence divine (2) Columbia
MS 6582; Music Guild MS 142
†Fete des belles eaux (3) Musical
Heritage Society MHS 821

MILHAUD, DARIUS
*La riviere endormie (3) Festival
FLD 76 (mono)
*†Suite for Ondes Martenot and piano
(3) Musical Heritage Society
MHS 821

MIMAROGLU, ILHAN
Agony (1) Turnabout TV 34046S
Le Tombeau d'Edgar Poe (1)
Intermezzo (1) Turnabout TV 34004S
Six Electronic preludes (1)
*Piano music for performer and
composer (1) Turnabout TV 34177
Duchess Music Corp.
Bowery Bum (1) Turnabout
TV 34004S
Unpublished

MIYOSHI, AKIRA
Ondine (3) Time 2058

MOROI, MAKOTO
Shosanke (3) Nippon Victor SJX 1004

MUMMA, GORDON
*Mesa (1) Odyssey 32160158
Music from the Venezia Space
Theater (1) Advance FGR-5 (mono)
*Peasant Boy (1) ESP Disk 1009
The Dresden Interleaf, 13 February
1945 (1) Jornadas de Musica
Experimental JME ME 1-2 (mono)
Unpublished

MUSICA ELETTRONICA VIVA
*Spacecraft (3) Mainstream MS 5002

NIKOLAIS, ALWIN
Aeolus (1)
Eruptions and Evolutions (1)
Fetish (1)
Fixation (1)
Glymistry (1)
Illusional Frieze (1)
Lyre (1)
Lythic (1)
Paraphrenalia (1)
Prismatic Forest (1)
Shivare (1) Hanover HM 5005
(mono)
Chroseonics Music

NILSSON, LEO
That Experiment HZS (3) Odeon
E061-34052

NITSCHKE, MANFRED
Ferdinands Zauberhauschen (3)
Litera (45 rpm, mono)

NONO, LUIGI
*La Fabrica Illuminata (1) Wergo
WER 60038
Schott/Belwin-Mills Publishing Corp.
*Ricorda cosa ti hanno fatto in
Auschwitz (1) Wergo WER 60038
Sinon N. V.

NORDHEIM, ARNE
*Epitaffio (3)
*Response I (3) Limelight LS 86061

NUOVA CONSONANZA GRUPPA
*Credo (3) Deutsche
Grammophon DGG 137007

*Improvisations (3) RCA Italiana
MILDS 20243

OLIVEROS, PAULINE
I of IV (3) Odyssey 32160160

ORAM, DAPHNE
Electronic Sound Patterns (3) His
Master's Voice 7EG 8762
(45 rpm, mono)

PARMEGIANI, BERNARD
Danse (3) Candide 31025
Bidule en Re (3)
Capture ephemere (3)
*Violostres (3) Philips (Fr.) 836889
DSY

PENDERECKI, KRZYSZTOF
Psalmus 1961 (2) Supraphon
DV 6221 (mono)
**Capriccio for violin and orchestra
(2) Nonesuch 71201
**De Natura Sonoris (2) Nonesuch
71201; Philips PHS 900184
**Dies Irae (Auschwitz Oratorio) (2)
**Polymorphia (2) Philips PHS
900184
**Passion according to St. Luke (2)
Philips PHS-2-901; RCA
Victrola VICS 6015
**Psalmen Davids (2)
**Anaklasis (2)
**Fluorescences (2)
**Stabat Mater (2) Wergo
WER 60020
**Quartetto per Archi (2) Deutsche
Grammophon DGG 137001
**Sonate for cello and orchestra (2)
Wergo WER 60020 or WER 60036

**Threnody for the Victims of Hiroshima (2) Philips PHS 900141 or PHS-2-901; RCA Victrola VICS 1239

PFEIFFER, JOHN
Electronomusic: 9 Images (2)
RCA Victrola VICS 1371

PHILIPPOT, MICHEL
Ambiance I (3) Boite a musique
BAM LD 070 (mono)
Ambiance II (3) Boite a musique
BAM LD 071 (mono)
Etude (3) Ducretet-Thomson DUC 9 (mono)
Etude III (3) Candide CE 31025
Maldoror (3) Boite a musique
BAM LD 705-6 (mono)
Rhinoceros (3) Vega T 31 SP 8003 (mono)

PIERCE, JOHN R.
Molto Amoroso (3)
Five against Seven (3)
Random Canon (3)
Melodie (3) Decca DL 79103
Stochatta (3)
Beat Canon (3)
Variations in Timbre and Attack (3)
Decca DL 79103; Bell 122227 (mono)

POPP, ANDRE
*Helsa Popping et sa musique siderante (3) Philips (Fr.) 680201 NL (mono)

POUSSEUR, HENRI
Electre (1) Universal Edition

UE 13500
*Jeu de Miroirs de Votre Faust (3)
Wergo WER 60026
*Rimes pour differentes sources sonores (3) RCA Victrola VICS 1239
Scambi (3) Limelight LS 86048
Trois visages de Liege (1)
Columbia MS 7051
**Madrigal III (1) Everest 3170
**Sept versets des psaumes de la penitence (1) Wergo WER 60026
Universal Edition/Theodore Presser

POWELL, MEL
Electronic Setting I (2) Son-Nova S-1
Events (2)
Second electronic setting (2)
CRI 228 USD

RAAIJMAKERS, DICK
Contrasts (2) Limelight LS 86055

RANDALL, JAMES K.
*Lyric Variations for Violin and Computer (1) Vanguard VCS 10057
Ryerson Music Publishing, Inc.

REA, JOHN
Synergetic Sonorities (1) Allied 16
Iroquois Press

REICH, STEVE
Come Out (1) Odyssey 32160160
It's Gonna Rain (1)
*Violin Phase (1) Columbia MS 7265
Unpublished

RIEDL, JOSEF ANTON
Daniel-Henry Kahnweiler-Erzahltes Leben (3) Deutsche Grammophon DGG 18738-9 (mono)

Zwei Studien für elektronische Klange (3) Supraphon DV 6221 (mono)

RILEY, TERRY
*A Rainbow in Curved Air (1)
*Poppy No Good and the Phantom Band (1) Columbia MS 7315
Reed Streams (1) Mass Art M-131 (mono)
Unpublished

ROBB, JOHN DONALD
Collage (2) Folkways FM 33436

RUDIN, ANDREW
Tragoedia (3) Nonesuch H-71198

RUDNIK, EUGENIUSZ
Dixi (3) Turnabout TV 34301

SAHL, MICHAEL
*Mitzvah for the Dead (1) Vanguard VCS 10057
Ryerson Music Publishing, Inc.
Tropes on the Salve Regina (3) Lyrichord LLST 7210

SALA, OSKAR
A fleur d'eau (3)
Der Fluch der gelben Schlange (3)
Metronome MEP 6043 (45 rpm, mono)
Berliner Kaleidoskop (3)
Das Magische Band (3)
Die Traume des Herrn Jules Verne (3)
Ici Mars (3)
Improvisation mit dem Rauschgenerator (3)
Stahl, Thema mit Variationen (3)
Unter der Oberflache (3) Gravesaner Blatter ML 308 (45 rpm, mono)

Five improvisations on magnetic tape (3) Westminster WST 14143

SALZMAN, ERIC
*The Nude Paper Sermon (2)
Nonesuch H-71231

SAUGUET, HENRI
Aspect sentimental (3) Boite a musique BAM LD 070 (mono)

SCHAEFFER, MYRON
Summer Idyl (with Arnold Walter and Harvey Olnick) (1)
Dance R4÷3 (1) Folkways FSS 6301
Alpha Film Music

SCHAEFFER, PIERRE
Etude aux animes (3)
Etude aux allures (3) Boite a musique BAM LD 070 (mono)
Etude aux objets (3) Philips (Eur.) 835487 AY
Flute Mexicaine (3)
Etude aux torniquets (3)
Le voile d'Orphee (3)
Etude aux chemins de fer (3)
Etude pathetique (3) Ducretet-Thomson DUC 8 (mono)
Interlude (Phedre) (3) Groupe de Recherches Musicales de L'O.R.T.F.
GRC 9071 (45 rpm, mono)
Les paroles degelees (3)
L'Oiseau RAI (3) Radiodiffusion-Television Francaise (mono)
Objets lies (3) Candide CE 31025

SCHAEFFER, PIERRE, and HENRY, PIERRE
Bidule en Ut (3) Ducretet-Thomson

DUC (mono), Radiodiffusion-
Television Francaise (mono)
Deux aspects de piano (3) Ducretet-
Thomson DUC 8 (mono)
Le Capitaine Nemo (3)
Orphee 51 (3) Radiodiffusion-
Television Francaise (mono)
Symphonie pour un homme seul (3)
Oiseau R.A.I. (3) Ducretet-Thomson
DUC 9 (mono)

SCHAEFFER, PIERRE, and
REIBEL, GUY
Solfege de l'objet sonore (3) Editions
du seuil ORTF-SR 2 (includes
selections by 8 composers of
musique concrète, mono)

SCHUBEL, MAX
f# (3)
Joyeux Noel (3) Opus One #7

SCHWARTZ, ELLIOTT
*Aria #4 (2) Advance FGR-7
(mono)

SHIBATA, MINAO
Improvisation (3) Nippon Victor
SJX 1004

SIKORSKI, TOMASZ
*Antyfony (3) Muza Warsaw Fest
212 (mono)

SMILEY, PRIL
Eclipse (3) Turnabout TV 34301

SOUFFRIAU, ARSENE
Extracts from works (3) Conroy
International Film Library (mono)
Etude en Galvanise (3)

Etude #1 sur piano prepare (3)
Impressions sur l'Electronic 30 (3)
Video Moods (mono)
Variations sur l'Electronic 30 (#s 1
and 5) (3)
Variations sur un son de piano (3)
Variations sur un son de tambour (3)
Alpha 1009 (45 rpm, mono)

SPEETTH, SHERIDAN D.
Theme and Variations (3) Decca
DL 79103

STEPHEN, VAL T.
Fireworks (1)
The Orgasmic Opus (1) Folkways
FM 33436
Alpha Film Music

STOCKHAUSEN, KARLHEINZ
Gesang der Jünglinge (1) Deutsche
Grammophon DGG 138811;
DGG LP 16133 or 17243 LPE (mono)
Hymnen (1) Deutsche Grammophon
DGG 139421/2
Kontakte (1) Deutsche Grammophon
DGG 138811; Candide CE 31022
*Mikrophonie I (1)
*Mikrophonie II (1) Columbia
MS 7355
*Momente (1) Nonesuch H-71157
*Prozession (1) Candide CE 31001
*Solo für Melodie-Instrument mit
Ruckkopplung (1) Deutsche
Grammophon DGG 137005
Studie I (1) Deutsche Grammophon
DGG LP 16133 or 17243 LPE
(mono)
Studie II (1) Deutsche Grammophon

260

DGG LPEM 19322 (mono);
DGG LP 16133 or 17243 LPE (mono)
*Telemusik (1)
*Mixtur (1) Deutsche Grammophon
DGG 137012
**Gruppen (1)
**Carre (1) Deutsche Grammophon
DGG 137002
**Klavierstucke I-XI (1) CBS
32210008
**Klavierstucke VIII (1) Candide
CE 31015; CBS 32110008
**Klavierstucke X (1) Mace 9091;
CBS 32110008
**Kontra-Punkte (1) RCA Victrola
VICS 1239
**Nr. 5 Zeitmasse (1) Odyssey
32160154
**Refrain (1) Mainstream MS 5003;
Time S8001; Candide CE 31022
**Zyklus (1) Mainstream MS 5003;
Time S8001; Columbia MS 7139;
Mace 9091
Universal Edition/Theodore Presser

STRANG, GERALD
Composition #4 (1) Jornadas de
Musica Experimental JME ME 1-2
(mono)
ACA

STRANGE, ALLEN
Two X Two (3) Capra 1201

SUBOTNICK, MORTON
Electronic preludes, interludes to
"2001" (2) Columbia MS 6167
Silver Apples of the Moon (2)

Nonesuch H-71174
Touch (2) Columbia MS 7316
The Wild Bull (2) Nonesuch H-71208

SWICKARD, RALPH
*Sermons of St. Francis (3) Orion
702

TAKEMITSU, TORU
Eurydice-La Mort (3)
Relief Statique (3) Universal
Recording (Japan) ALP 1009 (mono)
Sky Horse and Death (3) Nippon
Victor SJU 1515
Vocalism Ai (1) RCA Victrola
VICS 1334; Universal Recording
(Japan) ALP 1009 (mono)
Water Music (1) RCA Victrola
VICS 1334
**Coral Island (1) RCA Victrola
VICS 1334
Metric Music, Inc.
**Asterism (1)
Green (November Steps II) (1) RCA
Victor LSC 3099
**The Dorian Horizon (2) RCA
Victor LSC 3099; Columbia MS 7281
**Ki No Kyoku (1) Columbia
(Japan) OS 373-N
**November Steps (1) RCA Victor
LSC 7051
**Requiem for strings (1) RCA
Victor LSC 3099; King SKF 3004
C. F. Peters Corp.
**Textures (3) Odyssey 32160152

TALCOTT, DAVID
Trilogy (1)

Loop Number 3 (1) Folkways
FSS 6301
Alpha Film Music

TANENBAUM, ELIAS
*Improvisations and Patterns for
Brass and Tape (1) Desto
DC 6474-77
ACA

TENNEY, JAMES
Noise Study (3) Decca DL 79103

THIENEN, MARCEL VAN
*La relantie (3) Boite a musique
BAM LD 037 (mono)

TOGNI, CAMILLO
Recitativo (3) Compagnia generale
del Disco ESZ-3

TOYAMA, MICHIKO
*Aoi-no-Ue (1)
*Waka (1) Folkways FW 8881
(mono)
Alpha Film Music

TRYTHALL, GILBERT
*Entropy (1)
Golden Crest S-4085
Unpublished

USSACHEVSKY, VLADIMIR
Creation-Prologue (1) Columbia
MS 6566
Metamorphosis (1)
Linear Contrasts (1)
Improvisation #4711 (1) Orpheum
SN-3
Of Wood and Brass (1)

Wireless Fantasy (1) CRI 228 USD
Piece for tape recorder (1) CRI 112
(mono)
Sonic Contours (1) Desto DC 6466;
Folkways FX 6160 (mono)
Transposition (1)
Reverberation (1)
Composition (1)
Underwater Waltz (1) Folkways
FX 6160 (mono)
ACA

VAGGIONE, HORACIO
Cuentos infantiles (3) Fonotex
EDD 4001-3 (45 rpm, mono)
*Sonata IV (3) Jornadas de Musica
Experimental JME ME 1-2 (mono)

VANDELLE, ROMUALD
Crucifixion (excerpts) (3) Boite a
musique BAM LD 070 (mono)

VARESE, EDGARD
*Déserts (1) Columbia MS 6362
Poème Electronique (1) Columbia
MS 6146
**Ameriques (1) Vanguard
Everyman S-274
**Arcana (1) Columbia MS 6362;
RCA Victor LSC 2914
**Density 21.5 (1) Columbia
MS 6146; Candide CE 31028;
EMS 401 (mono); Coronet 1291
(mono); Wergo WER 60029
**Hyperprisms (1) Columbia
MS 6146; Candide CE 31028
**Ionisation (1) Columbia MS 6146;
Candide CE 31028; Urania 5106;

EMS 401 (mono); Folkways
FX 6160 (excerpt, mono)
**Nocturnal (1)
**Ecuatorial (1) Cardinal VCS 10047
**Octandre (1)
**Integrales (1) Columbia MS 6146;
Candide CE 31028
**Offrandes (1) Columbia MS 6362;
Candide CE 31028
Colfranc Music Publishing

VLAD, ROMAN
Ricercare elettronica (3) Compagnia
generale del Disco ESZ-3

WEHDING, HANS HENDRIK
*Concertino (3) Eterna 720205
(mono)

WHITE, RUTH
Seven Trumps from the Tarot Cards
(2)
Pinions (2) Limelight LS 86058
Flowers of Evil (2) Limelight
LS 86066

WHITTENBERG, CHARLES
*Electronic Study II with contrabass
(1) Advance FGR-1 (mono)
Associated Music Publishers, Inc.

WILSON, GALEN
Applications (3) Capra 1201

WILSON, OLLY
Cetus (3) Turnabout TV 34301

WISZNIEWSKI, ZBIGNIEW
3 Postludia electrone (3) Muza
Warsaw Fest 211 (mono)

WUORINEN, CHARLES
Time's Encomium (1) Nonesuch
H-71225
ACA

XENAKIS, IANNIS
Analogique A + B (3)
Concrete P.H. (3) Philips (Eur.)
835487 AY
Diamorphoses (3) Boite a musique
BAM LD 070 (mono)
Orient-Occident (3) Limelight
LS 86047
**Achorripsis (1) Angel S36656
Bote & Bock
Polla ta Dhina (3)
ST/10 = 1-080262 (3) Angel S36656
**Akrata (3) Angel S36656; Columbia
MS 7281; Nonesuch H-71201
**Atrees (3)
Morisma-Amorisma (3)
ST/4 (3)
Nomos Alpha (3) Angel S36650
**Herma (3) Angel S36655
**Metastasis (3)
Eonta (3) Vanguard VCS 10030
**Pithoprakta (3) Vanguard
VCS 10030; Nonesuch H-71201

YUASA, JOJI
Projection esemplastic (3) Nippon
Victor SJU 1515

ZELJENKA, ILJA
Studio 0,3 (3) Supraphon DV 6221
(mono)

ZIMMERMANN, BERND ALOIS
Tratto (1) Wergo WER 60031
Schott/Belwin-Mills Publishing Corp.

A SAMPLING OF ELECTRONIC POP

THE BEATLES
Sgt. Pepper's Lonely Hearts Club
Band (1)
Capitol SMAS 2653

JOSEPH BYRD and the
FIELD HIPPIES
American Metaphysical Circus (1)
Columbia MS 7317

THE COPPER-PLATED
INTEGRATED CIRCUIT
Plugged in Pop (1) (2)
Command 945-S

CYRKLE
Neon (1) (2)
Columbia CS 9432

ELECTRONIC CONCEPT
ORCHESTRA
Electric Love (1) (2)
Limelight LS 86072
Moog Groove (1) (2)
Limelight LS 86070

RICHARD HAYMAN
Genuine Electric Latin Love Machine
(1) (2)
Command S-947

DICK HYMAN
Age of Electronicus (1) (2)
Command S-946

GERSHON KINGSLEY and
JEAN-JACQUES PERREY
Kaleidoscopic Variations (1) (2)
Vanguard VSD 6525

ROLAND KIRK
Rip, Rag and Panic (1) (2)
Limelight 86027

LOTHAR and the
HAND PEOPLE
Capitol ST 2997 (1)
Space Hymn (1)
Capitol ST 247

J MARKS
Rock and Other Four-Letter Words
(1)
Columbia MS 7193

GIL MELLE
Tome VI (1)
Verve V6-8744

MOOG ESPANA
RCA Victor LSP 4195 (1) (2)

THE MOTHERS OF INVENTION
We're Only in It for the Money (1)
Verve 65045
Uncle Meat (1)
Bizarre 2MS 2024

VAN DYKE PARKS
Song Cycle (1)
Warner Brothers 1727

ROBERT POZAR
Good Golly, Miss Nancy (1)
Savoy 12189

SOFT MACHINE
Volume One (1) (2)
Probe 4500

Volume Two (1) (2)
Probe 4505

SPOOKY TOOTH/PIERRE HENRY
Ceremony (1)
A&M SP 4225

GILBERT TRYTHALL
Country Moog Switched-On
Nashville (1)
Athena 6003
Nashville Gold (1)

Athena 6004

UNITED STATES OF AMERICA
Columbia CS 9614 (1)

VELVET UNDERGROUND and
NICO
Verve 65008 (1)

FRANK ZAPPA
Lumpy Gravy (1)
Verve 6-8741

Appendices and Bibliography

Appendix A

THE MATERIAL IN THIS APPENDIX IS OF A SPECIALIZED NATURE, BUT of the highest interest to those seriously interested in electronic music.

Otto Luening, of course, has been in the vanguard of the development of electronic music, and has contributed here his history of the movement in Germany, supplied to him by Dr. Meyer-Eppler. This article was originally published in the *Music Educators Journal* for 1968, and I thank the Music Educators National Conference and Dr. Luening for permission to reprint here.

Dr. J. R. Pierce is a leading pioneer of computer music, and I thank the Bell Laboratories of New Jersey for permission to reprint his paper.

Hubert S. Howe of Queens College has an expertise in computer music that few other experimenters as yet have obtained, and his article may be studied with profit by anyone who wishes to learn more of this field.

A Documented History of the Cologne School by Otto Luening*

Several years before his untimely death, Werner Meyer-Eppler supplied me with a list of the important dates in the development of electronic music in Germany with an urgent request to keep the record straight by publishing it at an appropriate time. Meyer-Eppler was an eminent German physicist and director of the Institute of Phonetics at Bonn University. In 1948 Homer W. Dudley, a visitor from the Bell Telephone Laboratories in New Jersey, demonstrated for Meyer-Eppler the vocorder, a composite device consisting of an analyzer and an artificial talker. This instrument and the *Mathematical Theory of Communication* (1949) by Claude Shannon and Warren Weaver made a strong impression on Meyer-Eppler. He used a tape of the vocorder to illustrate his lecture, "Developmental Possibilities of Sound," given at the Northwest German Radio Music Academy in Detmold in 1949. During the lecture, Robert Beyer of the Northwest

*Reprinted with the kind permission of Mr. Luening and the *Music Educators Journal*, where this first appeared in 1968.

German Radio, Cologne, took notice of the new possibilities of producing sound. Beyer was known as the author of the stimulating article, "The Problem of the 'Coming Music'" (*Die Musik*, Vol. 19, 1928).

After the Detmold meeting, it was decided to prepare lectures on electronic music for the International Summer School for New Music in Darmstadt. These lectures were to be in the form of a report about known electronic instruments and the process of speech synthesis as stated in Meyer-Eppler's book, *Electronic Tone Generation, Electronic Music, and Synthetic Speech*. The term "electronic music" was therefore used to describe any kind of music that could be produced by electronic instruments.

Two lectures by Beyer and one by Meyer-Eppler on "The World of Sound of Electronic Music" were presented at the International Summer School for New Music in Darmstadt in August 1950. Among those attending were Edgard Varèse and Herbert Eimert.

In 1951 Meyer-Eppler made systematic examinations and produced models of synthetic sounds leading to the conclusion that the past limitations of sound could be considerably expanded. He used a "Melochord," invented by H. Bode, and an A.E.G. tape recorder to conduct his experiments. He presented these samples (with demonstrations) in a lecture, "Possibilities of Electronic Sound Production," in July at the International Summer School for New Music in Darmstadt. [Pierre] Schaeffer attended the lecture. Under the same auspices, Beyer discussed "Music and Technology" and Eimert lectured on "Music on the Borderline."

At the Tonmeister meeting in Detmold in October, Meyer-Eppler lectured on "Sound Experiments" with examples of sound; the demonstrations were received with reservations by some of the attending composers and with great enthusiasm by others. The term "authentic composition" was coined. Fritz Enkel, technical director of the Northwest German Radio, Cologne, was present.

On October 18, 1951, a night program of music called "The World of Sound of Electronic Music" was broadcast over the Cologne radio station. It was a forum with Beyer, Eimert, and Meyer-Eppler participating, the last providing the examples in sound. On the same day, a committee consisting of those gentlemen and also Enkel, Schulz, and a few others from the technical department recommended "following the process suggested by Dr. Meyer-Eppler to compose directly onto magnetic tape" and attacking the problem at the Cologne radio station. This recommendation was the upbeat for the creation of an electronic studio in the Cologne radio station. In December of that year, Meyer-Eppler lectured on "New Methods of Electronic Tone Generation" for an audience of about a thousand at a meeting of technical and scientific societies at the House of Technique in Essen.

In collaboration with Meyer-Eppler at the Institute of Phonetics at Bonn University in 1952, Bruno Maderna produced his *Musica su due Dimensioni* and performed it at the Darmstadt Summer School before an audience that included Pierre Boulez, Karel Goeyvaerts, Bengt Hambraeus, Giselher Klebe, Gottfried Michael Koenig, and Karlheinz Stockhausen. The program stated that the work was for flute, percussion, and loudspeaker, and Maderna wrote "*Musica su due Dimensioni* is a first attempt to combine the past possibilities of mechanical instrumental music with the new possibilities of electronic tone generation as presented by Dr. Meyer-Eppler in the Darmstadt Summer School for New Music in 1951."

In December 1952, Meyer-Eppler lectured at a technical *Hochschule* in Aachen on "Authentic Compositions." Samples of sound and models of sounds were presented, but no real compositions were played. However, H. Eimert in his article, "Electronic Music—a New World of Sound," had this to say: "... The idea of infinite tonal material is an age-old music dream. At the beginning of our century Busoni and Schönberg occupied themselves with such 'free compositional flights.' . . . They were stopped at the borders of instrumental mechanism, Busoni with his splitting of his tonal materials [Eimert neglected to mention Busoni's description of Cahill's "Dynamophone" and electric sound production as one way out of the dilemma!], Schönberg with his tone-color melodies. But both saw the problem in its present-day importance, even though Busoni said, 'For a generation it will not be possible of solution.' The technical solution today, thanks to electronic production of sound, is no longer a doubtful quantity. . . . It is also not a matter of fantasies about the future. The first problem is just as concrete as it is difficult. It is simply: 'Begin!' "

In 1953, Eimert and Beyer produced the first compositions using only electronically generated sounds with the technical assistance of Enkel, Bierhals, and Schuetz. Eimert and Meyer-Eppler gave samples of this program at the International Summer School in Darmstadt in July, and then Meyer-Eppler lectured at the International Acoustical Congress in Delft, The Netherlands, and Eimert at the Première Décade Internationale de Musique Expérimentale in Paris.

The Cologne radio presented a public concert in a small hall on October 19, 1954, in the series "Music of Our Time," using only electronically generated sounds by Stockhausen, Goeyvaerts, Pousseur, Gredinger, and Eimert. The new pieces were in strict serial technique. In spite of the previous concerts, it was attempted later to represent these works as the "first truly electronic compositions anywhere." In 1956, under the same auspices, a similar concert took place with works by the composers Hambraeus, Koenig, Heiss, Klebe, Stockhausen, and Krenek. In contrast to earlier presentations, it was concerned with space music that was fed through five separate channels and through groups of speakers distributed throughout the hall. Stockhausen joined the ranks of the lecturers, who now spread the new gospel to new cities and other European countries. Since then, many new works and some new studios have been developed in Germany.

Some Thoughts on Computers and Music by Dr. J. R. Pierce, Bell Laboratories

The proponents of electronic music have found themselves plagued with two chief problems. One of these has been the terribly time-consuming process of setting up equipment that generates or processes electronic sound, adjusting and using the equipment, and piecing bits of tape together to achieve an over-all result. The other limitation has been the lack of variety of sound. However strange electronic music may sound, it seldom sounds anything but electronic.

A great deal of skill, on the part of instrument-makers and composers, has gone into making conventional instruments and ensembles produce extremely various sounds. Still, the writer of music for conventional instruments is limited by the sounds that conventional instruments can be made to produce and by his reliance on the skill of the performer in executing his intentions. Haydn had instruments and orchestra at his beck and call, but today's composer must often wait a considerable time for an experimental verification of the effect he conceives and intends.

As long as the maker of electronic music simply creates new but limited instruments, he suffers the limitations of all instruments, whether they be mechanical or electronic. He may or may not rely on a performing artist, according to the techniques he uses, but he certainly has not escaped the challenges of manual skill and dexterity. A partial escape is illustrated by the RCA music synthesizer, now in use by Milton Babbitt and others at the Columbia-Princeton Electronic Music Center, which can be controlled by a punched tape.

The coming of the digital computer has, in principle, changed the situation. In 1936 the English logician, Turing, showed that a certain rudimentary type of computer, which we call a Turing machine, can compute any computable number. In simpler words, this means that a Turing machine can carry out any numerical process that one can specify explicitly. While modern digital computers are not Turing machines and have limitations that the idealized Turing, with its infinite memory, does not have, they are much more flexible and capable in a practical way than the machine Turing envisaged. In a very real sense, electronic computers are universal machines which can do anything that can be done mechanically. Limitations lie in the insight and skill of the programmer, not in the digital computer itself.

Digital computers produce numbers, not sounds. However, information theory, which C. E. Shannon launched on its course in 1948, tells us, even in its most elementary aspects, that the world of messages is a universal world, amenable to numerical representation and interpretation. The electronic wave which, by means of a microphone or a pickup, goes from an instrument or a recording into the speaker of a high-quality sound system can be specified with complete accuracy as a sequence of numbers. These numbers specify the amplitude of the wave at regularly spaced instants of time.

The number of numbers required per second is twice the bandwidth of the sound, or about 20,000 numbers per second for high-quality music. Furthermore, the numbers themselves need not be infinitely accurate, for the ear cannot detect small errors in amplitude. Thus, 20,000 three-digit numbers a second can describe not only any music that has ever been played, but any music that ever could be played, if only we are able to choose the right numbers.

Here is a powerful resource. A digital computer as a source of numbers, together with not very complicated equipment for turning this sequence of numbers into an electric wave that can drive a loudspeaker, is truly the universal musical instrument—the instrument which can, in principle, create any sound that can be created, any sound that can be heard by the ear. A composer equipped with a digital computer has no limitations except his own.

Over the past few years, workers at both the Massachusetts Institute of Technology and the Bell Telephone Laboratories have been experimenting with the digital computer as a source of musical sound. More recently, this work has been extended to Princeton University, and similar work is being carried on at the Argonne National Laboratory. Related studies of the analysis and synthesis of conventional musical sounds are being carried out at Yale.

What are the results? They are surprising and promising in some ways and discouraging in others. One discouraging aspect is that even the IBM 7094, which is a very fast computer, takes about five seconds to produce one sound of music. Time on the 7094 costs several hundred dollars an hour. This is a limitation that will be overcome as computers become faster and more economical.

The other discouraging aspect is that, while the sounds produced are often wild and weird, they lack the richness we are accustomed to hearing in conventional instruments, and more especially in large ensembles of instruments. Something is missing, and while we can guess at its nature, we cannot point to it in a precise and quantitative enough way so that we can tell the computer to produce the effect we seek.

Helmholtz made great strides in musical acoustics in the nineteenth century, but the science has not progressed at the same rapid pace as others. The user of a computer is free to specify the wave form or frequency content of the sound he produces; he can make these random or regular in any degree; he can introduce regular or random vibrato. He can control the "attack" and the duration of the notes. But, unlike the composer who has used a symphony orchestra as one huge instrument, he has neither years of tradition nor the skill of instrumentalists to rely on.

A little experimentation shows clearly that, while the harmonic content or frequency spectrum of the note has a strong influence on its quality, the attack has an even stronger influence. A rapid rise and gradual fall gives a plucked quality to a sound. A moderate rise, a sustained sound, and a moderate fall simulate a woodwind quality. A vibrato enhances the musicality of the sound. However, many things escape us. The brazen summoning of the trumpet is not easily evoked. Massed strings or voices must gain their effect through some degree of randomness in pitch or in attack. Yet, introducing randomness into computer music in simple ways makes it sound merely wobbly or noisy, rather than rich.

In all, the user of the computer is in somewhat the position of a musically talented savage when confronted with a grand piano. Certainly, wonderful things can come out of this box, but how is one to bring this about? Tuition, intuition, and practice are required, but there is no teacher and no one to guide the practice.

We are faced with an intriguing challenge. In principle, the computer *can* become the universal musical instrument. All that stands between us and all that was previously unattainable is an adequate grasp, scientific and intuitional, of the relevant knowledge of psycho-acoustics. Both by experimentation, and by careful measurement and analysis of musical sounds, we must find among the bewildering complexity of the world of sound what factors, what parameters are important, and in what degree, in achieving the effects we aim for: all the variations of sound that we hear from a skilled instrumentalist, all the characteristic sounds of instruments, the rich massed sound of the orchestra, and everything that can possibly lie beyond these familiar elements of music.

Men who are scientists or engineers only will never solve this problem. Its solution can come only through co-operation between those who understand something of the mechanism of hearing and psychoacoustics, those who understand the use of computers, and those who have real musical talent and creativity. Here is a chance for fruitful co-operation between science and the arts, rather than the phony invocation of scientific formulae and jargon that so often satisfies artists now.

It is heartening to know that the work at Princeton and at MIT is carried out in the departments of music by people who are musicians and who are knowledgeable about computers, and who have the full cooperation of computer-oriented people. It is also heartening to know that the computer study of the analysis and synthesis of musical sounds being carried out at Yale is supported by a grant from the National Science Foundation.

The worry perpetually raised about the status and support of the arts in our society seems, in this instance, allayed in an unexpected way. If good art can embody a valid contribution to good science, as it can in the relation between music and psychoacoustics (and also, for that matter, in the relation between music and architectural acoustics), then art can validly share, not only the fruits of science, but the support that society so rightly gives to science, for the practical contributions that science makes to our welfare as well as the intellectual and philosophical value of science itself.

Let me emphasize the universality of the computer. It can in principle produce any sound, not only any hearable sound, but any possible sound of limited bandwidth, whether or not the ear can distinguish that sound from other sounds.

Compared with this potential universality, the sounds we actually have produced cover a comparatively narrow range. Yet these sounds have seemed to us to have interesting, or we might say musical, qualities. The range of sounds produced overlaps the range of conventional musical sounds. The computer sounds exhibit some features which are not found in conventional music and, alas, conventional music exhibits many desirable features which we have not been able to produce by means of the computer.

Our procedure has been to generate various sounds and present them in simple man-made musical compositions. Just hearing a sound once is insufficient for us to make a judgment concerning it. Repeating a sound indefinitely is boring. Thus, we have felt that in exploring sounds it is best to put them in some simple, short musical context. Many of our experiments are available on a Decca record, *Music from Mathematics*.

The computer is a universal source of sound, without any of the specialization of the human voice or of musical instruments, either mechanical or electronic. A mathematical theorem, called the sampling theorem, tells us that if a musical or other sound contains no frequencies above the frequency B, the sound can be accurately and completely represented by and re-created from a series of 2B numbers per second, numbers which describe the amplitude of the sound wave at equally spaced *sampling times.*

Thus, if we want to use the computer to generate sound waves with frequencies no higher than 5000 cycles per second, we cause the computer to write 10,000 numbers per second on a magnetic tape. In order to produce a sound wave, these numbers are read out through a digital-to-analog converter. When the resulting sequence of pulses is passed through a low-pass filter whose bandwidth is 5000 cycles per second, the output will be a smooth wave, representing the sound. What numbers do we cause the computer to write? We program the computer to choose the numbers according to some rule; for instance, a very simple rule might be that the samples be ordinates of a sine wave of specified frequency and amplitude. We can go beyond this to other wave forms and to more complicated specifications.

To the musician and, especially, to the composer, the computer offers an instrument for sound production which is in principle infinitely flexible, though the exploitation of this flexibility calls for considerable knowledge and insight. The computer has no inherent scales, harmonic intervals, or timbres, and no limitations of rhythm, tempo, or dynamics—the composer can choose freely, accepting or rejecting tradition in any degree. But, if a composer is to use a computer, he can no longer call on the instrument maker or the performing artist for help. If he wants notes or intervals outside of a traditional scale, he must specify what frequencies he wants. If he wants a particular sound quality, he must supply the computer with an objective description of a wave form which will give the desired psychoacoustic effect. If he wants to achieve expressive effects through legato, staccato, crescendo, or ritardando, he must put these into his instructions to the computer. Yet the result may eventually be worth the difficulty. And, by assuming these responsibilities, a composer potentially can go beyond the capabilities of any instruments or of any performers. Here is a challenge to composers, old and young, to master a new musical language in order to make use of a new mode of expression.

To the student of music the computer, with careful psycho-acoustic experimentation, makes it possible to attack many problems experimentally which have in the past been approached chiefly "philosophically"; that is, with heated debate and disagreement. The way of science is not to seek agreement on arbitrary questions, but to discover in what range of experience we are forced into agreement by experiments which can be replicated. I think that psychoacoustics, together with the computer, can put us on firmer ground in a number of respects.

Some aspects of the question as to what "rules" of music should be attributed to acculturation and what to the nature of the human being—to the limitations and capabilities of his hearing and to his ability to remember sequences of sounds—are certainly amenable to experiment. Indeed, recent experiments by Plomp and Levelt seem to me to show the inescapability of Helmholtz's theory that consonant intervals are those in which the harmonics of the two tones coincide or are adequately separated in frequency. Moreover, this work casts further light on the question of consonance.

The use of the computer in producing with great ease accurate tonal and rhythmic patterns opens the way to all sorts of interesting investigations. Among these could be whether the procedures of twelve-tone composition do give an acoustic as well as a numerical unity to compositions. In plainer terms, is the sort of orderliness that twelve-tone composers introduce into their compositions apparent to the listener? (The fact that music judged as good is orderly does not imply that music which is orderly need be judged as good.)

Whatever computer generation of musical sounds can mean to composers and to students of music, it is pertinent to my work for what it means to the science and technology of acoustics. Sound quality and the problems of understanding vocal sounds and generating high-quality artificial speech are all central to communication. To arrive at an understanding of the quality of sounds calls not only for sharp minds, but for sharp ears. I feel that a strong effort on the part of musicians in the understanding and synthesis of good musical sounds will be invaluable to psychoacoustics in other fields, including that of communication.

The Composer and Computer Music by Hubert S. Howe, Jr.

Director, Electronic Music Studio, Department of Music, Queens College, City University of New York

Computers have had a profound impact on all aspects of contemporary life, but we are likely not to realize how deep this impact is until we learn about some of the creative fields in which computers are currently being used. Because of its completely abstract nature, music has perhaps felt a greater effect from computers than have the other humanities. Today there are numerous instances of computers being used in music history, theory, analysis, and bibliography as well as in the direct synthesis of music and even in musical composition.

When the computer is used in electronic music, it is actually used as a *performing instrument*—that is, as a means of synthesizing the sound of a composition of electronic music. The composer ultimately decides all the qualities of sound that will be used in a piece, when events will begin and end, what notes will be used, etc. In short, the composer composes the composition and the computer performs it. The difficulty—perhaps it is better described as the temptation—is that the way in which these instructions are conveyed to the computer allows the composer to specify not necessarily *what* notes the computer is to play but *how* to choose these notes from a given set of possibilities. And so we are left with the complication of deciding who wrote the piece: the composer or the computer.

The way in which a computer is instructed to decide how to choose the notes of a musical composition is very important, which makes it possible for us to investigate the many facets of a compositional method, and ultimately even the creative process itself. We will return to these questions at the end of this essay. What is important for us to realize at this time is that "composing" the piece is only a part of what computers do when they are used to synthesize a composition of electronic music. Let us look into the other aspects of computer sound synthesis in more detail.

It is difficult to imagine how a computer can be used to create music, and in reality this difficulty is both technical and intuitive.

Computers are *digital* devices: they operate upon one number at a time, and all the data fed into a computer must be rounded off to the closest value if they do not come within the range of values accepted by the computer. Music, on the other hand, is an *analog* phenomenon: it is a continuous function of time. If time is to be represented in a computer, it must be broken up into tiny intervals that it is to be hoped will be so closely spaced that we will not recognize the difference between the discrete and the continuous forms.

This is precisely the way in which music, as well as any other analog function, is represented in a computer. The process of transforming a continuous function into a discrete representation is called *analog-to-digital conversion*, and the reverse process is called *digital-to-analog conversion*. This operation requires a special component called a *converter* which very few computers now have.

The process of conversion between analog and digital forms involves the assumption that the digital representation or *quantization* of the analog phenomenon be accurate enough that we will not recognize the difference. If this is not the case, then *distortion* will be introduced. In order to evaluate the accuracy required of the digital representation, we must first have some idea of the range of response of the human ear and the kinds of signals to which it reacts.

There are two different qualities to consider in measuring the response of the human ear: one is *amplitude*, the other *frequency*. Figure 1 shows an analog sound wave and a digital representation of it. The amplitude response of the ear will determine *how high a signal* the digital representation should be capable of measuring, and the frequency response will determine *how many time-intervals* one second of sound will be broken into. The frequency response of the human ear varies with different listeners, but most people cannot hear a tone above 15,000 or 16,000 cycles per second. Since the representation of one vibration requires at least two impulses, a tone of 15,000 cycles per second requires 30,000 discrete values or *samples* per second. Without going into all the technical details of amplitude, a rather loud sound consisting of several separate tones requires at least approximately 4,000 to 8,000 levels, and it would be better to have even more.

These, then, are the technical specifications that are required

Figure 1.   *Digital Representation of a Sound Wave*

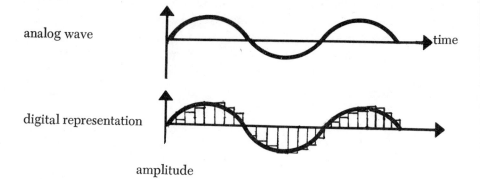

analog wave .... time

digital representation

amplitude

for digital-to-analog conversion of sufficient quality to represent music. What is immediately apparent from these factors is that computing all the numbers to represent one second of music is a very complicated task which a human being would never attempt to carry out without the aid of a computer. In order to be fairly flexible and to provide a means of dealing with complicated sounds that might be the equivalent of an entire orchestra playing, a very fast and large general-purpose computer is required.

Such a computer, if it is equipped with a digital-to-analog converter, is so powerful that it can synthesize or analyze virtually any sound or combination of sounds imaginable. That is precisely the machine's limitation: the user's imagination and knowledge of what he wants it to do. In order to get the machine to do what he wants, he must have a knowledge of programming, and that is the next area we will consider.

One of the first things a composer learns in an electronic music studio is how to make interconnections between different kinds of signal generating and processing equipment. Normally these interconnections are made by patch cords, which are simply wires that carry the signal from one device to another, although sometimes switches are used. The important point about this procedure is that, in order to build up a complex sound—complex in the sense that it has many independent characteristics, as do most sounds produced on musical instruments—it is necessary to process the sound in several ways. When all of the patches are complete, the sound can be played and different control settings can be tried until the desired result is obtained.

There are two steps in producing a sound that a composer uses in an electronic music composition: one is making the connections between all of the different devices to be used, and the other is providing all the proper control information to produce just that sound. This procedure is somewhat analogous to that used in live music: first the composer chooses the instrumental combination he wants, and then he provides a score showing the performers what to do.

A computer program which generates electronic music works in just the same way, except that all of the manual operations of connecting together the appropriate devices and setting the controls are simulated through programming. There are two quite distinct parts, which are named by analogy with live music: the composer provides an "orchestra" consisting of "instruments" of his own specifications; and then he provides a "score" consisting of "notes" which "play" the instruments at the appropriate times and with the appropriate variable data. The output of the computer program is a digital tape ready for conversion to sound by means of a digital-to-analog converter.

One of the most important considerations about computer music from the composer's point of view is that, in general, he really does not have to have more than a vague notion of the internal workings of the program or of programming in general. He must understand a few things about the broad outlines of the program and what parts go where. What he needs to understand most of all is how to structure instruments out of the available units in the program, and he must be able to express to the program very precise details about how to produce the qualities of sound that he wants to use in his music.

This kind of knowledge can be acquired only by experience, but it is not difficult to describe how the composer expresses these details to the program. "Instruments" for computer music are assembled through programming, by connecting together "unit-generators" (or simply "units"), which are subprograms that simulate electronic signal generating and processing devices like those found on an electronic music synthesizer. Each unit-generator has one or more *inputs* and one *output*, which may be used as an input by a subsequent unit-generator.

There are some important differences between the units in a computer program and those on an electronic music synthesizer, however. For one thing, there are, in general, no limitations as to the number of units available in a particular orchestra. It is quite common to find composers using hundreds of units at a time. For another thing, there are no restrictions on the rhythmic complexity of the music, whereas most of the equipment on an electronic music synthesizer has to be controlled by manual devices operated in real time. The primary advantage of this feature is not just that a computer can be used to generate very complicated and difficult rhythms, but that it can generate an entire composition or passage at one time. Most composers working with electronic music synthesizers must be content to produce just one "line" or succession of sounds at a time, and then employ intricate methods to combine all of their separate sources into the finished composition.

The unit-generators in a computer program or on an electronic music synthesizer can be classified on the basis of the kinds of operations they perform, or the acoustical functions they simulate. *Generators* are units that initiate signals of various descriptions; *processors* are units that modify one or more input signals in a particular way. Sometimes it is necessary to distinguish between *signal* generators and processors and *control* generators and processors. Signals are actual sounds themselves and controls are signals which determine the operating characteristics of the signal generators and processors. With computer programs and with certain electronic music synthesizers such as the Moog Synthesizers, the same signals can be used for both purposes. In other systems different kinds of signals employ different electrical characteristics.

Signal generators include a variety of units like *oscillators* or *white noise generators*, which initiate musical tones. *White noise* is mainly used for percussive effects. *Oscillators* are distinguished on the basis of the kind of *waveform* which they produce. A *sine wave oscillator* generates a single tone with no overtones. Other types of oscillators, such as *sawtooth, square wave* or *pulse wave* oscillators, produce a series of harmonic partials usually with an infinite number of overtones. In these instances the original signal is meant to be modified by other devices, for the original tones are raspy and have a "buzz-like" quality. Sometimes each overtone is available as a separate output; such a unit is usually called a *harmonic generator.*

Signal generators which are simulated through computer programming are usually much more versatile than their analog components. In the first place, there is usually no restriction on the kind of waveform they produce. Second, they cannot output an infinite series of frequencies because of a feature of digital-to-analog conversion known as "fold-over"; but this feature makes it possible to generate frequency shifting and non-harmonic overtone spectra from a simple oscillator. Third, some signal generators include a variety of signal processing within the unit itself, so that it is possible not only to obtain any musical timbre but also to include an adjustment which compensates for the uneven response of the human ear to different frequencies—in other words, to generate tones of the same or different timbres but the same *subjective* loudnesses. Finally, signal generators can also be used with complete compatibility as control generators.

Signal processors include many different units such as filters, mixers, envelope generators, reverberators, spatial separation devices, and other units which modify tones in various ways. Each of these devices needs to be discussed separately in relation to the musical function which it is used for.

A *filter* is a device which modifies the *overtone spectrum* or *timbre* of a sound. A *lowpass* filter "cuts off" high frequencies beginning at a specified cutoff frequency; in other words, it "passes" low frequencies. A *highpass filter* cuts off low frequencies and passes high frequencies beginning at a certain point. A *bandpass filter* cuts out everything except a specified area or "band" of frequency. An important characteristic of a filter is whether its frequency response characteristics are *fixed* or *variable*—that is, whether its cutoff points may be varied over the course of a tone. All kinds of filtering can be accomplished with computer programs, and here one of the important considerations is the endless amount of "equipment" available on the computer.

A *mixer* is a device which combines two or more signals into one sound. On the computer, this device is simulated through *addition.*

Other kinds of arithmetic operations can also be used to produce a variety of results. *Multiplication* or *division* by a constant, for example, is simply a way of rescaling the amplitude of a tone; but multiplication of two waveforms produces *ring modulation*. Multiplication by -1 produces 180-degree *phase shifting*.

Envelope is a term covering the *attack* and *decay characteristics* of a sound, but its more general application encompasses any dynamic variations in musical characteristics. For example, each of the overtones of a complex sound may have separate envelopes, or a single envelope may be applied to the entire sound. An envelope may also be used to produce a dynamic variation of *pitch* instead of amplitude.

Reverberation or "echo" is a complicated process which mechanically corresponds to what happens in a natural environment when a sound bounces off the walls and returns to mix with the portion of the signal coming toward the listener directly from the source. Its variable characteristic is the *reverberation time*, which is the time it takes a sound to die away in a given environment.

Channel separation devices produce a variety of spatial effects ranging from isolating sounds in different speakers to travelling between speakers. In this context it is unfortunate that most installations are presently equipped only to handle stereophonic playback, whereas much electronic music employs dazzling spatial effects which can be duplicated only with four- or eight-track tape recorders.

Random units include a number of devices that produce values anywhere within a specified range. They can be applied to any musical characteristics either partially or totally. Sometimes these units are used for various compositional purposes, such as producing a series of random pitches, for example.

Many other kinds of units are available, but those we have discussed are probably the most common. It is important to remember that the outputs of units in a computer program can be used for signals and for control functions.

The procedure that a composer must follow in order to produce a sound he wants, then, is first to design an instrument and then to provide the appropriate data for the sound. Figure 2 shows the design of a simple instrument which has just one oscillator, filter, and envelope generator, terminating in an "OUT" unit which "plays" the tone. The "oscillator," abbreviated "OSCIL" in the diagram, has two inputs and one "function," which is indicated inside the unit. "P4," the left input, specifies that the instrument is to take its *amplitude* from parameter field 4 of an instrument card in the score. The right input, "PITCH (P5)," specifies that the *pitch* of the instrument is to be determined by converting a number in parameter field 5 of an instrument card to the appropriate value. Parameter field 5, as the example of data for the instrument shows, specifies "8.01." This number is interpreted in the "octave point pitch-class" form, which means that the part before the decimal point specifies the octave and the part after the decimal point specifies the pitch-class for the desired tone. "8.01" specifies octave 8 and pitch-class 1, which calls for a C# above middle C. The inputs to the filter, P6 and P7, determine the center frequency and bandwidth of the filter. The values "500" and "100" on the instrument card specify a bandpass filter with center frequency of 500 and bandwidth of 100 cycles per second. The envelope generator has an

Figure 2. *Design of a Simple Instrument*

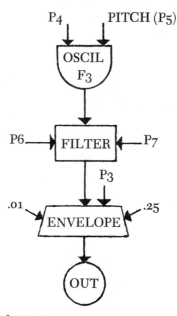

Example of data for this instrument:

P1	P2	P3	P4	P5	P6	P7
I 1	11	4	1000	8.01	500	100

attack time of .01 and decay time of .25 seconds, with a duration (also in seconds) specified in parameter field 3. The remaining parameter fields on the instrument card, P1 and P2, specify the instrument number and starting time for the note indicated.

A more complicated instrument structure is shown in Figure 3. This instrument contains two oscillators with amplitudes which vary so that one starts at maximum amplitude and goes to zero while the other starts at zero and goes to the maximum over the course of a note. The pitch of both oscillators is the same, and they are mixed together immediately; so the effect of this portion of the instrument is to produce a timbre variation from one extreme to the other over the course of a note. The resulting mixture is sent to a reverberator, and then both the reverberated and unreverberated signals are sent through separate amplitude modification units, mixed together again, and sent to an envelope generator. The final sound is made to travel from one speaker to another over the course of a note by the two units which are combined in the right output of the OUT unit.

A single note on this instrument, first of all, will have the timbre variation described above. Second, the mixture of reverberated and unreverberated signals will be modified over the course of the note, and the envelope will be applied to the result. Finally, the sound will travel from one speaker to the other over the course of the note. Thus, there are three separate components of the tone which vary over the course of its duration: the timbre, the mixture of reverberation, and the spatial location.

This last example is somewhat more typical of the kind of programming composers of computer music are likely to engage in themselves. A certain amount of this kind of experience is necessary to be able to make use of the full resources of the medium.

Once the instruments for a particular composition are defined, the composer has to provide the notes to play the instruments at the appropriate times and with the appropriate data. At this point the computer can be asked to assist the composer in writing the notes. There are actually many different ways in which the computer can assist the composer, and not all of them need to be thought of as "computer composition."

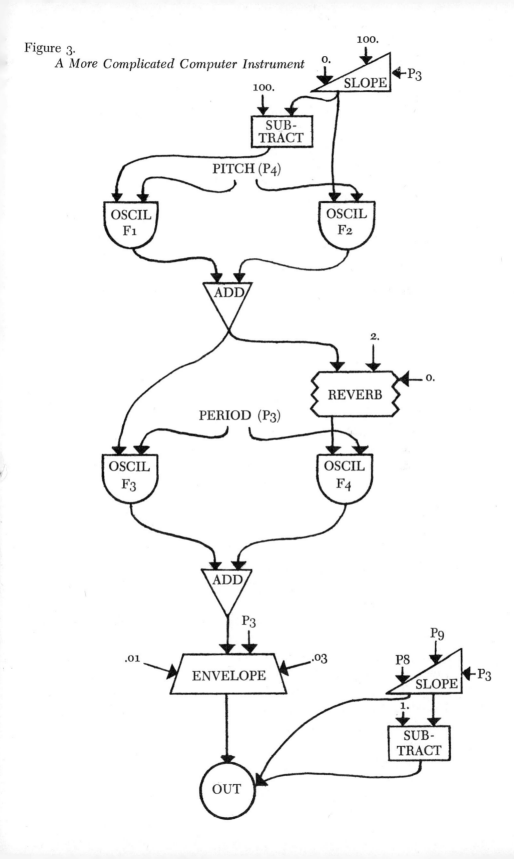

Figure 3.
A More Complicated Computer Instrument

Perhaps the easiest way in which the computer can assist the composer is in performing some very simple but tedious task which the composer doesn't want to waste his time doing. For example, if a group of notes must be repeated 100 times, the composer could physically duplicate them himself and include them in his score; but it is simple to ask the computer to duplicate them 100 times, and much effort is thereby spared the composer. Examples like this, however important they might be when actually using the computer, are uncontroversial because the computer is not being employed to make *decisions*.

There are several kinds of decisions which a computer can make that also do not necessarily mean it is "composing" music. For example, a composer can write a group of numbers from 1 to 4 to indicate "timbre," and the computer can decide that each number means such and such filter bandwidths and center frequencies, etc. In a more complicated situation, a composer can write a procedure like the following: if all of the other instruments playing at the time when a given note begins are very soft, then play this note softly too; but if the other instruments are playing loudly, then reduce their amplitudes so that this note will have prominence. In this example the computer is actually deciding what the amplitudes of a group of notes will be on the basis of contextual information. The composer doesn't even have to know where this particular adjustment takes place, nor does he have to worry about its numerical details (except when writing the program to carry out the procedure); the important thing is that he thinks in terms of the *principle* which applies to his music.

Many similar principles can be written as compositional sub-programs. They might be applied to qualities as simple as the loudness of a passage or as complicated as the pattern of consonance and dissonance in a melody. As these procedures increase in complexity, the compositional purpose of the computer becomes more and more central to the investigation, and it becomes less likely that the computer will also be used to synthesize the sound at the same time.

At the extreme end of computer composition we find composers encoding their own procedures for choosing notes and rhythms as computer programs and investigating what results are obtained in different situations. Once these procedures are codified in this manner, it is possible to study them in great depth and determine whether they make sense when used in various ways. An analogy can be made to the process of expressing a scientific theory of some observable phenomenon as a computer program in order to explore its inner structure and interpret its implications when confronted with various forms of experimental data. If a composer obtains some musical effect which he doesn't want, it is his procedures which are at fault, not necessarily his taste.

Any compositional procedure can be investigated in this way: for example, the rules of harmony and counterpoint which are often given in textbooks on the subject can be tested for their validity or completeness. On the frontiers of this activity, the proposals of speculative musical theory can be examined and reformulated as new results are obtained.

Once computer composition of music is explained in these terms, it becomes understandable but loses much of its mystery. For it is always clear exactly what the computer has done in each of these circumstances; there is no mystery about decisions based upon the values of certain numbers. Like the problem of whether computers can "think," the mystery has to do with understanding how composers decide to choose the notes in their music, as in the case of thinking it has to do with understanding what goes on in the human brain. If we all understood both of these things, we might be much better off, but we would be living in a different world.

Appendix B:

A Glossary of Electronic Terms

Acoustics—The science of sound; more specifically, the study of the production, transmission, and reception of sound. Psychoacoustics is the study of the effects of sounds on humans.

Amplifier—A device that increases the voltage, power, or current of a signal.

Amplitude—Refers to the maximum value of power, voltage, or current of a specific signal.

Amplitude Modulation—The alteration of signal amplitude. The periodic variation of amplitude, or the process by which this is achieved.

Analog Computer—A device to perform calculations about real systems by constructing a (usually electrical) model or "analog" of a system and making measurements on it. (In digital computers, however, numbers or numerical representations are manipulated to effect computation.)

Analog Tape—A magnetic tape on which information may be stored in continuous form as magnetic densities. The standard tape employed in tape recording is an analog tape.

Atonality—Music without a defined tone center.

Attack and Decay—Wave forms beginning and ending a sound or pulse.

Audio Generator—An electronic device that produces complex signals. The terms oscillator and generator are often used interchangeably; however, an oscillator refers to a generator of sine waves, whereas a generator is a device which produces other than sine waves.

Audio Oscillator—A device that produces sinusoidal signals at frequencies between 20 and 20,000 Hz, usually for purposes of testing, or sound synthesis.

Audio Spectrum—The frequency range of sound potentially hearable.

Bandpass Filter—This term applies to a filter that allows a restricted range of signal frequencies to be transmitted.

288

Band-Elimination (Reject Filter)—A filter that attenuates a particular band of frequencies, while allowing other frequencies to pass and be heard.

Bandwidth—The range of frequencies in a band.

Bell Gate—An envelope generator, especially one that produces replicas of percussive envelopes.

Binary—A characteristic property or condition in which there are two possible alternatives. The binary code used in computers is expressed in terms of one and zero, representing on and off.

Bit—Common abbreviation for binary digit; used also as a unit of measurement of information in the use of computers in music.

Center Frequency—The center frequency of a passed or rejected band.

Colored Sound—Signal being or resembling white sound that has been processed by a filter or equalizer. (Compare with *White Noise*.)

Computer—An information-storage and processing device.

Contact Microphone—A microphone which is placed in physical contact with a vibrating violin, guitar, etc., thereby transforming vibrations into electrical signals.

Conversion—The process by which digitally stored information is transformed into analog information, or vice versa.

Decay—Those amplitude characteristics that apply to the ending of a sound or signal.

Digital Tape—Magnetic tape on which information is stored in discrete, numerical form (as opposed to analog tape).

Digital-to-Analog Interface—An auxiliary device converting output information from a digital computer to a form suitable as the input to an analog device.

Doppler Effect—This term, used in physics, refers to the effect, principally an apparent shift or frequency, due to relative motion between a sound source and the listener.

Drift—Any gradual or accidental (and usually undesired) drifting away from a desired sound value, usually because of equipment deficiencies.

Driver—An electrical to mechanical transducer.

Echo—The discernible repetition of a sound, usually at a lower amplitude. (See *Reverberation.*)

Electronic Switch—A device employed to produce a periodic interruption of a signal.

Electrosonics—A nice term, which is used rather airily to cover the entire field of electronically produced sounds, including sonic experiments, music, sound effects, etc.

Envelope—The loudness-time contour of a sound. Those characteristics of amplitude which determine the growth and decay of a signal.

Envelope Generator or Transient Generator—An instrument that produces a transient control voltage which, when used to control the gain of a voltage-controlled amplifier, imparts an envelope to a steady sound.

Envelope Follower—An instrument that derives a voltage proportional to the envelope of the sound which is fed into it.

Equalizer—A device for increasing or decreasing signal strength in selected portions of the audible spectrum.

Erase Head—The leadoff head of a tape recorder that erases previously recorded material on the tape prior to its passing the record head.

Event (often referred to as a "sound event")—This is a single musical entity in the totality of its dimensions—that is, pitch, duration, loudness, timbre, and so on.

Feedback—Return of a signal to a controller indicating the result of an action taken by that controller and used to determine further actions. As generally used in electronic music, the term refers to the practice of sending a portion of the playback signal from a tape recorder back around to the input while the machine is running in the second mode. The consequent effect is that of a series of echoes of the original sound, either diminishing or increasing, depending on the loop gain of the feedback system.

Filter—A modifier that emphasizes certain frequencies and attenuates others. A lowpass filter lets through all frequencies below its "cutoff frequency," and attenuates all frequencies above cutoff; a highpass filter lets through all frequencies above its cutoff frequency, and attenuates all frequencies below cutoff. A bandpass filter passes one particular band of frequencies. An equalizer is a filter that is generally designed to correct for nonuniform frequency response.

Filter Bank—A group of filters.

Fletcher-Munson Curve—A diagram of equal contours that displays the relationship between intensity and loudness (perceived intensity) at varying (sinusoidal) frequencies. A group of sensitivity curves made of the human ear showing its characteristic for different intensity levels between the threshold of hearing and the threshold of feeling.

Four-Track Tape—Recording tape on which four separate sound paths can be utilized at the same time for recording and playback.

Frequency—Vibrations per second of a signal. The repetition rate which determines the pitch of a sound.

Frequency Counter—A device that measures the frequency of a signal by literally counting the individual oscillations that occur during a particular time interval.

Frequency Modulation—The periodic variation of signal frequency affecting pitch; the alteration of signal frequency. (Compare with Amplitude Modulation.)

Frequency Response—The effect of a device through which information passes on the amplitude plotted as a function of frequency.

Frequency Shift—A change in frequency of an input signal made possible by a multiplier-type modulator or frequency shifter. (See *Klangumwandler*.)

Formant—An emphasized region of the audible spectrum characteristic of a particular timbre.

Gain—A quantity expressing the degree of amplification of an amplifier or similar device.

Gate—A device for controlling the amplitude of a signal path. The term, as used in electronic music, is synonymous with voltage-controlled amplifier.

Generator—An instrument that originates a signal.

Half-Track Recorder—A tape recorder that records and plays on half of a one-fourth-inch magnetic tape. Two-track or stereo recorders are often referred to as "half-track" if the width of each channel is actually one-half of the tape width. Usually, however, half-track recorders are monaural.

Half-Track Heads—The heads on a half-track tape recorder.

Harmonic—An overtone, or frequency component present in complex sounds. The frequency of a harmonic is an integral multiple of the fundamental frequency, which is the lowest frequency partial present in a given sound. All harmonics are necessarily partials.

Hertz—The unit of frequency in general use, equal to one cycle per second. Hertz (Hz) derives from the name of the German scientist Heinrich Rudolph Hertz, who was first to detect, create, and measure electromagnetic waves.

Heuristics—Techniques by means of which the individual (or machine) can be equipped to solve problems. When the heuristics are applicable, they will provide a shortcut to the goal (used in computer work).

Input—A signal fed into a circuit or device.

Input Language—The code employed to convey instructions when programming an electronic device. An encoding language such as FORTRAN or COBOL.

Interface—An instrument that enables two other instruments of dissimilar modes of operation to function in combination.

Jack—A plug-in type terminal such as is found on telephone switchboards. A socket-type connector to which temporary connections can be made with patch cords.

Key Punch—A device for punching information on computer data cards.

Klangfarbenmelodie—Timbre melodies, in which various timbres function like pitches in a linear melody. A succession of musical events generally having different instrumental timbres associated with each event. The use of timbre as the primary compositional material; timbre used thematically. "Klangfarben" is a fragmented style of instrumentation, especially associated with Webern, whereby each note of a melody may be given a different instrumental color. Schönberg, however, first used it in his *Harmonliehre* in 1911.

Klangumwandler—A ring modulation-like device in which one set of resultant frequencies is suppressed.

Linear Control—A device for continuously varying properties of sound. As manufactured by the Moog Company, fingertips are moved along gold contact wires to vary electrical current.

Magnetic Tape—Iron-oxide-coated plastic tape used in magnetic recordings. Standard widths are one-quarter, one-half, and one inch.

Manual Controller—A controller whose control voltage outputs respond to hand movements.

Microtonel—Interval smaller than a semitone.

Mixer—An instrument which permits the controlled combination of signals and their routing to other instruments.

Modifier—An instrument that alters a signal in a specified manner. Modifiers are extremely useful for altering the tone quality of sounds.

Modulation—The process in which a characteristic of a waveform is (usually periodically) varied.

Modulator—A modifier that alters a given characteristic of one signal in response to the variations of a second signal.

Monitor—A device used for checking audio signals, usually during the recording process.

Musique Concrète—Electronic music in which natural or instrumental sounds, rather than electronically generated sounds, are used as source material.

Mutation—The transformation of sound by radical change.

Noise—Undesired sound. (See *White Noise*.)

Oscillator—A generator that produces periodic or regularly repeating wave forms. Oscillators produce pitched sounds.

Oscilloscope—An instrument that reproduces on the screen of a cathode-ray tube a graphical representation of signals as voltages with respect to time. Used to determine amplitude, frequency, and other wave-form characteristics.

Output—The signal that comes out of a circuit or device.

Parameter—A variable quantity that can be measured. In computer work, a discrete characteristic of a system.

Partial—A frequency component, not necessarily harmonically related to other components.

Patch Cord—A cord with a plug at both ends, used to establish a temporary connection between two jacks, usually an output and an input.

Peak—The maximum value of amplitude, or a momentary value considerably higher than the average.

Permutation—The alteration or changing of variables in sounds or structures.

Pitch Succession—The consecutive sounding of two or more tones.

Potentiometer (abbreviated POT)—A device used for the precise measurement of voltages by comparison of an unknown voltage with a reference voltage. Often used to describe a volume control on audio equipment.

Programming—The directions for the sequential behavior of an electronic system, particularly a computer.

Punched Paper Tape Programmer—A device that stores information by means of coded holes in a paper tape.

Quarter-Track Recorder—A tape recorder that uses one-quarter (rather than one-half, or all) the width of the tape for each recording. Stereo recording requires simultaneous recording on two of the four tracks. Many "four-track" recorders should rightly be called quarter-track, as the term "four-track" should be reserved for machines capable of simultaneous use of all four tracks on the tape.

Random Generator (also called *White Sound Source* or *White Noise Generator*)— A generator that produces a signal in which there is no predictable relation between any two parts of the waveform. The sound is completely pitchless and sounds like rushing air.

Reverberation—Repetitions of sound that are so minutely spaced in time that they cannot be distinguished individually. The effect produced by multiple overlapping echoes in a room or concert hall.

Reverberation Unit—A modifier that adds a series of closely spaced echoes to a signal, thereby imparting a sense of liveliness and space to sound material.

Ring Modulator—An analog multiplier circuit used to combine signals in such a manner that the output consists of sums and differences of all the input frequency components.

Recording Head—An electromagnetic transducer used to implant magnetized patterns on recording tape.

Sawtooth Wave—Information whose waveform resembles a sawtooth. A signal consisting of a fundamental frequency and all harmonics, with the intensities of the harmonics inversely related to frequency. (See *Wave Form*.)

Sel-Sync—A term used by Ampex Corporation for their sync-head recorders.

Sequencer—A device that is used to produce a preset voltage sequence for the purpose of controlling a series of events with voltage-controlled equipment.

Sequential Controller—A controller whose control voltage outputs consist of sequences of present (programmed) voltages.

Signal—Electrical analog of sound. The variations of an electrical current which constitute the flow of information.

Signal Generator—The source of sound; an oscillator or, sometimes, a tape recorder in a very general sense.

Sine Wave—The waveform corresponding to a single frequency oscillation, a pure and simple tone. Its waveform is identical to the graph of the mathematical sine function of the angle.

Sound—Pressure waves of a frequency audible by the human ear. The properties of sound are frequency, amplitude, duration, and timbre or waveform. When frequency of vibration is regular or stable, pitch results; when unstable, noise results.

Sound-on-Sound—A method of recording a second signal on top of a previously recorded track of a tape. The erase head of the tape recorder must be disconnected or disabled to prevent erasure of the first signal during the process of recording the second. The results are usually quite poor in terms of signal quality.

Sound Wave—The periodic compression and rarefaction of the atmosphere at frequencies discernible to the human ear.

Source—The entity that supplies signals. The element at the start of a signal path.

Spectrum—A frequency representation of the (audio) signal which plots amplitude against frequency; the conversion from the waveform to the spectrum representation is achieved mathematically by a Fourien transformation.

Splice—The connection of two segments of magnetic tape, usually with the help of special splicing tape.

Square Wave—A signal consisting of fundamental frequency and all odd-numbered harmonics with the intensities of the harmonics inversely related to frequency.

Steady-State—That portion of a sound or signal that lacks significant perceived variations.

Synchronization—Coordinating one set of events with another with regard to time.

Synthesizer—A system of generators, modifiers, and controllers for the production and control of sound.

Tape Deck—The tape transport and heads portion of a tape recorder.

Tape Music—Sounds assembled on magnetic tape and then formed to make a composition. It has to be played over a loudspeaker.

Tempophone—A device used in tape recording to increase or decrease performance speed without altering pitch. The reverse operation is also possible, so that pitch may be altered without altering speed.

APPENDIX B: A GLOSSARY OF ELECTRONIC TERMS

Timbre—The recognizable quality of sound distinguishing one instrument or voice from another. It is a complex function of the relative amplitudes and frequencies of the component partial tones.

Timbre Modulation—The alteration of timbre.

Time Delay—The time lapse or a device for its production for an event to be transmitted or repeated.

Tonality—Strictly speaking, the relationships between tones that are inherent in acoustical facts, so that the term covers all scale systems, or rather formulae, from the pentatonic to the chromatic. In practice, however, the word tonality has become associated with the tempered diatonic (major and minor) scales of European music in the eighteenth and nineteenth centuries. The terms atonality and pantonality are used to define the breakdown of that system. (See *Atonality*.)

Tone Control—A device for the regulation of signal intensity portions of the audible spectrum.

Transient—Any nonperiodic component of information, as characteristic response occurring during the start or end of a given signal but not present during the stable steady-state condition.

Transient Generator—A generator that produces a wave form of defined but nonrepetitive shape.

Transient Overtones—Overtones (harmonics) momentarily present, usually during the attack of a sound. (See *Steady-State*.)

Transistor—A device made from semiconductor materials that can act as an electrical insulator or conductor, depending on the electrical charges placed upon it. Transistors are used in amplification and oscillation as a substitute for vacuum tubes.

Tremolo—Amplitude or loudness variation at a frequency of from about 4 to 8 Hz; the repetition of a note at a frequency rate of from about 4 to 12 Hz.

Triangular Wave—Information whose waveform is characterized by being comprised exclusively of alternate straight lines of equal and opposite slope. Synonym: delta wave.

Trigger—A signal which has only two possible states and which is used to initiate transient waveform.

Variable Speed Unit—A device used to control the speed of a tape recorder motor.

Variable Width—With reference to a rectangular wave, the ability to control the duty cycle.

Variac—A variable AC transformer, sometimes used to control the speed of a tape recorder motor by reducing the 117-volt line voltage. This system, however, often shortens the life of the motor.

Vibrato—Cyclic pitch change of less than a minor second at a frequency in the range from 4 to 8 Hz. (See *Tremolo*.)

Voltage Control—The control of the operating characteristics of an instrument by the variation of an externally applied voltage called the "control voltage." A voltage-controlled oscillator is an oscillator in which the frequency of the waveform is voltage-controllable. A voltage-controlled filter and a voltage-controlled amplifier offer, respectively, voltage-controllable cutoff frequency and gain.

Vocoder—Developed in the early 1950s to break down complex vocal sounds into digital bits of information for transmission over narrow bandwidths by wire or by radio.

Voltage-Controlled Amplifier—An amplifier whose gain is made variable by means of a change in voltage.

Voltage-Controlled Filter—A filter whose characteristics, such as bandwidth and frequency, are made variable by means of a change in voltage.

Volume Control—A device for the regulation of signal intensity.

Wave Form—The graph of an electrical variation versus time. The shape produced by one complete cycle of a periodic signal when its amplitude is plotted as a function of time.

White Noise—Signal theoretically comprised of infinitely random occurring frequencies throughout the audible spectrum which are of statistically equal intensities. By analogy with light, a signal that may be considered to contain all audible frequencies, with amplitudes randomly distributed. Colored noise, analogously, is noise in which one or more bands of frequencies are suppressed.

Selected Bibliography

BOOKS

Barzun, Jacques, *Music in American Life*. New York, Doubleday & Company, 1956.

Bassart, Ann Phillips, *Serial Music: A Classified Bibliography of Writings on Twelve-Tone and Electronic Music*. Berkeley, California, University of California Press, 1961.

Beckwith, John, and Kasemets, Udo, eds., *The Modern Composer and His World*. A report from the International Conference of Composers, Stratford, Ontario, 1960. Toronto, Canada, University of Toronto Press, 1961.

Boulez, Pierre, *Notes of an Apprenticeship*. New York, Alfred A. Knopf, 1968. Essays, containing the famous manifesto, "Schönberg Is Dead."

Busoni, Ferruccio, *Sketch of a New Aesthetic of Music*. New York, Dover Publications, 1962.

Busoni, Ferruccio, *The Essence of Music, and Other Papers*. New York, Philosophical Library, 1957.

Cage, John, *A Year From Monday*. Middletown, Conn., Wesleyan University Press, 1967.

Cage, John, *Silence*. Middletown, Conn., Wesleyan University Press, 1961.

Chavez, Carlos, *Toward a New Music*. New York, W. W. Norton & Co. 1937.

Cohn, Arthur, *Twentieth Century Music in Western Europe*. Philadelphia, J. B. Lippincott Company, 1965.

Collaer, Paul, *A History of Modern Music*, trans. by Sally Abeles. Cleveland, World Publishing Co., 1961.

Cowell, Henry, *New Musical Resources*. With supplementary notes by Joscelyn Godwin. New York, Small Publishers Co., 1969. This prophetic book from 1930 forecast many subsequent musical innovations.

Cross, Lowell M., ed., *A Bibliography of Electronic Music*. Toronto, Canada, University of Toronto Press, 1967.

Crowhurst, Norman H., *Electronic Musical Instrument Handbook.* Indianapolis, Sams, Howard W., & Company, 1962.

Davies, Hugh, ed., *International Electronic Music Catalog.* Cambridge, Massachusetts, M.I.T. Press, 1968.

Dorf, Richard H., *Electronic Musical Instruments.* Mineola, N.Y., Radiofile, 1963.

Douglas, Alan, *The Electrical Production of Music.* London, MacDonald, 1957; New York, Philosophical Library, 1957.

——, *The Electronic Musical Instrument Manual,* 3rd ed. London and New York, Pitman Publishing Corp., 1962.

Eimert, Herbert, ed. *Electronic Music.* Philadelphia, Theodore Presser Publishers, 1958.

Gerhard, Roberto, "Concrete and Electronic Sound Composition," in *Music Libraries and Instruments* (London, Hinrichsen Edition, 1961).

Guy, Percival J., "Musique Concrete and Radiophonics," in *Practical Tape Recording Handbook.* London, 1964.

Handel, Samuel, ed., *A Dictionary of Electronics.* Baltimore, Maryland, Penguin Books, 1962.

Hiller, Lejaren A., and Isaacson, Leonard M., *Experimental Music.* New York, McGraw-Hill Book Company, 1959.

Judd, F. C., *Electronic Music and Musique Concrete.* London, Neville Spearman, 1961.

Helmholtz, Herman L. F., *On the Sensations of Tone as a Physiological Basis for the Theory of Music,* Trans. and with notes and an appendix by Alexander J. Ellis. 6th ed., New York, Peter Smith, 1948.

Kostalanez, Richard, *John Cage.* New York, Praeger Publishers, 1970.

Lewer, S. K., *Electronic Musical Instruments.* London, Electronic Engineering, 1948.

Machlis, Joseph, "Electronic Music," in *Introduction to Contemporary Music* (New York, 1961).

Marcuse, Sibyl, *Musical Instruments: A Comprehensive Dictionary.* Garden City, N.Y., Doubleday & Company, 1964.

Mathews, Max V., and Miller, Joan E., *Music IV Programmer's Manual.* Murray Hill, N.J., Bell Telephone Laboratories, 1965.

Olson, Harry F., *Musical Engineering.* New York, McGraw-Hill Book Company, 1952.

Puellette, Fernand, *Edgard Varèse.* New York, Orion Press, 1968. A conscientious biography.

Partch, Harry, *Genesis of a Music.* Madison, Wisc., University of Wisconsin Press, 1949.

Peyser, Joan, *The New Music.* New York, Delacorte Press, 1971. Excellent for Schönberg and his school.

Pierce, John R., *Electrons, Waves, and Messages.* Garden City, N.Y., Hanover House, 1956.

Reichardt, Jasia, *Cybernetic Serendipity, the Computer, and the Arts.* New York, Praeger Publishers, 1969. A fascinating survey with articles by Cage, Hiller, Pierce, etc.

Salzman, Eric, *Twentieth Century Music: An Introduction.* Englewood Cliffs, N.J.: Prentice-Hall, Inc., 1967. An incisive and literate survey.

Schillinger, Joseph, "Electronic Instruments," in *The Schillinger System of Musical Composition,* Book XII, Vol. II (New York, 1941), Chapter 5.

Schwartz, Elliot, and Childs, Barney, *Contemporary Composers on Contemporary Music.* New York, Holt, Rinehart & Winston, Inc., 1967. Indispensable essays by Busoni, Varèse, Partch, Luening, etc.

Seashore, Carl E., *Psychology of Music.* New York and London, McGraw-Hill Book Company, 1938.

Stuckenschmidt, H. H., *Twentieth Century Music.* New York, McGraw-Hill Book Company, 1969. Extremely good material on electronic music, for the non-specialist.

Stravinsky, Igor, "Electronic Music," in *Conversations With Igor Stravinsky.* Garden City, N.Y., Doubleday & Company, 1960.

Taylor, C. A., *The Physics of Musical Sounds.* London, English University Press, 1965.

Tenney, James, *Meta (+) Hodos: A Phenomenology of Twentieth-Century Musical Materials and an Approach to the Study of Form*. New Orleans, Tulane University, 1964.

Ussachevsky, Vladimir A., "Notes on a Piece for Tape Recorder," in Paul Henry Lang, ed., *Problems of Modern Music*. New York, W. W. Norton & Co., 1962.

———, *Electronic Musical Instruments*, a bibliography, 2nd ed. London, Tottenham Public Libraries and Museum, 1962.

PERIODICALS

Babbitt, Milton, "An Introduction to the R.C.A. Synthesizer." *Journal of Music Theory*, Vol. B (Winter, 1964), p. 251.

———, "Who Cares If You Listen?" *High Fidelity*, Vol. 8 (February, 1958), p. 38.

Backus, John, "Die Reihe—a Scientific Evaluation." *Perspectives of New Music*, Vol. 1 (Fall, 1962), p. 160.

Brown, Clement. "How to Make Electronic Music." *Popular Science*, Vol. 176 (April, 1960), p. 184.

Carter, Elliott, and Ussachevsky, Vladimir, "Reel vs. Real." *American Symphony Orchestra League Newsletter*, Vol. 11 (July, 1960), p. 8

Ciamaga, Gustav, "Some Thoughts on the Teaching of Electronic Music." *Yearbook of the Inter-American Institute for Musical Research*, Vol. 3 (1967), p. 69.

Cowell, Henry, "Composing With Tape." *Hi-Fi Music at Home*, Vol. 2 (January-February, 1956), p. 23.

Davies, Hugh, "A Discography of Electronic Music and Music Concrete." *Recorded Sound*, No. 14 (April, 1964), p. 205.

De la Vega, Aurelio, "Electronic Music, Tool of Creativity." *Music Journal*, Vol. 23 (September, 1965), p. 52; (October, 1965), p. 61; and (November, 1965), p. 52.

———, "Regarding Electronic Music." *Tempo*, Vol. 75 (Winter, 1965–66), p. 2.

Dockstader, Tod, "Inside-Out: Electronic Rock." *Electronic Music Review*, No. 5 (January, 1968), p. 15.

Forte, Alan, "Composing with Electrons in Cologne." *High Fidelity*, Vol. 6 (October, 1956), p. 64.

Goeyvaerts, Karol, "The Sound Material of Electronic Music." *Die Reihe*, Vol. 1 (1958), p. 41.

Hamilton, Donald, "A Synoptic View of the New Music." *High Fidelity*, Vol. 18 (September, 1968), p. 44.

Hiller, Lejaren A., "Acoustics and Electronic Music in the University Music Curriculum." *American Music Teacher*, Vol. 12 (1963), p. 24.

Hunkins, Arthur B., "First Creative Encounter with Electronic Music." *American Music Teacher*, Vol. 16 (1967), p. 29.

Judd, F. C., "The Composition of Electronic Music." *Audio and Record Review*, Vol. 1 (November, 1961), p. 78.

Kelly, Warren E., "Tape Music Composition for Secondary School." *Music Educators Journal*, Vol. 52 (June-July, 1966), p. 86.

Lawrence, H., "Music Criticism in the Electronic Age." *Audio*, Vol. 44 (October, 1960), p. 78.

————, "Splitting the Tone." *Audio*, Vol. 41 (November, 1957), p. 78.

Luening, Otto, "Karlheinz Stockhausen." *Juilliard Review*, Vol. 6 (Winter, 1958-59), p. 10.

————, "Some Random Remarks About Electronic Music." *Journal of Music Theory*, Vol. 8 (Spring, 1964), p. 89.

Meyer, Leonard B., "Art by Accident." *Horizon*, Vol. 3 (September, 1960), p. 30.

Mumma, Gordon, "An Electronic Music Studio for the Independent Composer." *Journal of the Audio Engineering Society*, Vol. 12 (June, 1964), p. 240.

Pierce, J. R., "Portrait of the Machine as a Young Artist." *Playboy*, Vol. 12 (June, 1965), p. 124.

Pousseur, Henri, "Calculation and Imagination in Electronic Music." *Electronic Music Review*, No. 5 (January, 1968), p. 21.

Rabb, B., "Electronic Music Is Valid!" *Music Journal*, Vol. 19 (October, 1961), p. 60.

Salzman, Eric, "Music from the Electronic Universe." *High Fidelity*, Vol. 14 (August, 1964), p. 54.

Schuller, Gunther, "The New German Music for Radio." *Saturday Review*, Vol. 45 (January 13, 1962), p. 62.

Seawright, James, "What Is Electronic Music?" *Radio-Electronics*, Vol. 36 (June, 1965), p. 36.

Stockhausen, Karlheinz, "Electronic and Instrumental Music." *Die Reihe*, Vol. 5 (1961), p. 59.

————, "Music in Space." *Die Reihe*, Vol. 5 (1961), p. 67.

"Swurpledeewurpledeezeech!" *Time*, Vol. 88 (November 4, 1966), p. 68.

Technische Hausmitteilungen des Nordwestdeutschen Rundfunks, Vol. 6, 1-2 (1954). Special issue on electronic music, trans. by National Research Council of Canada, Technical Translations 601-612, 1956. Articles by Eimert, Enkel, Stockhausen, and others.

Ussachevsky, Vladimir, "Music in the Tape Medium." *Juilliard Review*, Vol. 6 (Spring, 1959), p. 8.

————, "Notes on a Piece for Tape Recorder." *Musical Quarterly*, Vol. 46 (April, 1960), p. 202. Also in *Problems of Modern Music*, Paul Henry Lang, ed. New York, W. W. Norton & Co., 1962.

————, "The Process of Experimental Music." *Journal of the Audio Engineering Society*, Vol. 6 (July, 1958), p. 202.

Wen-Chung, Wen, "Varèse: A Sketch of the Man and His Music." *Musical Quarterly*, Vol. 52 (April, 1966), p. 151.

"Writings on the Use of Computers in Music," *College Music Symposium*, Vol. 6 (1966), p. 143.

Essays, Lectures, and Collected Articles

"Electronic Music." Originally published as the November, 1968, issue of the *Music Educators Journal* by the Music Educators National Conference, 1201 16th Street N.W., Washington, D.C. 20036. Valuable articles by Milton Babbitt, Otto Luening, Vladimir Ussachevsky, Morton Subotnick, etc.

"Music and Technology in the Europe of 1970" by Werner Kaegi, UNESCO Pamphlet, Paris, 1970.

"Syncopation by Automation," in Data from ElectroData. Pasadena, California. Burroughs Corporation (ElectroData Division). August, 1956.

Technische Hausmitteilungen des Nordwestdeutschen Rundfunks, Vol. 6, 1-2 (1954). Special issue devoted to electronic music, translated by National Research Council of Canada, Ottawa, 1956. Articles by Adams, Bode, Eimert, Enkel, Stockhausen, etc.

"The Electronic Sound Studio of the 1970's" by M. V. Mathews, Bell Telephone Laboratories, New Jersey.

Koenig, Gottfried Michael, "The Use of Computer Programmes in Creating Music." Utrecht University (UNESCO Pamphlet, Paris, 1970.)

"Unijunction Organ (Unitone) Tone Generator," *Electronic Components Hobby Manual.* Owensboro, Kentucky, Electronic Components Division of General Electric (1965), p. 91.

Encyclopedia Articles

"Electronic Music," *The International Cyclopedia of Music and Musicians,* 9th ed. New York, Dodd, Mead and Company, 1964, p. 594.

"Musique Concrète," *The International Cyclopedia of Music and Musicians,* 9th ed. New York, Dodd, Mead and Company, 1964, p. 1432.

Searle, Humphrey, "Concrete Music," *Grove's Dictionary of Music and Musicians,* 5th ed., Vol. 9, Appendix 2. London and New York, The Macmillan Company, 1954. Supplementary Volume, 1961. See also his article on "Electrophonic Music."

Unpublished Material

Bahler, Peter Benjamin. "Electronic and Computer Music: An Annotated Bibliography of Writings in English." Unpublished M.A. dissertation. University of Rochester, 1966.

Index